THE FOOD TRUCK COOKBOOK
NO. 2

A RANDOM HOUSE BOOK published by Random House New Zealand
18 Poland Road, Glenfield, Auckland, New Zealand

For more information about our titles go to www.randomhouse.co.nz

A catalogue record for this book is available from the
National Library of New Zealand

Random House New Zealand is part of the Random House Group
New York   London   Sydney   Auckland   Delhi   Johannesburg

First published 2013

© 2013 text Michael Van de Elzen; images Babiche Martens

The moral rights of the author have been asserted

ISBN 978 1 77553 411 2

This book is copyright. Except for the purposes of fair reviewing no part of this publication
may be reproduced or transmitted in any form or by any means, electronic or mechanical,
including photocopying, recording or any information storage and retrieval system,
without permission in writing from the publisher.

Design: Kate Barraclough
Cover photograph: Babiche Martens www.babichemartens.com

Printed in China by Everbest Printing Co Ltd

Thanks to Richard Linton (www.lintonphoto.com), Chris Coad (www.chriscoad.co.nz),
Craig Robertson (www.fullframe.co.nz) and Jim Tannock (www.jimtannock.co.nz) for additional
game day photographs.
Thanks for the loan of props to: Alison of Aunty Mavis, Auckland; Simonne of Let's Go Retro,
Swanson; Sandy and Ian of Rainbow Relics, Oratia; and Peter and Maria of Real Time, Ponsonby.

THE FOOD TRUCK COOKBOOK NO. 2

Michael Van de Elzen

PHOTOS BY BABICHE MARTENS

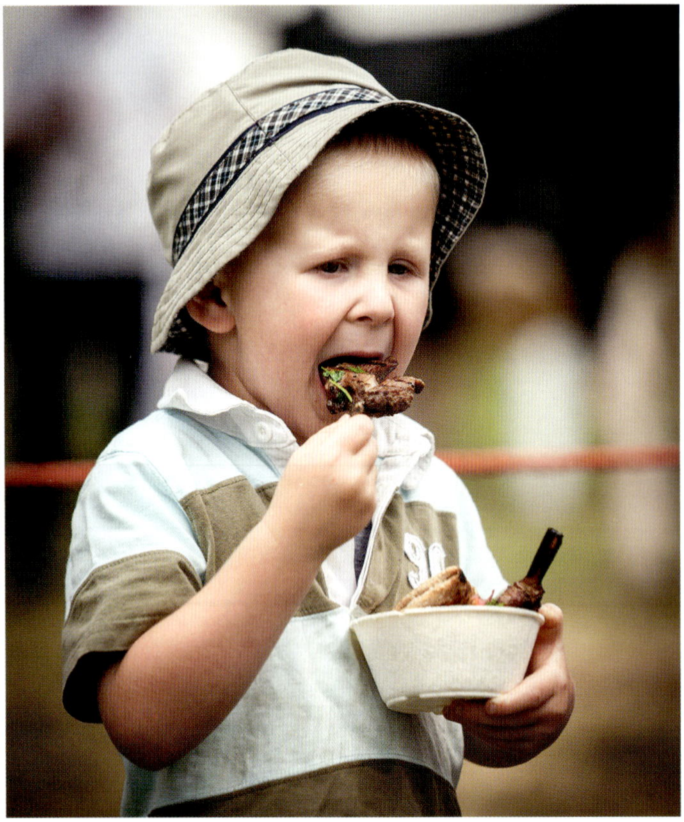

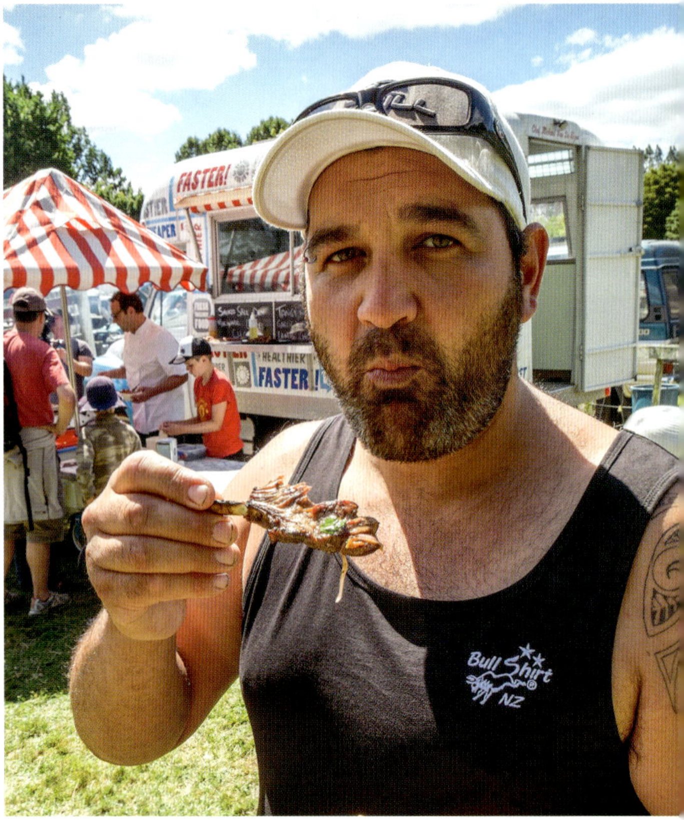
FASTER!
FASTER
Bull Shirt
NZ

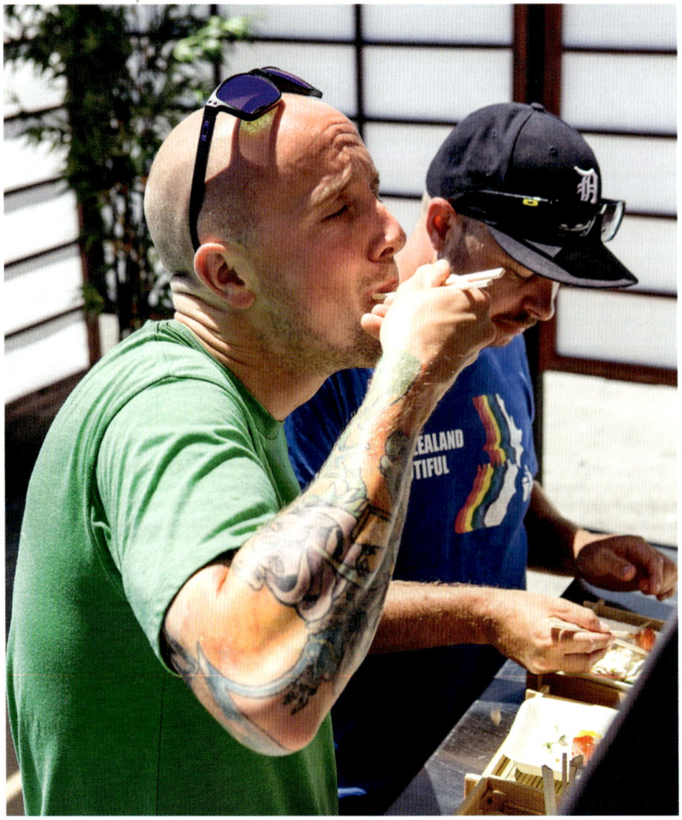

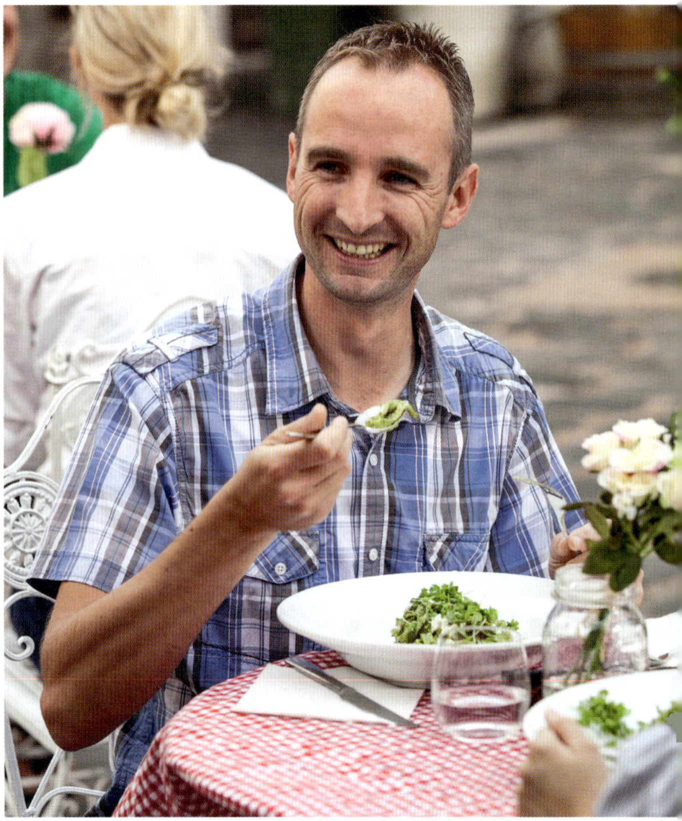

Chef Michael Van De Elzen

THE FOOD TRUCK

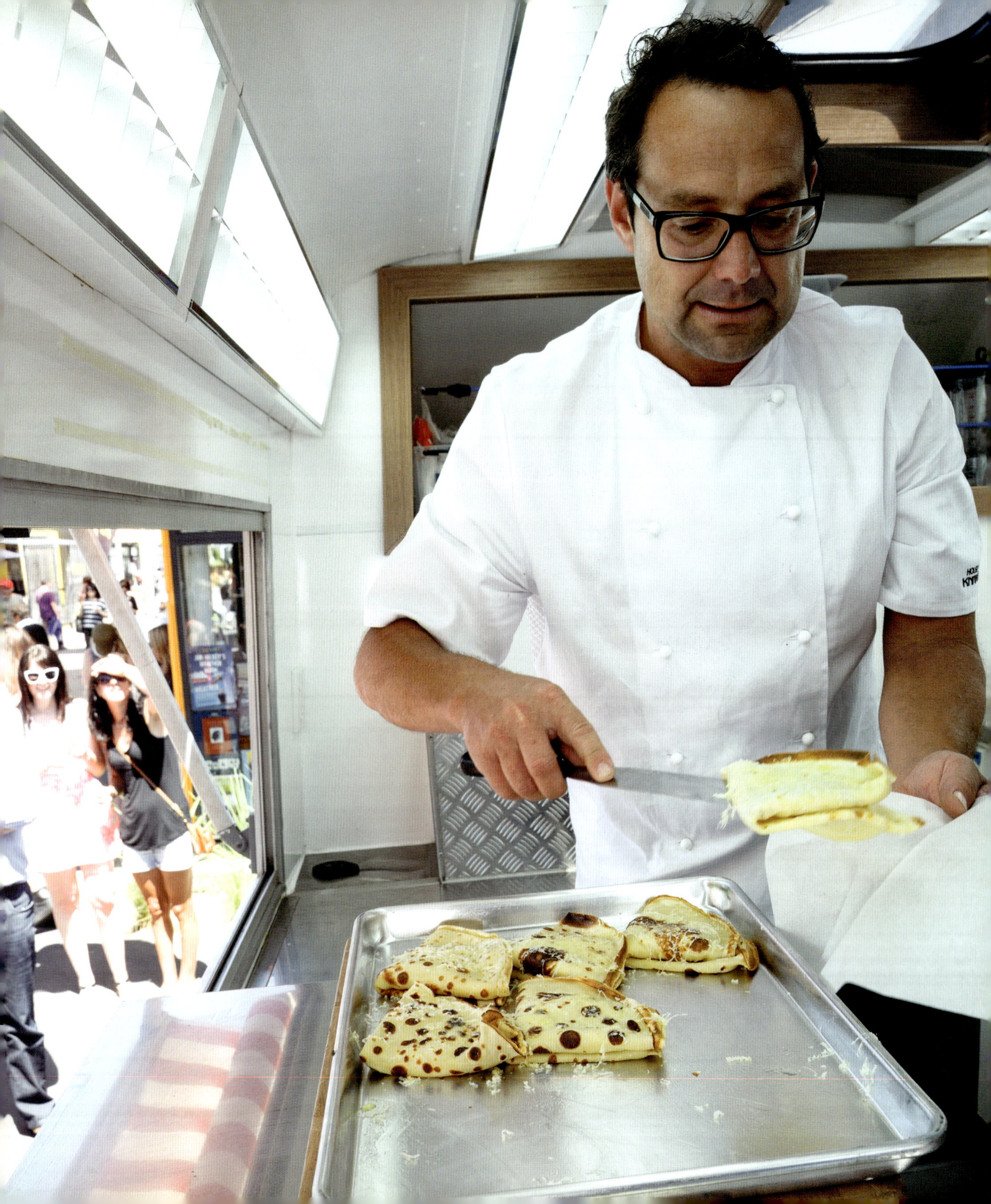

Contents

A few words from Mike
09

Ole!
Spanish and Argentinian
14

Mexican Standoff
42

The East
Chinese, Japanese and Thai
50

Easy Vietnamese
84

Europe
French, Italian and German
96

Home Favourites
Burgers, Pizzas, Pies and More
130

Middle Eastern Feast
168

A short history of food trucks and street food
182

Healthy options
186

Credit roll
189

Index
190

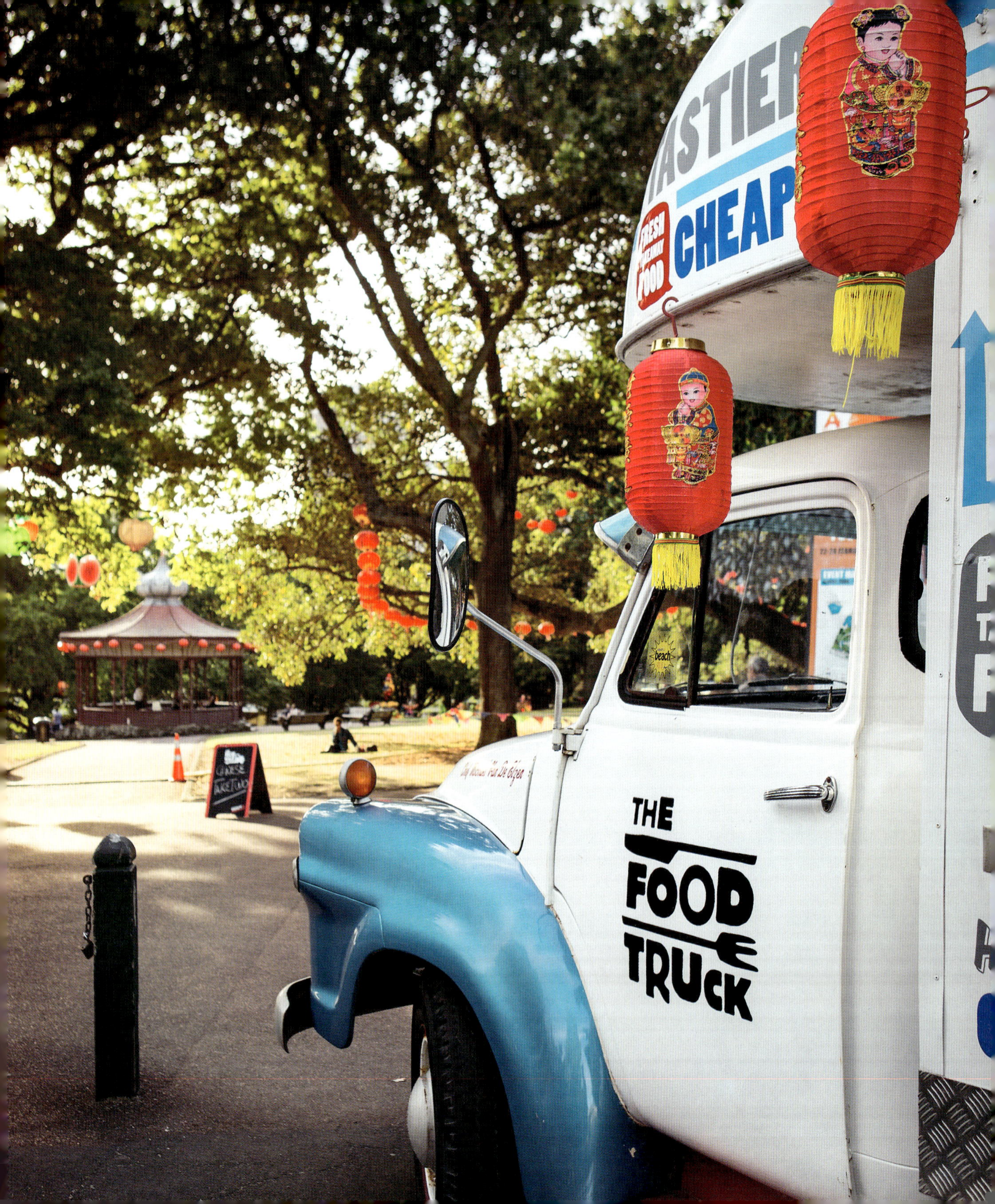
CHEAP
THE
FOOD
TRUCK

A few words from Mike

It started with the very first Food Truck customer to ask for her money back. I was at a rodeo just out of Whangarei and I'd decided on an American theme, seeing as I was, temporarily at least, in cowboy country. Triple blueberry doughnuts: blueberries baked in the dough, blueberries injected in the centre, then the doughnuts rolled in freeze-dried blueberries. An extravaganza. Yum. Or so I thought.

I'd made some the day before because I figured that I'd be really busy and that I should have some ready to go the moment I pulled up the roller blind on the side of the truck. Big mistake. They were hard and had a texture like bread. I should not have served them. And when not one but two ladies complained and asked for their money back, it made me question the whole Food Truck philosophy. How could I make a healthy doughnut anyway? It's deep-fried dough rolled in sugar! What was I thinking?

I have to confess I thought about throwing the tea towel in. Why do it all again? Why go through three months of being stuck in a stinking hot food truck? Why had I sold the restaurant? But I got a grip. Had a good talk to myself. Because for those two ladies who didn't like the doughnuts (and fair enough), there were 30 enthusiastic young people who did. The Food Truck was back in business!

The first two *Food Truck* television series and the first *Food Truck Cookbook* were runaway successes. I was so delighted that people really enjoyed the food they bought from the truck, and that they appreciated the bonus of it being fresh, flavoursome and healthy. And it's great that Kiwis are trying it themselves at home, using the book and discovering how easy it is to get a delicious fast-food meal that everyone loves.

As I've said before, there's nothing wrong with nipping down to the chippie or Maccas for some takeaways — I like doing that as much as the next person. (In fact a couple of times when we were making series three and I was just *so* hungry, I was spotted ducking in to a café to grab a hot pie. It was a little bit embarrassing to realise that people were asking each other 'Was that the healthy food guy?') It's when we eat takeaways too often that it becomes a problem. The recipes in my first book were all about having the option to make fast food at home — and having it taste better.

I knew we'd have to make series three of the show even bigger and better than the first two, and

> *My mission hasn't changed. Taking the Food Truck to festivals and events is still about convincing Kiwis that the fast food they love can be healthy and fresh and taste terrific.*

that I'd have to challenge myself even more to make and sell fantastic food. We did! There are more episodes and, importantly, we got around a lot more of the country. Everywhere we went, from Christchurch to Whangarei, Blenheim to Wellington, the crowds were huge. Everyone's happy to have been part of the Food Truck story.

I was really pleased to be able to take my food to the rest of the New Zealand, and in particular it meant a lot to be in Christchurch, in the Re:Start Mall for the World Buskers Festival, doing our little bit to get life back into the city. That day the power cable to the truck went down and I had to use my neighbour's pizza oven to toast my crêpes — I loved the spirit of everyone helping each other. The creativity of Christchurch invigorated me for the three-month challenge ahead.

My mission hasn't changed. Taking the Food Truck to festivals and events is still about convincing Kiwis that the fast food they love can be healthy and fresh and taste terrific. And that they need to start thinking about what's in their takeaway meals because it's one of the reasons for our dreadful health statistics.

High fat, high salt, high sugar, high MSG, low fibre . . . it's all a big part of the reason for our high obesity, diabetes and heart-disease rates.

I'm totally committed to doing something about this. I won't give this up.

It's a high-pressure world in the back of Beddy. During New Zealand's hottest summer for 75 years the temperature got close to unbearable. And if you think making and serving food to queues of hungry, expectant people is hard, what about actually talking to the camera as you go? I can't remember how many times I mangled the word Vietnamese. Or how many times I could never say chorizo. Or melting. It drove the director crazy!

And if it's hard yakka making tasty fast food under pressure in the confines of a truck, then it's just as hard coming up with the ideas in less than a week, week after week, for 13 of them. (Oh, and did I mention that just before we started filming my wife Belinda and I had our second daughter and I was getting hardly any sleep?) That's why my recipes are quick and straightforward to prepare (well, most of them); they have to be. But just like the recipes in the first book, they don't rely on deep-frying and lots of fat for their flavour. You can do things quickly with healthy techniques, by

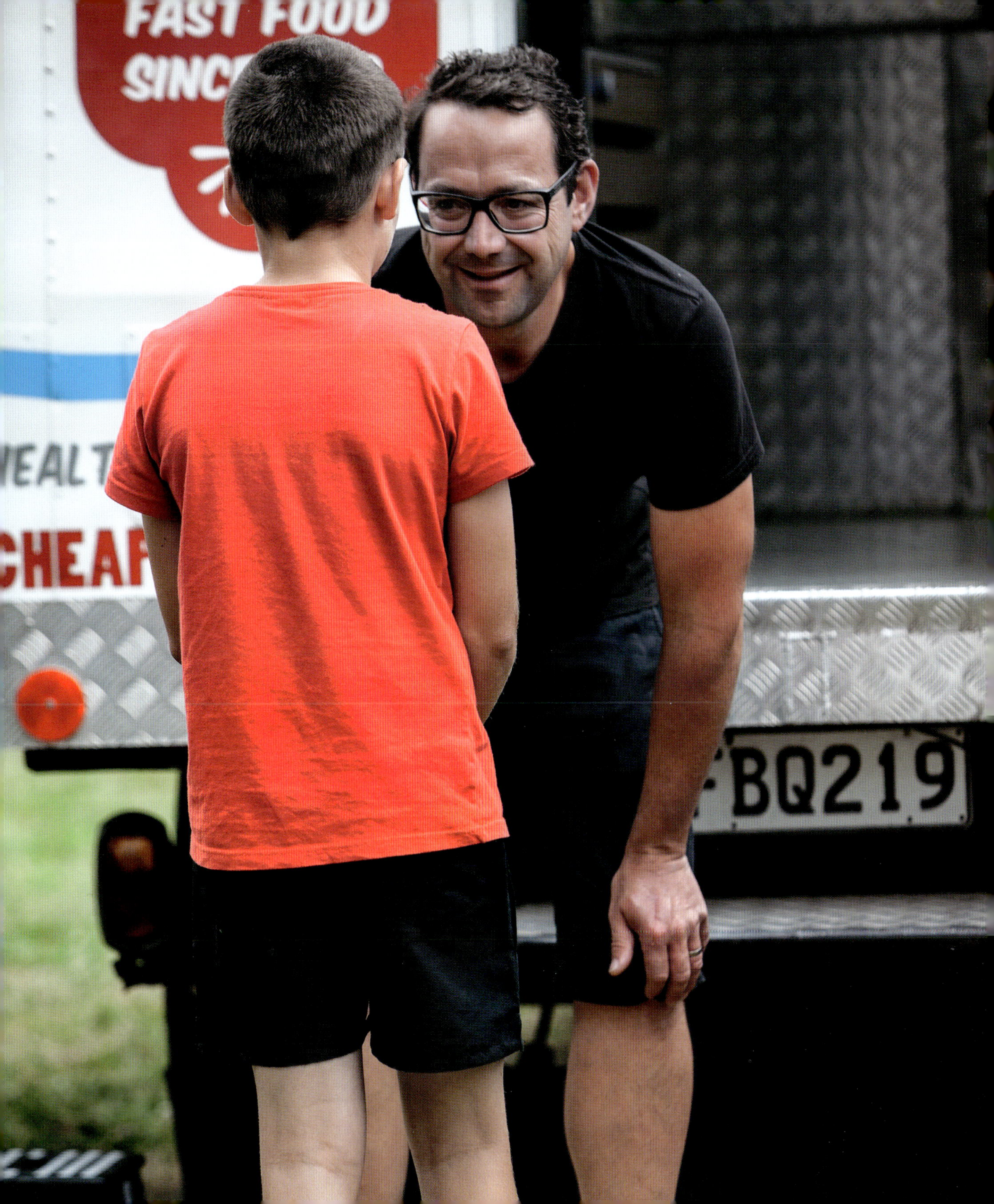
FAST FOOD
FBQ219

> *Above all, it really galvanised me to see how people just loved my food and how open Kiwis are to new tastes and textures.*

baking rather than frying, for example. It's not rocket science.

And, boy, is the food packed with flavour! The recipes in this book are very international, reflecting the broader 'world food' approach of series three. World food tastes terrific because it has *amazing* ingredients — chilli, lime, coriander, pungent spices. It's so fresh and zesty.

These days I can't travel to any of the countries where you get this stuff on the street — I've got kids, a mortgage and a job — but I can dream about them, and transport myself there through my kitchen. As you can, too.

This series extended my repertoire even further and I've met such fantastic chefs and cooks on the challenges. They really inspired me. Whether they are Japanese or Turkish, German or Pacific, their recipes, adapted by me to be healthier, will easily fit into *your* home-cooking repertoire.

Above all, it really galvanised me to see how people just loved my food and how open Kiwis are to new tastes and textures. It was especially exciting to see the reaction young people have to the truck. They, in turn, motivate me to keep doing it, because if they can change the way they eat anyone can. The day I saw kids ordering choy sum dippers — boxes of green veges — I knew there was hope!

This new book has recipes inspired by cuisines from around the globe, more salads and wraps, and there are also recipes for burgers, pizzas and pies. They have all been tested by me (and on you, the general public), each one has a prep and cooking time, and once more I give a nutritional analysis for each one.

This book clusters the recipes from series three into themes: 'Ole!' which is Spanish and Argentinian; 'The East', which is Chinese, Japanese and Thai; and 'Europe', which is French, Italian and German. There's also 'Home Favourites', which is where you will find recipes from the series for American-style foods such as doughnuts, almond shakes and burgers, Polynesian dishes that PI New Zealanders love, and some extra recipes for pizza, pies and sweet treats that I know you will really enjoy. There's even a recipe for a great broccoli snack! Finally, there's a bunch of Mexican, Vietnamese and Middle Eastern 'feasts' from the TV series.

Enjoy!

Mike Van de Elzen

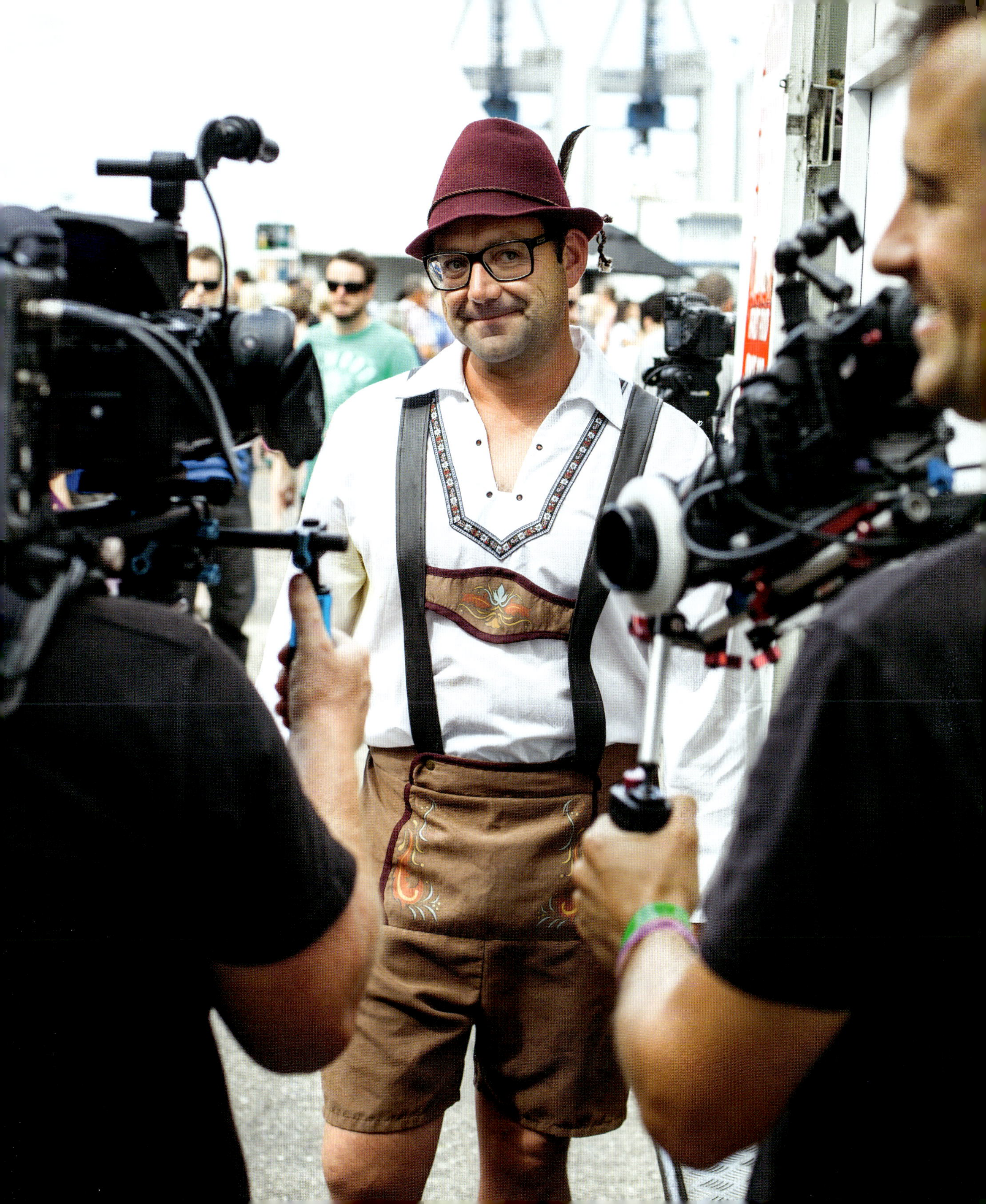

OLE! SPANISH AND

ARGENTINIAN

Find it difficult to pass on anything crumbed? These healthy baked-in-the-oven tuna croquettes are just the ticket.

Energy KJs	Protein	Total fat
690	7g	8.5g

Saturated fat	Carbohydrate	Sodium
1g	18g	158mg

Tuna Croquettes

Makes 12 • Preparation time 45 minutes • Cooking time 10 minutes

CROQUETTE MIXTURE

100ml grapeseed oil
50g flour
50g wholemeal flour
100ml low-fat milk
pinch salt and white pepper
2 tablespoons freshly grated Parmesan
150g blanched spinach, chopped (about 8 bunches)
4 spring onions, finely chopped
100g tuna in spring water, drained
1 teaspoon gelatine dissolved in 2 teaspoons water

CRUMB MIXTURE

3 egg whites, beaten with 1 teaspoon water
4 wholemeal pita breads, toasted until dry, finely crumbed

FOR THE CROQUETTES

1. Melt oil in a small heavy-based saucepan and add flours. Stir well to combine and place over a medium heat. Cook until flours are a straw colour.
2. Whisk in milk and continue cooking, whisking constantly, until the sauce is very thick. Season with salt and white pepper.
3. Add Parmesan, spinach, spring onions, tuna and dissolved gelatine. Mix well, then leave to cool.
4. Using a piping bag fitted with a large plain nozzle, pipe mixture into long rolls on to a baking tray lined with baking paper, or simply shape by hand. Cover and place in refrigerator to set mixture for at least 1 hour.
5. Meanwhile, preheat oven to 180°C.
6. Remove mixture from refrigerator and cut into 5cm long croquettes.
7. Dip croquettes in egg white, then pita crumbs. Repeat once more. Place back on to lined baking tray.
8. Place in oven and cook for 10 minutes until hot.

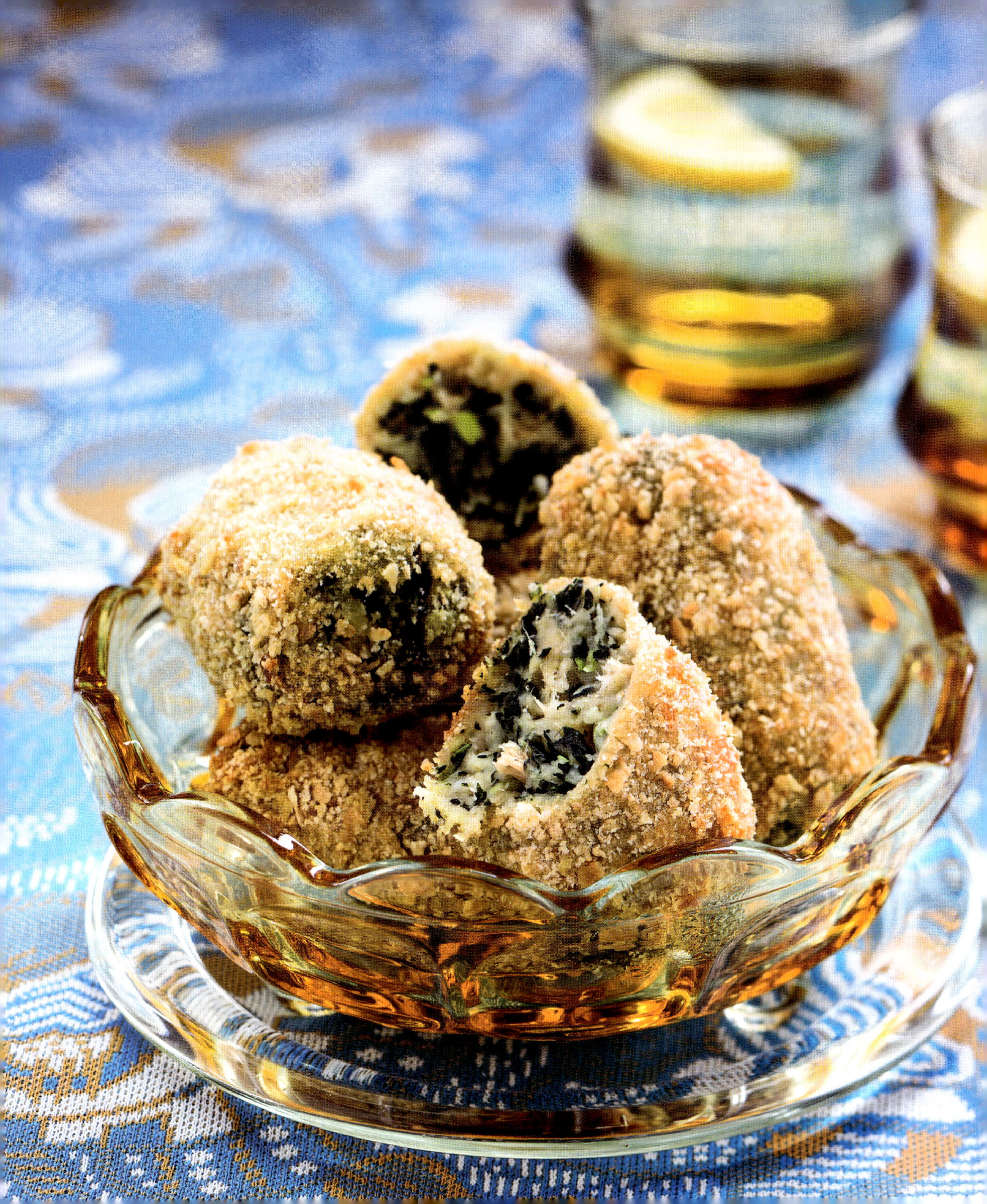

Romesco sauce is a Spanish tomato-based sauce. The ingredients list can differ from cook to cook but it's always a great accompaniment to meat, vegetables, and in this case, seafood.

Energy KJs	Protein	Total fat
673	7g	12g

Saturated fat	Carbohydrate	Sodium
1.3g	6g	112mg

Squid Skewers with Romesco Sauce

Makes 12 • Preparation time Marinate squid 1 hour • Cooking time 1 minute

ROMESCO SAUCE

MAKES: 1½ CUPS

1 bulb garlic, lightly smashed
1 large tomato
2 red peppers, chargrilled, skinned, deseeded and roughly chopped (see page 36)
1 small red chilli, deseeded and chopped
½ cup almonds, dry-roasted
½ cup hazelnuts, dry-roasted and skinned (see page 98)
1 slice wholemeal bread, broken into pieces
50ml dry sherry
50ml olive oil

SQUID

12 pieces raw pineapple-cut squid or 3 small squid tubes
12 skewers
2 tablespoons dry sherry
1 tablespoon grapeseed oil
½ tablespoon smoked paprika
1 clove garlic, crushed
zest of 1 orange

FOR THE SAUCE

1. Preheat oven to 180°C. Line a roasting dish with baking paper.
2. Place garlic and tomato in roasting dish and roast for 20–30 minutes. Remove from oven and discard tomato skins. Squeeze soft garlic from its skin. If garlic is not quite soft, return to oven for a little longer.
3. Place all remaining sauce ingredients in a blender, except olive oil. Blend until smooth, slowly pouring in oil as you blend. If necessary, add a little water to thin. Transfer to a bowl, cover and refrigerate.

FOR THE SQUID

1. If using small squid tubes, open and score on a 45-degree angle on both sides. Cut each into quarters.
2. Thread squid onto skewers. Place in a shallow ceramic dish.
3. Mix together sherry, oil, paprika, garlic and orange zest. Pour over squid, cover with plastic wrap and refrigerate overnight. If short on time, marinate for at least 1 hour.
4. Preheat barbecue grill to very hot.
5. Grill squid skewers quickly for 1 minute, turning after 30 seconds.
6. Serve with a small quenelle of romesco sauce on top of each squid skewer.

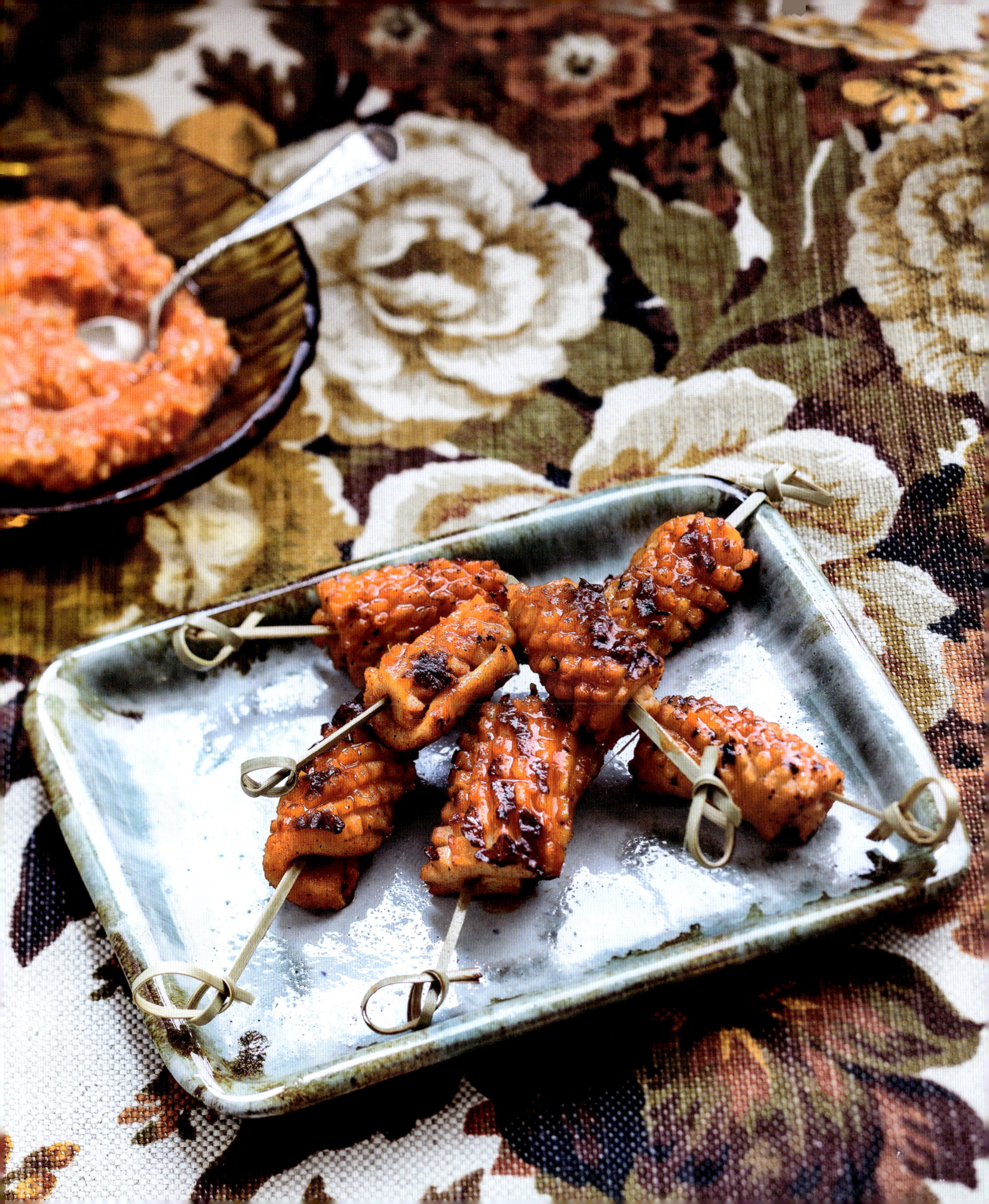

So simple but so good. Remember to cut the potatoes larger than you would naturally think to do as they shrink during roasting.

Energy KJs	Protein	Total fat
250	1g	3g

Saturated fat	Carbohydrate	Sodium
.5g	8g	34mg

Patatas Bravas

Makes 12 • Preparation time 15 minutes • Cooking time 20 minutes

3 large Agria potatoes, peeled and cut into 3–4cm dice
4 cloves garlic, lightly smashed
4 sprigs rosemary, lightly smashed
2 tablespoons olive oil
pinch salt and freshly ground black pepper
12 skewers
12 cherry tomatoes
zest of 1 lemon
olive oil spray

1. Preheat oven to 200°C.
2. Place diced potatoes in a shallow roasting dish, add garlic, rosemary, oil, salt and pepper. Toss well to coat.
3. Roast potatoes for 20 minutes or until just cooked.
4. Skewer one potato, one cherry tomato, one potato. Repeat until you have used all potatoes.
5. Grate over zest of lemon and lightly spray with olive oil.
6. Return to oven and reheat until tomato skins begin to split.

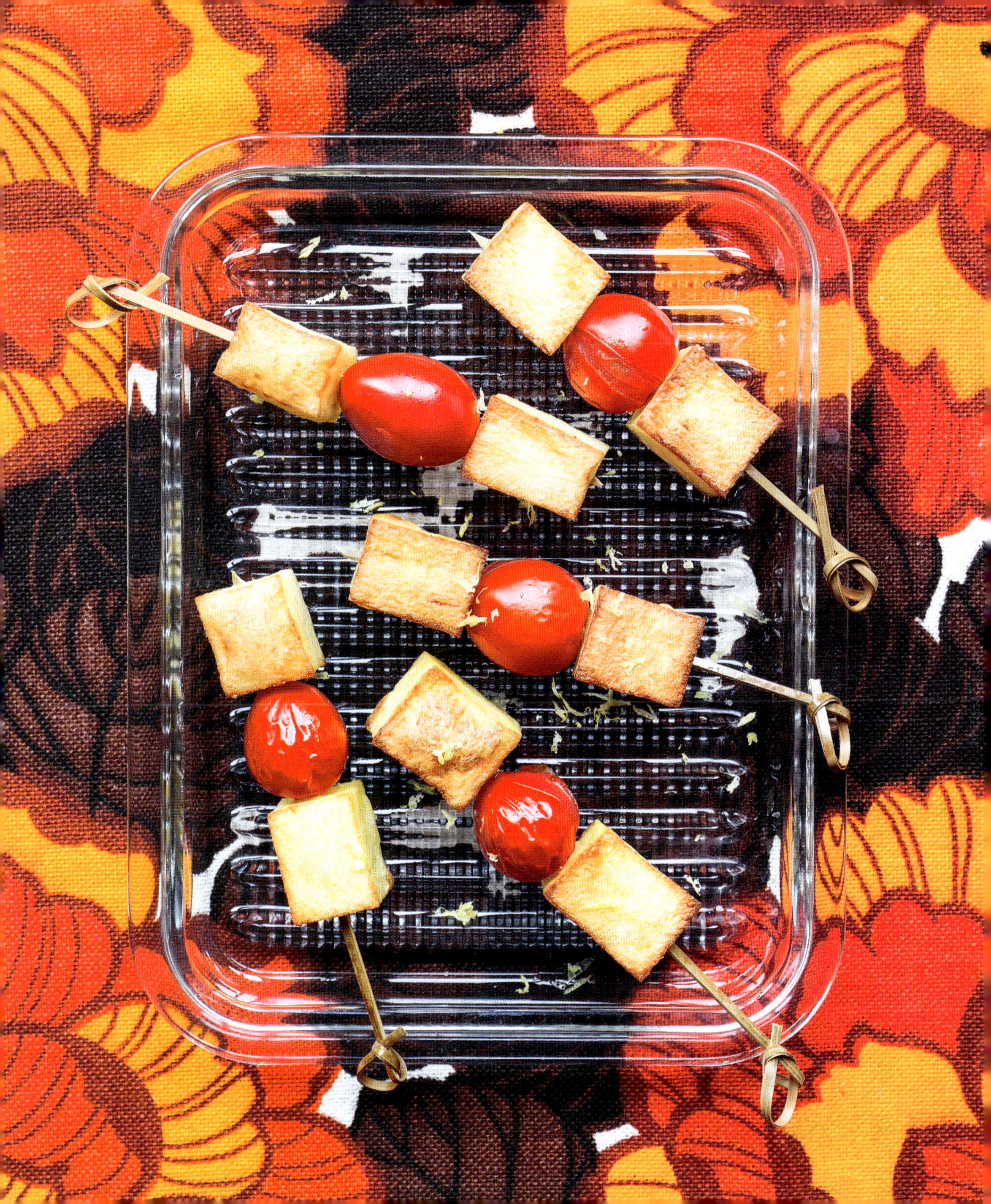

Peppers are a great vehicle for stuffing. You can put just about anything in them.

Energy KJs	Protein	Total fat
225	1g	1.2g

Saturated fat	Carbohydrate	Sodium
.4g	9g	117mg

Chorizo Paella 'n' Stuffed Peppers

Makes 24 • Preparation time 20 minutes • Cooking time 35-40 minutes

- 1 Spanish chorizo sausage, cut into small dice
- 1 cup paella rice
- 2 tomatoes, chopped
- ½ onion, chopped
- 2 cloves garlic, chopped
- ½ teaspoon paprika
- pinch saffron
- 2 cups vegetable stock
- ¼ cup chopped curly parsley leaves
- 24 tiny sweet peppers
- olive oil spray
- 24 skewers

1. Preheat oven to 180°C.
2. Pour a dash of olive oil into a paella pan or large frying pan and add chorizo. Cook for 1 minute.
3. Add paella rice, tomatoes, onion, garlic, paprika, saffron and vegetable stock. Bring just up to the boil, lower heat and cook for 25–30 minutes. Test a grain of rice to see if cooked. Stir in parsley.
4. Slice top or side off sweet peppers to form a cavity. Remove any seeds and fill with paella mixture. Replace top or side. Place filled sweet peppers on a shallow baking tray and spray with olive oil spray.
5. Place in oven for 10 minutes. Skewer to serve.

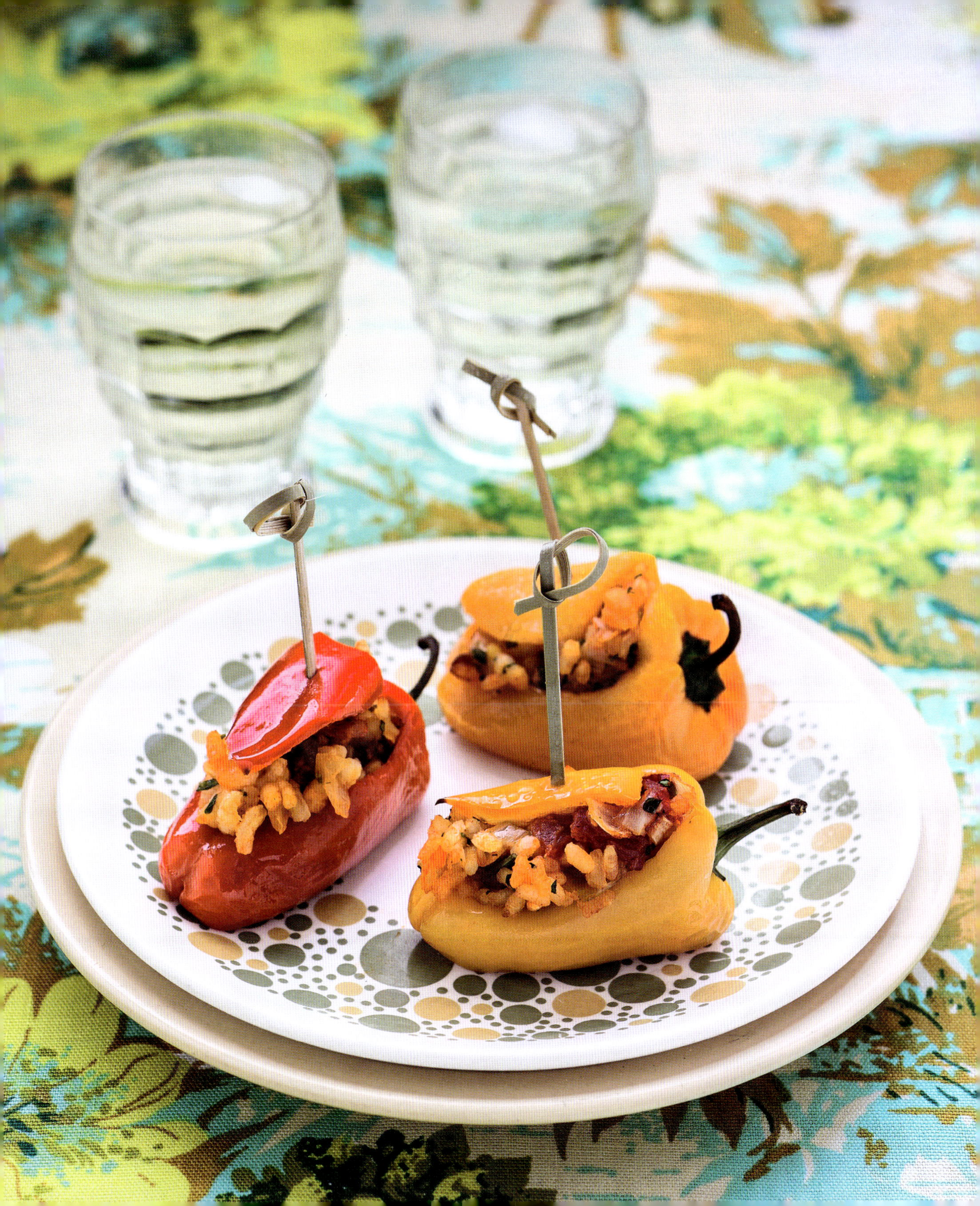

I love this recipe so much. The meatball mix could be used for other, larger, patties.

Energy KJs	Protein	Total fat
425	4.6g	8g

Saturated fat	Carbohydrate	Sodium
1.4g	3g	55mg

Healthy meatballs

Makes 12 • Preparation time 45 minutes • Cooking time 5 minutes

TOMATO WHITE BEAN SAUCE
MAKES: 1 CUP
100ml olive oil
2 sprigs rosemary
1 x 225g can Spanish butter beans, drained
150ml tomato juice

MEATBALLS
200g chicken mince
1 cup grated courgette
1 cup grated pumpkin
1 spring onion, finely chopped
1 tablespoon smoked paprika
½ teaspoon cayenne pepper
½ teaspoon mustard powder
pinch salt
½ teaspoon white pepper
12 skewers

FOR THE SAUCE
1. Place oil and rosemary in a small saucepan and heat until very hot but not boiling. Turn off immediately and leave to cool, then remove rosemary.
2. Place butter beans and tomato juice in a blender and blend, then slowly pour in infused oil until you have a sauce. Set aside.

FOR THE MEATBALLS
1. Mix all ingredients together and form into small balls (30g each).
2. Pan-fry in a dash of olive oil until golden brown on all sides and hot in the centre.

TO ASSEMBLE
1. Place a little sauce in 12 shot glasses, skewer meatballs and place across top of each glass.

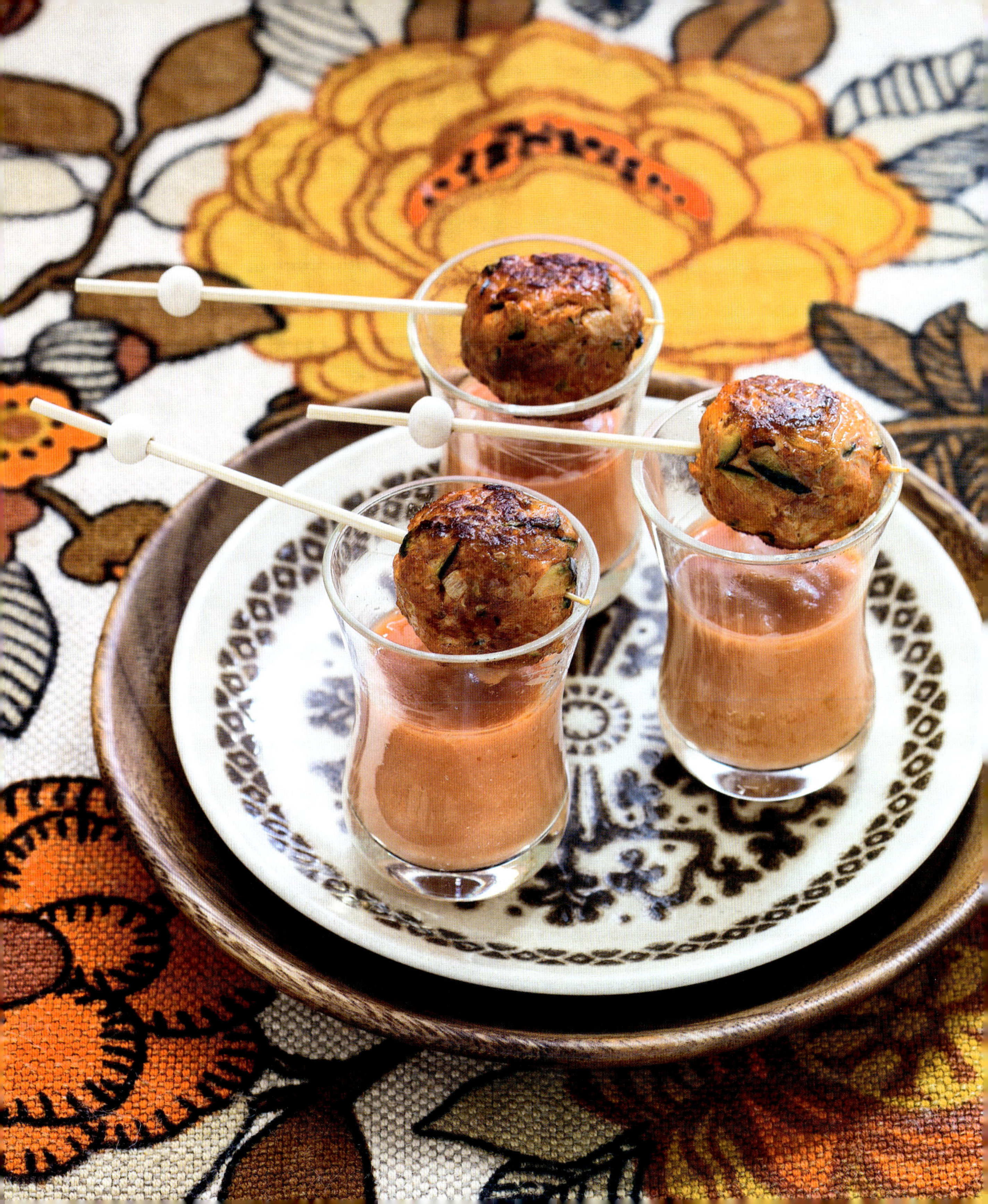

The tortilla is a Spanish staple, but, as always, I just had to mess with it a little. Simply by adding some kumara, parsnips and beetroot you end up with a more exciting dish with wicked colour.

Energy KJs	Protein	Total fat
354	2.8g	1.8g

Saturated fat	Carbohydrate	Sodium
.4g	15g	52mg

Vegetable Tortilla

Makes 12 • Preparation time 40 minutes • Cooking time 10 minutes

2 medium-sized kumara, unpeeled
2 medium-sized Agria potatoes, unpeeled
2 small parsnips, peeled and grated
2 small onions, very finely chopped
1 beetroot, peeled and grated
2 eggs
1 wholemeal French stick, sliced
12 slices Manchego cheese
12 black olives, pitted

1. Preheat grill to hot.
2. Place kumara and Agria potatoes in a saucepan of cold water. Bring to the boil, then remove from heat and drain. When cool enough to handle, peel if wished, then grate into a large bowl.
3. Add parsnip, onion, beetroot and eggs.
4. Add a dash of olive oil to a 26cm ovenproof frying pan. Add vegetable mixture and cook over a medium heat until golden brown on underside. (This allows time for the raw vegetables to cook). Transfer to oven and grill for a further 4 minutes.

TO ASSEMBLE

1. Slice vegetable tortilla and place on slices of French stick. Top with slices of Manchego cheese and scatter around olives.

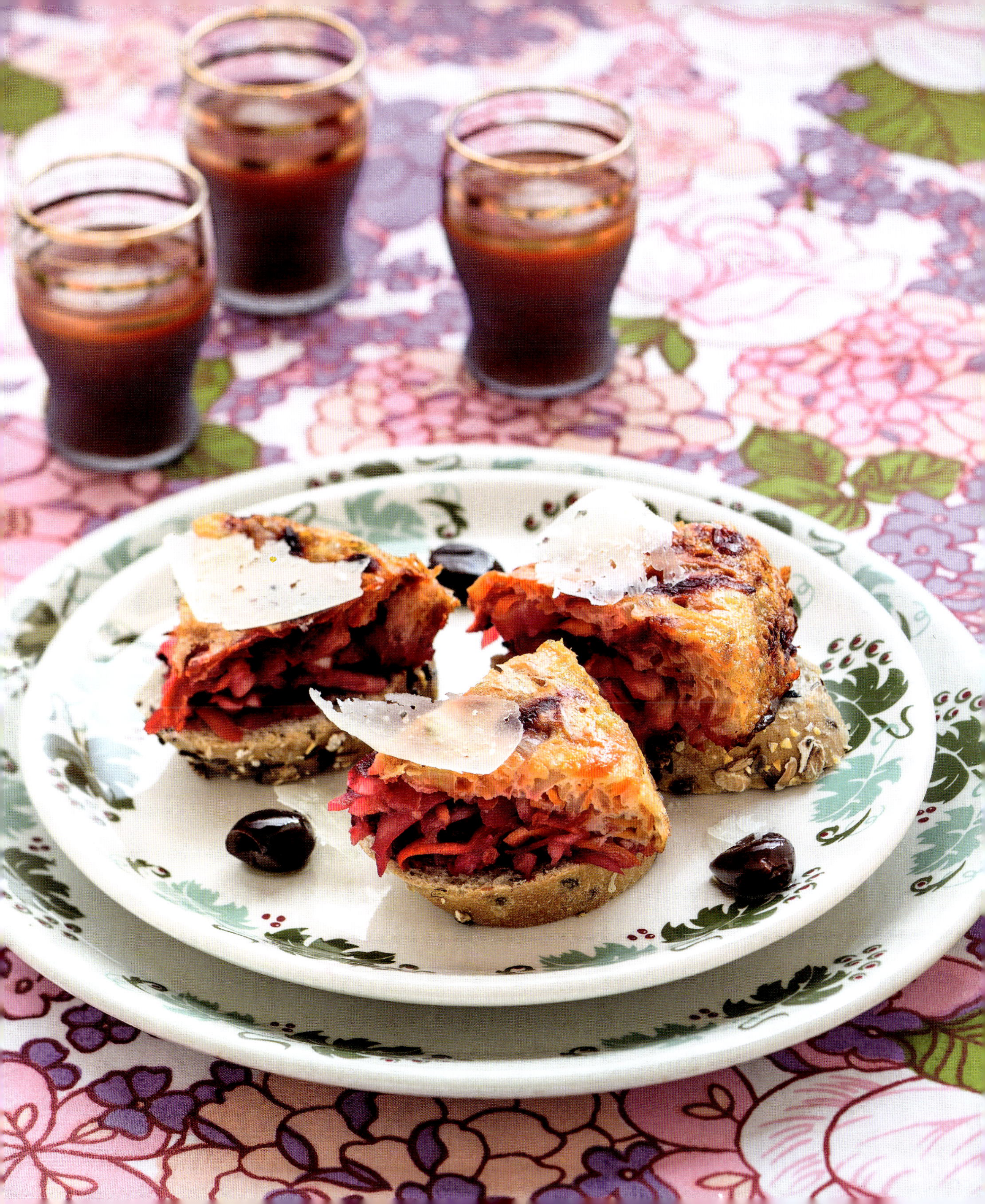

This one surprised me. The contrasting flavours of the olive and the cherries is amazing. One of my favourites.

Energy KJs	Protein	Total fat
281	**.5g**	**4g**

Saturated fat	Carbohydrate	Sodium
.6g	**8g**	**10mg**

Cherries with Olive Caramel

Makes 8 skewers • Preparation time 20 minutes

½ cup black olives, pitted
2 tablespoons honey
24 cherries, stoned
8 skewers

1. Blend black olives and honey using a stick blender.
2. Using a piping bag fitted with a small nozzle, pipe olive mixture into stoned cherries, or carefully fill using handle of a teaspoon.
3. Thread 3 cherries onto each skewer.

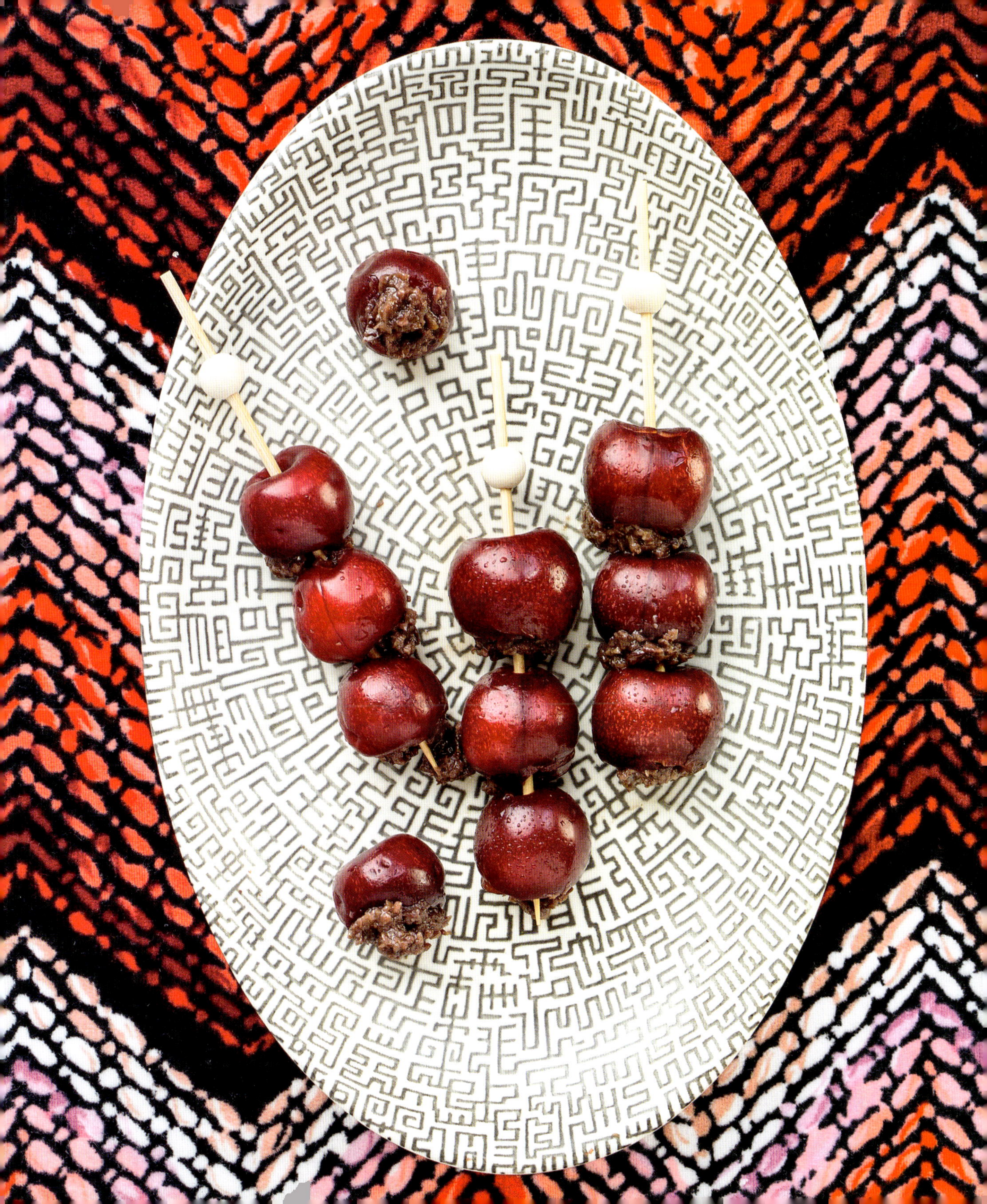

I love this because it just tastes of summer. The freshness of the melon combined with the spiced yoghurt is delicious. A great cocktail party recipe.

Energy KJs	Protein	Total fat
189	1.4g	.6g

Saturated fat	Carbohydrate	Sodium
.2g	9g	34mg

melon Balls *with Crispy Serrano Ham and Spiced Yoghurt*

Makes 12 • *Preparation time* 30 minutes

SPICED YOGHURT
100ml thick plain yoghurt
½ vanilla pod, seeds scraped
½ tablespoon sherry vinegar
½ tablespoon honey
¼ teaspoon smoked paprika

TO ASSEMBLE
¼ watermelon, seeds removed
½ small honeydew melon, seeds removed
½ small rockmelon, seeds removed
12 skewers
2 slices Serrano ham, grilled until crisp and lightly crushed in your fingertips

FOR THE YOGHURT
1. Mix yoghurt, vanilla seeds, vinegar, honey and paprika together.

TO ASSEMBLE
1. Using a melon baller, make 12 melon balls from each type of melon.
2. To serve, spoon spiced yoghurt into 12 shot glasses and sprinkle with crushed Serrano ham.
3. Skewer three different melon balls onto each skewer and place across the top of each shot glass.

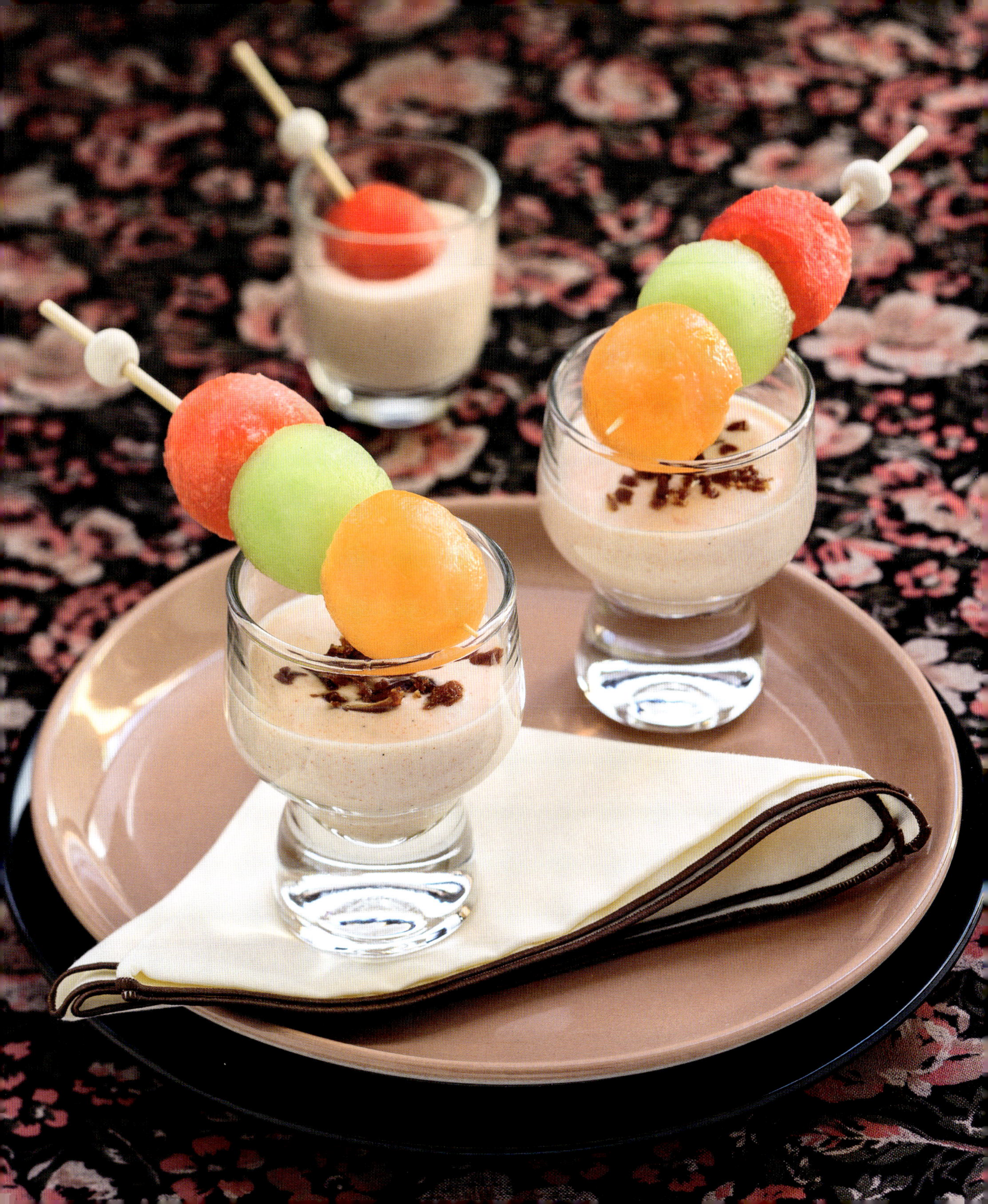

Cooking Argentinian food on the BBQ at the Rotorua A&P show was unlike anything I'd done before. I didn't have the truck to hide in, and being on the front line was both terrifying and exhilarating! The marinade is one of the simplest I know. It will work a treat on any red meat. The longer you leave it the better.

Energy KJs	Protein	Total fat
1214	27g	18g

Saturated fat	Carbohydrate	Sodium
6g	12g	165mg

Chargrilled Lamb Shoulder Chops
Wet Rub

Serves 6 • **Preparation time** *Marinate overnight* • **Cooking time** *12 minutes, 2 minutes resting time*

WET RUB
3 large lemons, roughly chopped
6 sprigs rosemary, remove some leaves
6 cloves garlic, crushed
3 tablespoons olive oil
pinch salt
1 teaspoon black pepper

LAMB
3 lamb shoulder racks
olive oil for brushing

1. Mix together wet rub ingredients in a shallow ceramic or glass dish.
2. Add in lamb shoulder racks and rub well with wet rub mixture. Cover and place in refrigerator overnight. Alternatively, if short on time, allow to marinate for at least 1 hour.
3. Remove marinated lamb from refrigerator and let stand to bring up to room temperature.
4. Preheat barbecue grill to hot. Preheat oven to 200°C.
5. Brush or rub in a little olive oil and place on hot grill. Grill for 2 minutes on presentation side only.
6. Remove lamb racks to a shallow roasting dish and place in oven for 10 minutes. Remove from oven, cover loosely and leave to rest for at least 2 minutes before slicing into cutlets.
7. Serve with chimichurri salad (see recipe on page 36) and breads.

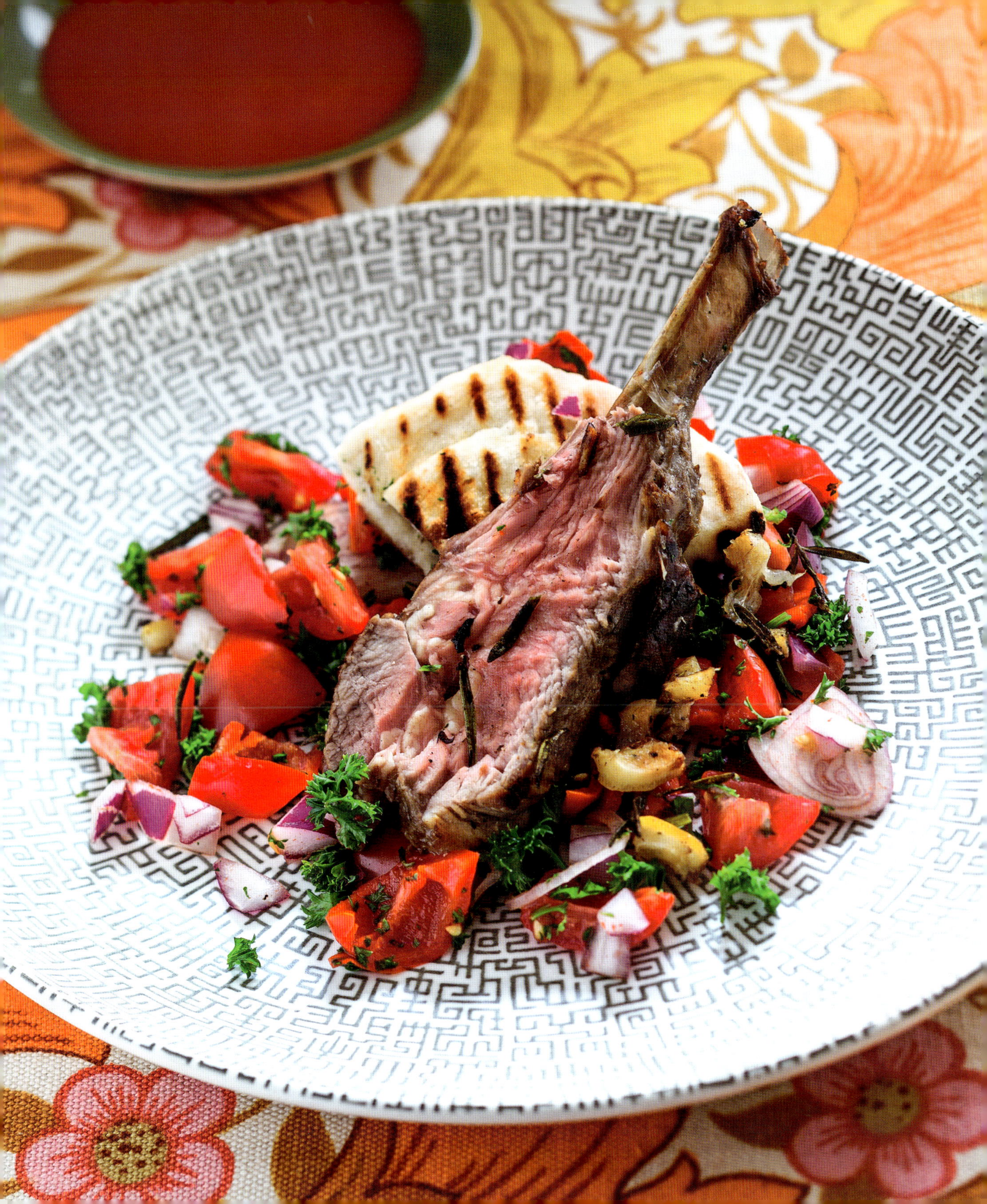

You'll need to raid your spice cupboard to make this dry rub but you won't regret it. The mix of spices gives you a smoky taste, as if the meat has been cooking on an open flame for hours. It can be made in bulk and stored in a container. It lasts for ages and can be used in practically anything.

Energy KJs	Protein	Total fat
930	26g	12g

Saturated fat	Carbohydrate	Sodium
5g	48g	589mg

Chargrilled Lamb Shoulder Chops Dry Rub

Serves 6 • *Preparation time* 5 minutes • *Cooking time* 8 minutes, plus 2 minutes resting time

DRY RUB
1 tablespoon dried oregano
1 tablespoon dried thyme
1 tablespoon dried rosemary
1 tablespoon smoked paprika
1 tablespoon dried chilli flakes
½ tablespoon freeze-dried, ground garlic
½ tablespoon smoke salt
1 tablespoon white pepper

LAMB
3 lamb shoulder racks, cut into cutlets
olive oil for brushing

1. Preheat barbecue grill to very hot.
2. Mix together dry rub ingredients and rub a little into each lamb cutlet.
3. Brush cutlets with olive oil and place on hot grill. Grill for 4 minutes on each side. Remove from grill and place on a large platter. Loosely cover and leave to rest for 2 minutes.
4. Serve with chimichurri salad (see recipe on page 36) and breads.

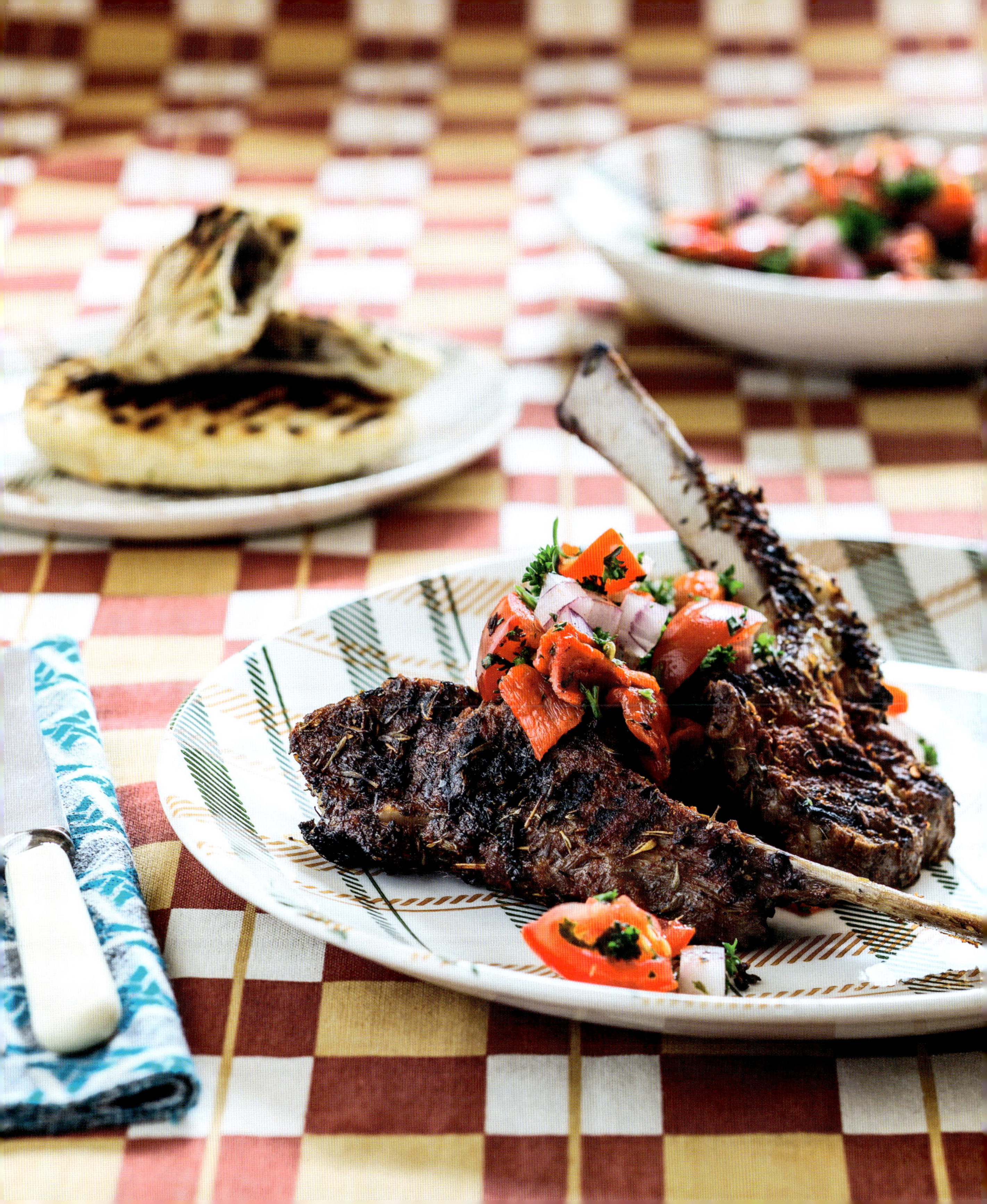

I have never tasted a more perfect accompaniment to smoky lamb than the famous South American sauce, chimichurri. This recipe takes those spices and puts them into a super-healthy salad.

Energy KJs	Protein	Total fat
522	2g	8g

Saturated fat	Carbohydrate	Sodium
1.2g	14g	135mg

Chimichurri Salad

Serves 6 • *Preparation time* 30–40 minutes

SALAD

2 red peppers
1 teaspoon olive oil
pinch salt
4 ripe tomatoes, cut into 1cm dice
10 preserved mild whole sweet piquante peppers, cut into quarters
3 shallots, thinly sliced
1 red onion, cut into 1cm dice
2 cloves garlic, crushed
1 cup roughly chopped curly parsley leaves

DRESSING

1/3 cup red wine vinegar
3 tablespoons olive oil
1 tablespoon smoked paprika
½ tablespoon honey
pinch salt
¼ teaspoon white pepper

FOR THE SALAD

1. Rub red peppers with oil and salt and chargrill over an open flame. Place in a bowl, cover with plastic wrap and leave to steam and cool. Skin, remove seeds and cut into 1cm dice.
2. Place chopped peppers and remaining ingredients in a bowl and toss gently. Cover and place in the refrigerator while grilling the lamb chops (see pages 32 and 34). Dress just before serving.

FOR THE DRESSING

1. Place all dressing ingredients in a clean screw-top jar and shake well.

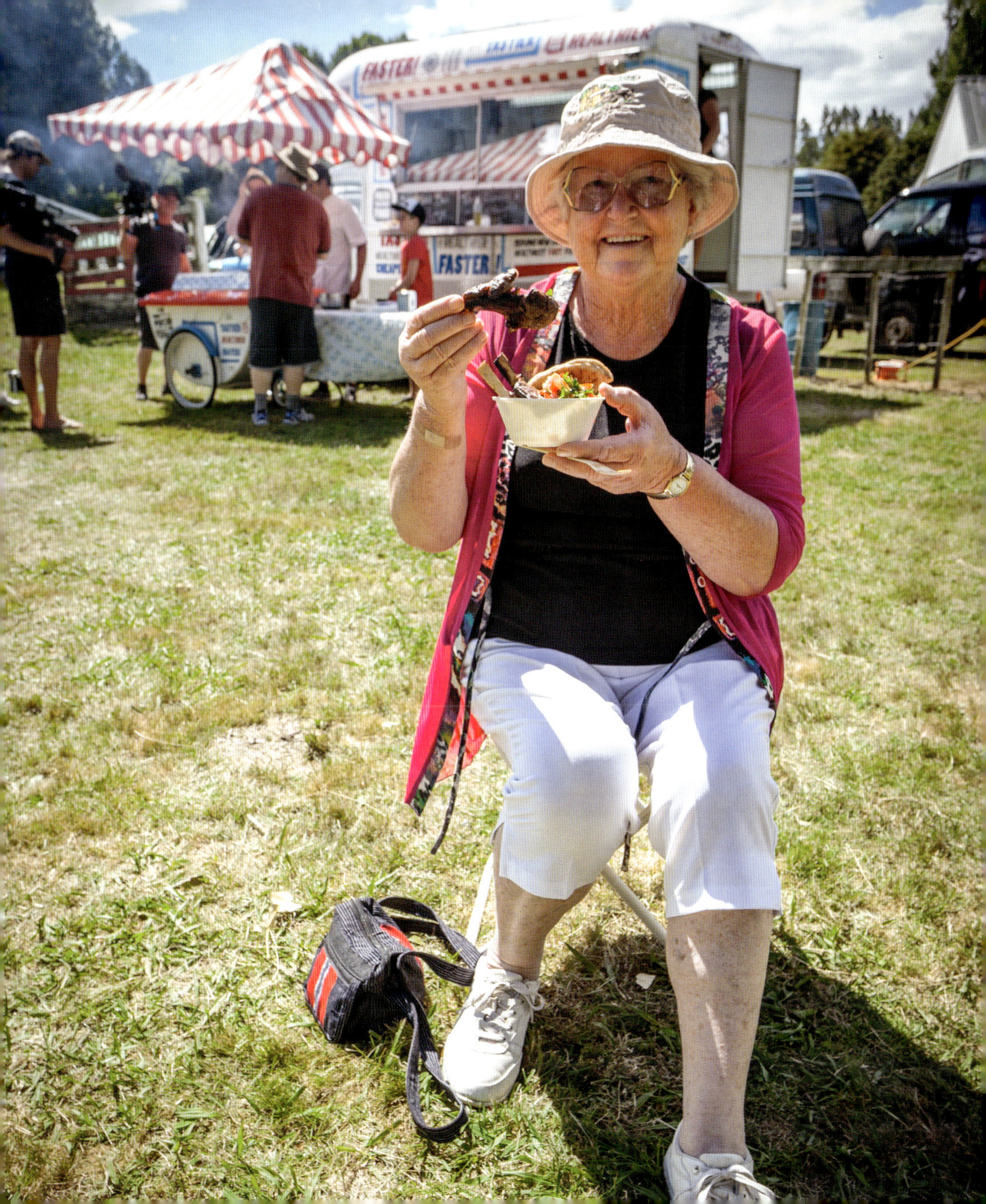
FASTER!
FASTER

This is my take on a South American empanada. You can stuff this bread with just about anything! Once you've got the hang of smoking things either in a smoker, the oven or a frying pan, you will never look back. Add two tablespoons of your favourite tea leaves to the rice for flavour.

Energy KJs	Protein	Total fat
576	6g	.7g

Saturated fat	Carbohydrate	Sodium
.1g	29g	72mg

Smoked Mushroom and Garlic Breads

Makes 6 • *Preparation time* 1 hour and 45 minutes • *Cooking time* about 6 minutes

WHOLEMEAL PIZZA DOUGH

150g high-grade or strong white flour
50g wholemeal flour
pinch salt
60ml low-fat milk
60ml water
7g dried yeast
¼ teaspoon sugar

SMOKED MUSHROOM AND GARLIC FILLING

1 cup rice for smoking
2 tablespoons tea leaves
300g mushrooms, peeled
1 bulb elephant garlic or 2 bulbs garlic

FOR THE DOUGH

1. Follow steps 1–4 on page 140.
2. Knead again and rest for 20 minutes before using.
3. Divide dough into six pieces, roll each piece out to a thin round, 12cm in diameter.

FOR THE FILLING

1. Preheat oven to 200°C. Place some rice and tea leaves in the bottom of a roasting dish.
2. Scrunch some aluminium foil, place on rice then add mushrooms, gill side down. Break open garlic a little to allow smoke to penetrate and place beside mushrooms. Cover dish with foil and cook until smoke fills the dish.
3. Once smoked and soft, chop mushrooms and squeeze out garlic flesh and combine.

TO ASSEMBLE

1. Divide filling mixture between rounds, placing filling in the centre. Fold over to enclose filling (as you would a calzone) and seal edges well using a fork.
2. Place on hot barbecue grill and cook until dough has puffed and is covered in grill marks.

COOL STORY, BABE.
Now go make me a sandwich
FASTER!
TASTIER
HEALTHIER
FASTER!
AgriSea
NEW ZEALAND
BBQ

Corra Anselmi
El Sizzling Chorizo

Corra is an authentic Argentinian gaucho (cowboy) and a master in the art of asado, the traditional Argentinean barbecue pit. After demolishing a whole cow with a chainsaw he showed me the art of slow cooking meat over an open fire for an entire night. You can taste his sensational meats and home-made chorizo at El Sizzling Chorizo in Ponsonby, Auckland.

thighs $30
(a taste of everything over 600gr $20
 $30

Provolone cheese with BBQ veges $26
chimichurri

El Sizzling CHORIZO

ARGENTINIAN BBQ

mexican standoff

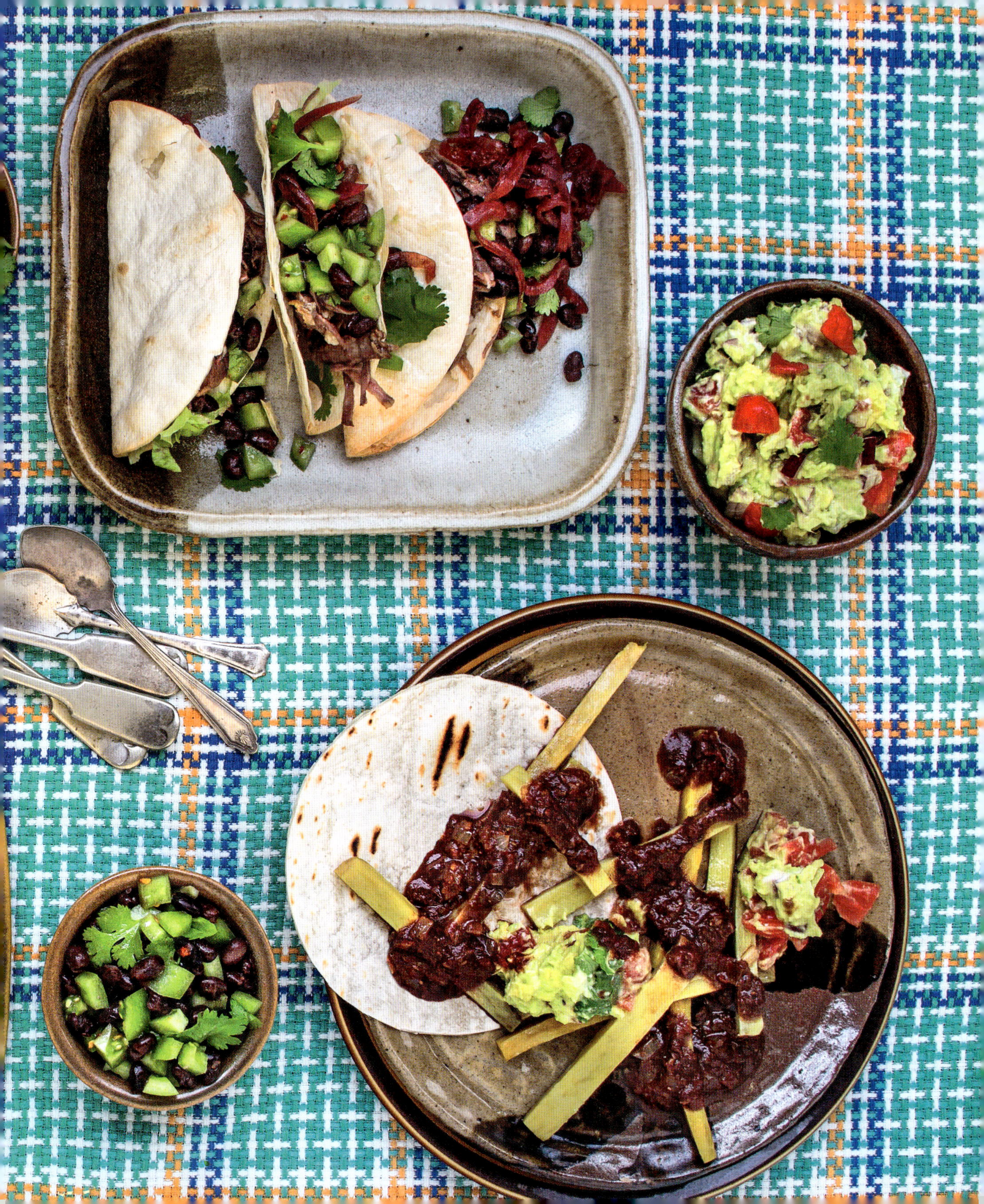

Golden kumara mole

Serves 6 • Preparation time 45 minutes • Cooking time 30 minutes

Energy KJs	Protein	Total fat
2424	9g	25g

Saturated fat	Carbohydrate	Sodium
4g	82g	500mg

MOLE
1 tablespoon olive oil
1 onion, finely diced
2 cloves garlic, crushed
1 x 400g can chopped tomatoes in juice
2 tablespoons dark cocoa powder
1 tablespoon brown sugar
1 tablespoon dry-roasted and ground cumin seeds
1 teaspoon dried oregano
¼ teaspoon each ground nutmeg, cinnamon and cloves
1 cup vegetable stock
1 cup water
¼ cup Mexican picante sauce

GOLDEN KUMARA
1kg golden kumara, peeled

GUACAMOLE
2 avocados, halved, stoned and peeled
2 tomatoes, skinned, halved, seeds removed and roughly chopped
½ red onion, finely chopped
juice of 1 lemon
1 tablespoon Greek yoghurt
pinch salt and white pepper

TO ASSEMBLE
6 soft corn or flour tortillas
¼ cup Greek yoghurt
¼ cup dry-roasted sunflower seeds
1 handful coriander leaves
few sprigs dill, roughly chopped

FOR THE MOLE
1. Heat oil in a medium-sized saucepan over a low heat and add onion and garlic. Cook for 5 minutes until soft.
2. Add remaining ingredients and simmer mole for 25–30 minutes until thick.

FOR THE KUMARA
1. Preheat oven to 170°C.
2. Cut golden kumara into long batons about 1cm thick. Place in a roasting dish, cover and roast for 30 minutes until tender.

FOR THE GUACAMOLE
1. Place avocados in a mortar and pestle (in Mexico they would use a molcajete), and lightly pound, leaving avocado still a little chunky. Alternatively, avocado can be lightly mashed using a fork. Stir through tomatoes, red onion, lemon juice and Greek yoghurt. Season with salt and white pepper.

TO ASSEMBLE
1. Heat tortillas in a large frying pan until the surface colours a little and begins to blister.
2. Fill with golden kumara, spoon over some mole and finish with guacamole, Greek yoghurt, sunflower seeds and herbs. (Add some shredded iceberg lettuce, if wished). To serve — see dish at lower right on page 43.

Tequila Chicken Tortillas

Serves 6 • Preparation time 45 minutes • Cooking time 1 hour

Energy KJs	Protein	Total fat
3499	47g	60g

Saturated fat	Carbohydrate	Sodium
15g	31g	540mg

TEQUILA-POACHED CHICKEN
1.5kg chicken
1½ litres vegetable stock
¼ cup tequila
3 stalks coriander root, crushed with a large knife

CORN SALSA
3 corn cobs, husks on
3 shallots, sliced into thin rings
60g sheep's feta, crumbled

LIME EMULSION
2 eggs, soft boiled for 5 minutes, peeled
zest and juice of 2 limes
100ml grapeseed oil
pinch salt and white pepper
vegetable stock to thin, if needed

TO ASSEMBLE
6 soft flour tortillas
¼ iceberg lettuce, shredded
1 handful coriander leaves

FOR THE CHICKEN
1. Place chicken in a large saucepan and cover with stock, tequila and coriander stalks.
2. Bring just to the boil, reduce heat to low and poach chicken for 1 hour. Leave chicken to cool a little in liquid. When cool enough to handle, pull chicken meat off bones and shred.

FOR THE SALSA
1. Preheat oven to 180°C.
2. Place corn in a roasting dish and roast for 30 minutes. Remove from oven and pull away husks and silks.
3. Stand cob on its end on a board and, using a sharp knife and cutting downwards, cut the kernels as close to the cob as possible. Repeat with remaining cobs.
4. Place kernels in a bowl and toss through shallots and feta.

FOR THE EMULSION
1. Place soft-boiled eggs and zest and juice of 1 lime in a food processor. Process for 30 seconds. Very slowly drizzle in oil through feed tube until you have an emulsion. Season with salt and white pepper, adding extra lime juice to taste. If necessary, thin with vegetable stock.

TO ASSEMBLE
1. Heat tortillas in a large frying pan until the surface colours a little and begins to blister. Mix a little lime emulsion through corn salsa to moisten. Top tortillas with shredded chicken, shredded lettuce, corn salsa and finish with coriander leaves. Serve extra lime emulsion separately. To serve — see dish at top left on page 42.

I made these for the taco challenge with Mexikai. The slow-cooked beef is full of flavour and shreds beautifully. Cooking the beef may take some time but if you make it in bulk you'll be able to eat these delicious tacos for a week! Freeze if you need a break.

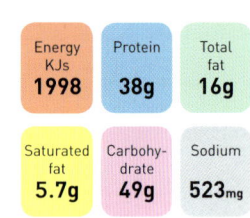

Energy KJs	Protein	Total fat
1998	38g	16g

Saturated fat	Carbohydrate	Sodium
5.7g	49g	523mg

Tacos with Shredded Beef

Serves 6 • Preparation time 1 hour • Cooking time 3–4 hours

BEEF
1 onion, chopped
1 carrot, peeled and chopped
1 small leek, white part only, sliced
1.2kg beef short rib
1 tablespoon Mexican chipotle sauce
1 cup vegetable stock
2 stalks coriander root, crushed with a large knife

CHIPOTLE CARAMELISED ONIONS
2 red onions, very thinly sliced
4 tablespoons red wine vinegar
2 tablespoons agave nectar
1 tablespoon Mexican chipotle sauce

FOR THE BEEF
1. Preheat oven to 160°C.
2. Place vegetables in the bottom of a roasting dish that will fit short rib snugly.
3. Heat a frying pan over high heat. Rub a little oil over short rib and brown on all sides. Transfer to roasting dish.
4. Spread Mexican chipotle sauce over short rib, pour in stock and scatter around crushed coriander stalks.
5. Cover roasting dish and place in oven and braise for 3–4 hours until meat is falling off the bone. Remove and shred meat using two forks.

FOR THE ONIONS
1. Place all ingredients in a heavy-based saucepan, cover with a lid and place over low heat.
2. Simmer for 20 minutes, remove lid and continue to cook for a further 20 minutes, stirring occasionally, until onions are caramelised and all the liquid has reduced.

Recipe continued over page . . .

TASTIER HEALTHIER FRESH TAKEAWAY FOOD

SERVING UP DELICIOUS HEALTHY, RESTAURANT QUALITY FAST FOOD SINCE 2010

Tacos with Shredded Beef continued . . .

TOMATILLO SALSA
4–6 fresh tomatillos, husks removed, halved, cored and cut into small dice
1 x 400g can black beans, rinsed and drained
¼ cup chopped coriander leaves
juice of 3 limes
2 teaspoons grapeseed oil
pinch salt
pinch chilli flakes

TO ASSEMBLE
6 soft corn tortillas
¼ iceberg lettuce, shredded
1 handful mint leaves

FOR THE SALSA
1. Combine all ingredients in a bowl. Cover and refrigerate until ready to use.

TO ASSEMBLE
1. Heat a chargrill or large frying pan until hot. Cook each tortilla for 15 seconds on each side, and then for a further 15 seconds on the first side.
2. Place some lettuce in a tortilla, top with beef, caramelised onion and salsa, and finish with mint leaves. Repeat with remaining tortillas. To serve — see dish at top right on page 43.

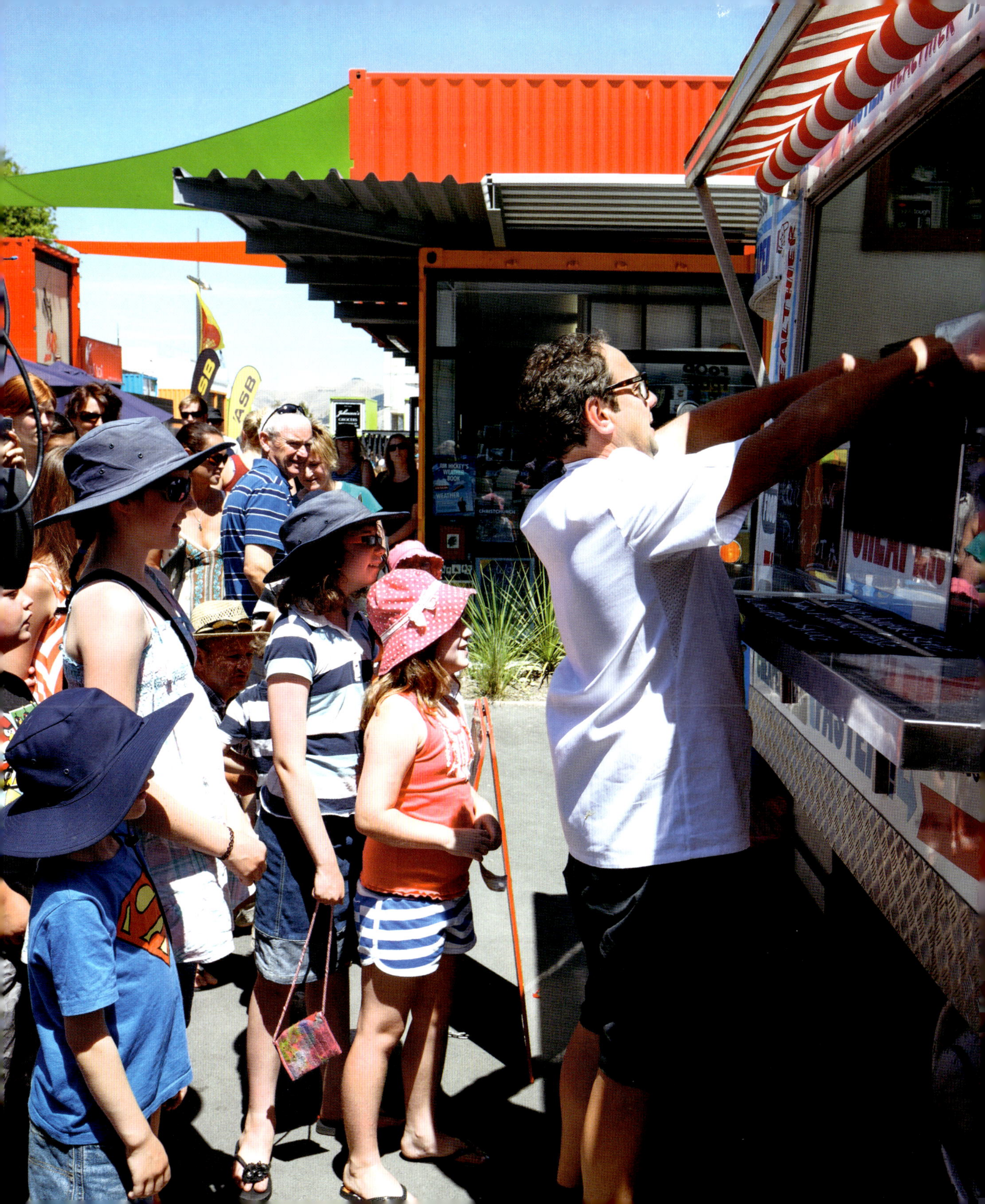
ASB

THE EAST CHINESE

JAPANESE AND THAI

You can buy your dumpling wrappers from an Asian supermarket or try the freezer aisle in your local supermarket. You can pretty much put anything in them — here is a vegetable version.

Energy KJs	Protein	Total fat
330	3g	.7g

Saturated fat	Carbohydrate	Sodium
0g	17g	128mg

Vegetable Dumplings

Makes 12 dumplings • Preparation time 45–50 minutes • Cooking time 20 minutes

VEGETABLE DUMPLINGS

1 onion, finely chopped
4 cloves garlic, finely chopped
2 bunches baby bok choy white stems, finely sliced
2 bunches baby pak choy white stems, finely sliced
200g Chinese white turnip, peeled and cut into very small dice
100g shiitake mushrooms, finely sliced
1 tablespoon low-salt soy sauce
2 bunches baby bok choy green leaves, sliced
2 bunches baby pak choy green leaves, sliced
12 dumpling wrappers

FOR THE DUMPLINGS

1. Place onion and garlic in a frying pan with a dash of oil and cook until soft, about 5 minutes. Add finely sliced white stems of bok choy and pak choy, turnip and shiitake mushrooms. Cook for a further 5 minutes, then stir in soy sauce. Transfer to a plate to cool.
2. In the same pan over a high heat, cook sliced green leaves of bok choy and pak choy until just wilted. Place in a clean tea towel and squeeze well to remove all moisture, if necessary. Combine all filling ingredients and leave to cool.
3. Hold one dumpling wrapper in the palm of your hand. Place a good tablespoon of vegetable mixture in the middle and with your finger or a brush moisten edges with a little water. Fold over to form a crescent, crimping well to seal the edges together.
4. Place on bench top, standing upright, then tuck one end in and crimp, then tuck and crimp the other end. Repeat with remaining dumpling wrappers.
5. Have your steamer ready to go.

Recipe continued over page . . .

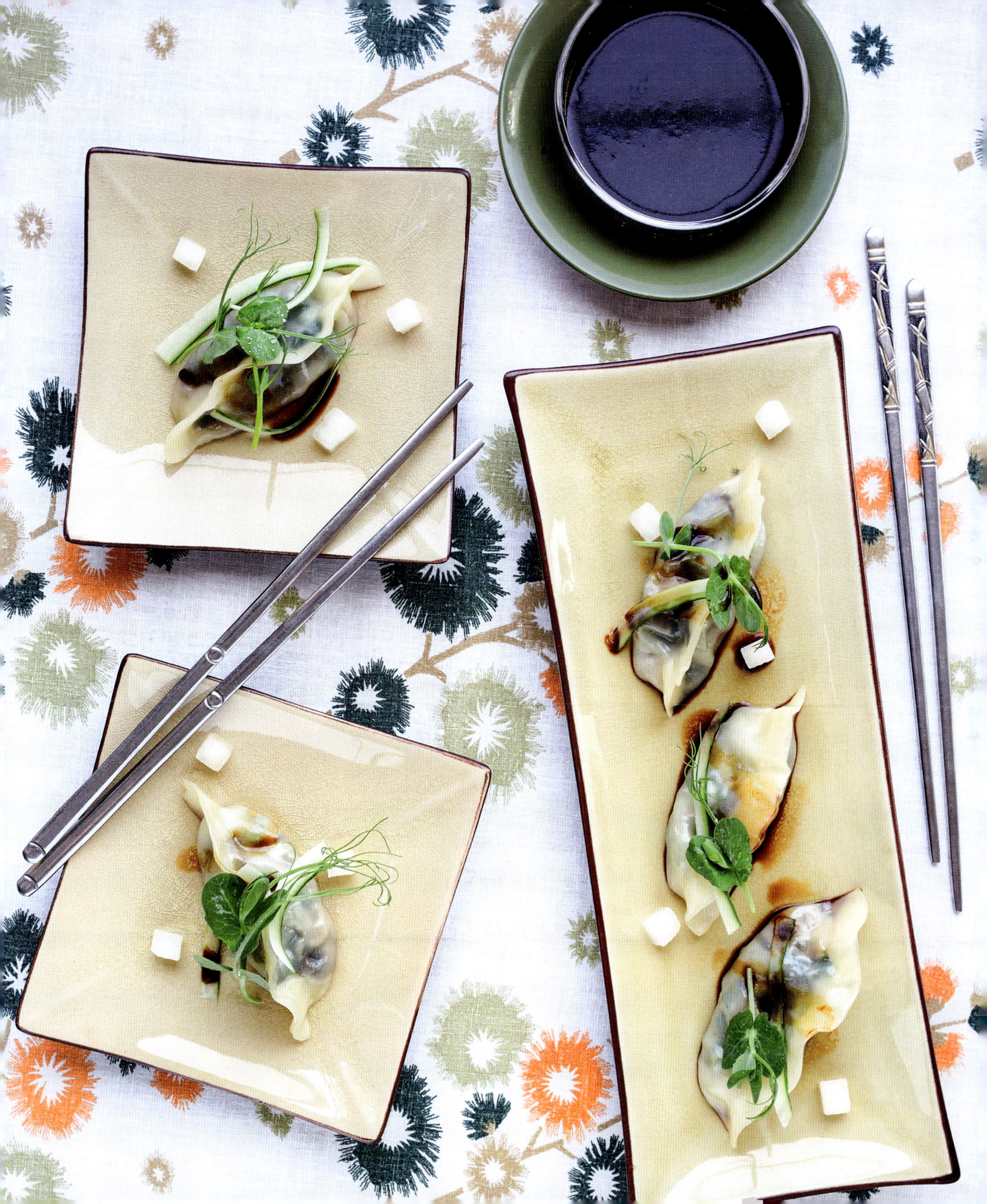

Vegetable Dumplings continued . . .

BLACK VINEGAR DRESSING

4 tablespoons black vinegar
1 teaspoon toasted sesame oil
1 teaspoon honey
½ teaspoon low-salt soy sauce

CUCUMBER AND NASHI PEAR

1 Lebanese cucumber, cut in half lengthwise and deseeded
1 nashi pear, peeled and cut into small dice
juice of 1 lemon

snow pea shoots and Asian micro greens

FOR THE DRESSING

1. Combine ingredients in a small sauce bowl and set aside.

FOR THE CUCUMBER AND NASHI PEAR

1. Use a vegetable peeler to peel off thick ribbons of cucumber.
2. Place diced nashi pear in cold water with a good squeeze of lemon juice to prevent browning.

TO ASSEMBLE

1. Place dumplings in a steamer and steam for about 5 minutes or until soft.
2. Serve garnished with cucumber ribbons, diced nashi pear, snow pea shoots and Asian micro greens. Serve with black vinegar dressing.

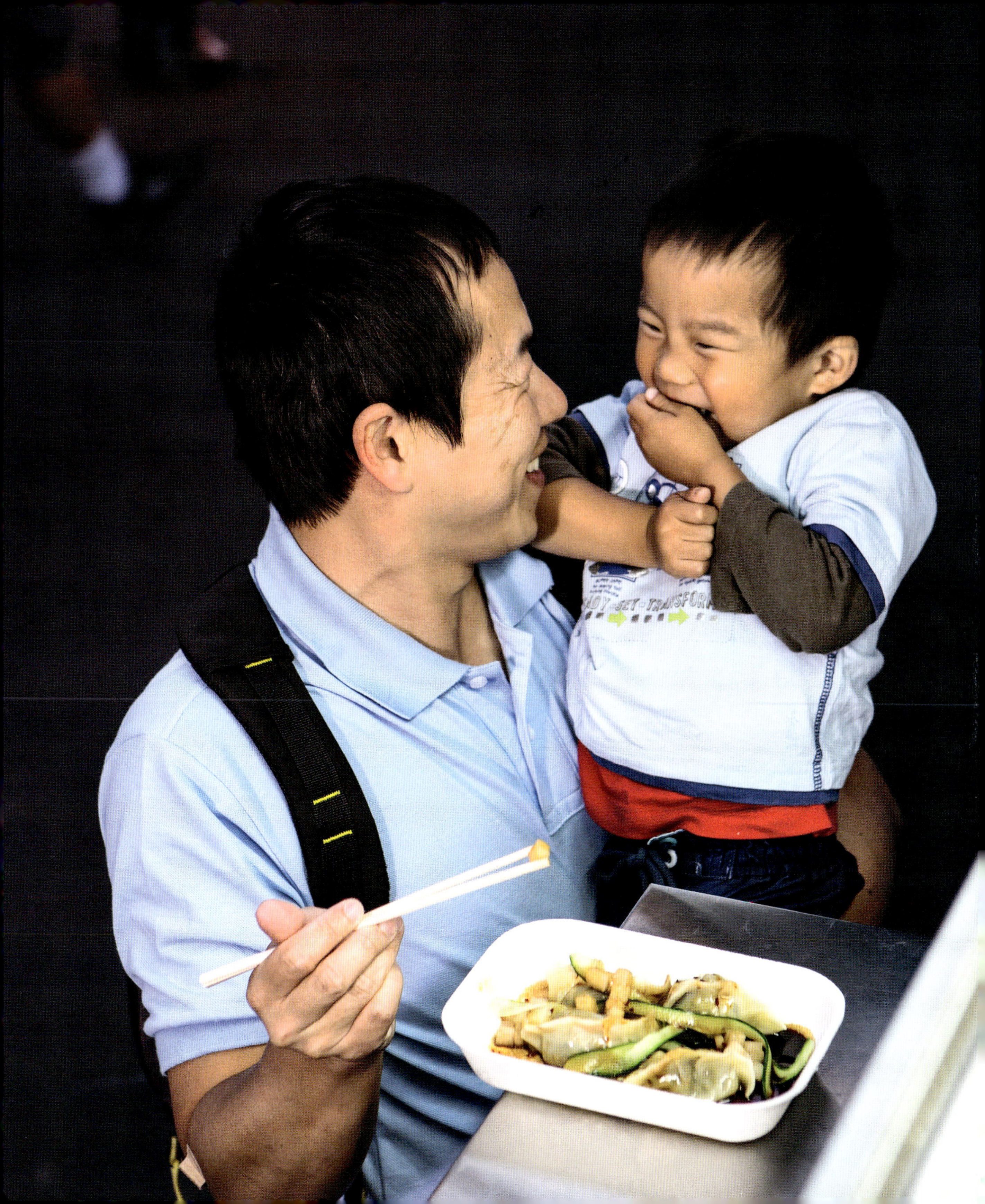

This is my Chinese take on a raw energy salad. It's chock-full of goodness and is great with shredded chicken for a meal in itself.

Energy KJs	Protein	Total fat
517	6.5g	6.4g

Saturated fat	Carbohydrate	Sodium
.7g	13g	139mg

Asian-inspired slaw

Serves 6 • Preparation time 35 minutes

DRESSING
10cm knob fresh ginger, peeled
juice of 2 small mandarins
1 tablespoon low-salt soy sauce
1 tablespoon honey
pinch white pepper

SALAD
¼ Chinese cabbage (wong bok), very finely shredded
2 stems Chinese broccoli (gai laan), very finely shredded
2 carrots, peeled and julienned
1 beetroot, peeled and julienned
small bunch chive flower shoots, snipped
250g shredded tofu
½ cup dry-roasted almonds, roughly chopped
2 tablespoons toasted sesame seeds

FOR THE DRESSING
1. Grate ginger, then squeeze for juice, discarding ginger fibre. Place juice in a small bowl with remaining ingredients. Set aside, then whisk before using.

FOR THE SALAD
1. Place Chinese cabbage, Chinese broccoli, carrot, beetroot, chive flower shoots, tofu and almonds in a large serving bowl.
2. Toss with dressing, sprinkle with sesame seeds and serve.

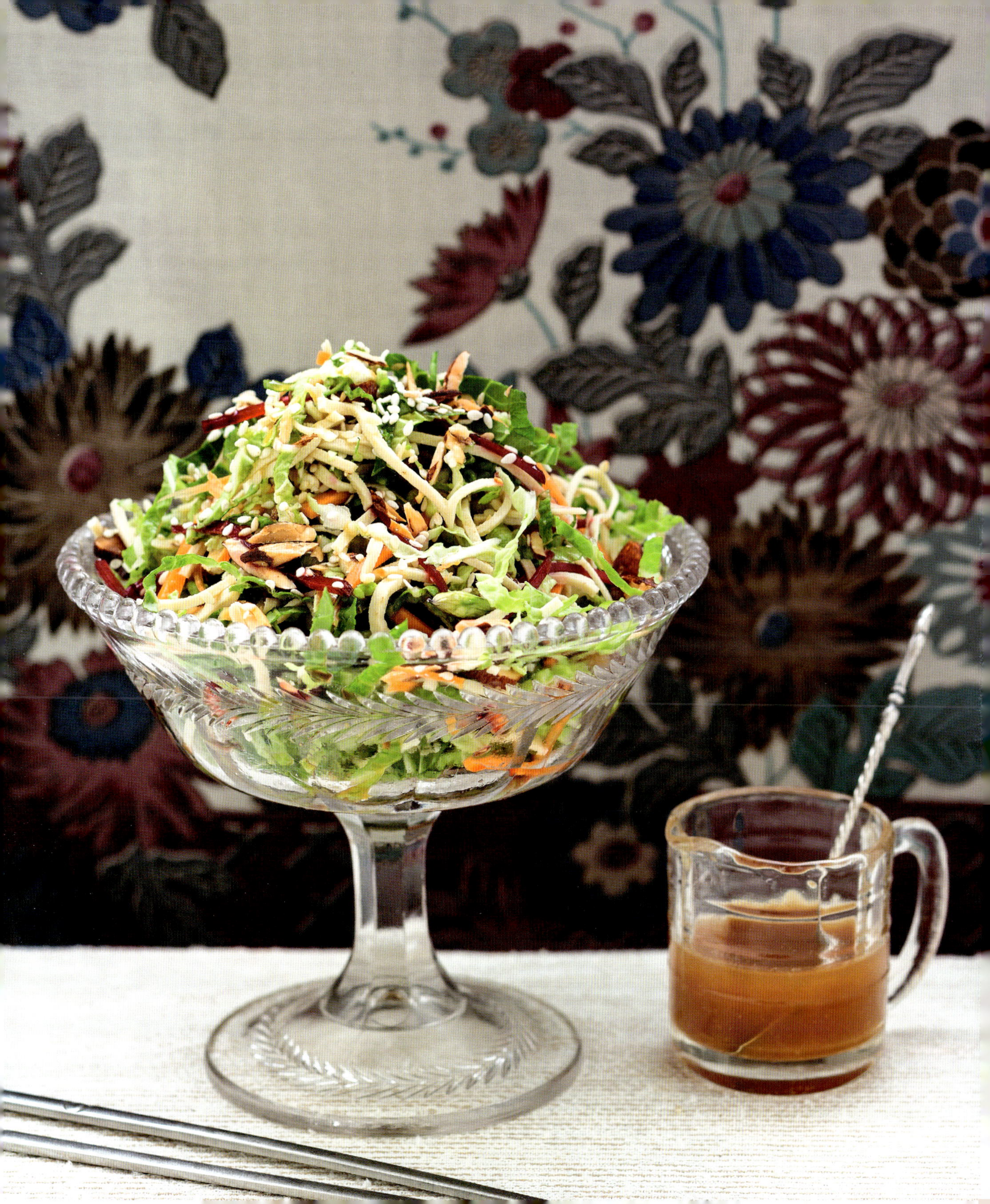

This fresh oyster sauce works with just about any Chinese green — choy sum, bok choy, pak choy — if it's green, it's a dream!

Energy KJs	Protein	Total fat
207	5.6g	1g

Saturated fat	Carbohydrate	Sodium
.2g	5g	335mg

Choy Sum with Oyster Sauce

Serves 6 • Preparation time 20 minutes • Cooking time 12 minutes

OYSTER SAUCE

1 onion, finely chopped
6 cloves garlic, finely chopped
1 tablespoon thyme leaves
150g fresh oyster meat
3 tablespoons water
1 tablespoon low-salt soy sauce
½ tablespoon dark soy sauce

CHOY SUM

12 small or 6 large stems choy sum
1 star anise
small piece cinnamon stick

FOR THE SAUCE

1. Place onion in a small saucepan with a dash of oil and cook until soft. Add garlic and thyme and cook for a further 1 minute.
2. Add oyster meat and water and cook on a low heat for 5 minutes.
3. Place in a blender with soy sauce and dark soy sauce and blend until smooth.
4. Transfer to a bowl, cover and refrigerate.

FOR THE CHOY SUM

1. Cook choy sum in boiling water infused with star anise and cinnamon until just tender, 1–2 minutes. Alternatively, steam, with the star anise and cinnamon in the water, until just tender.

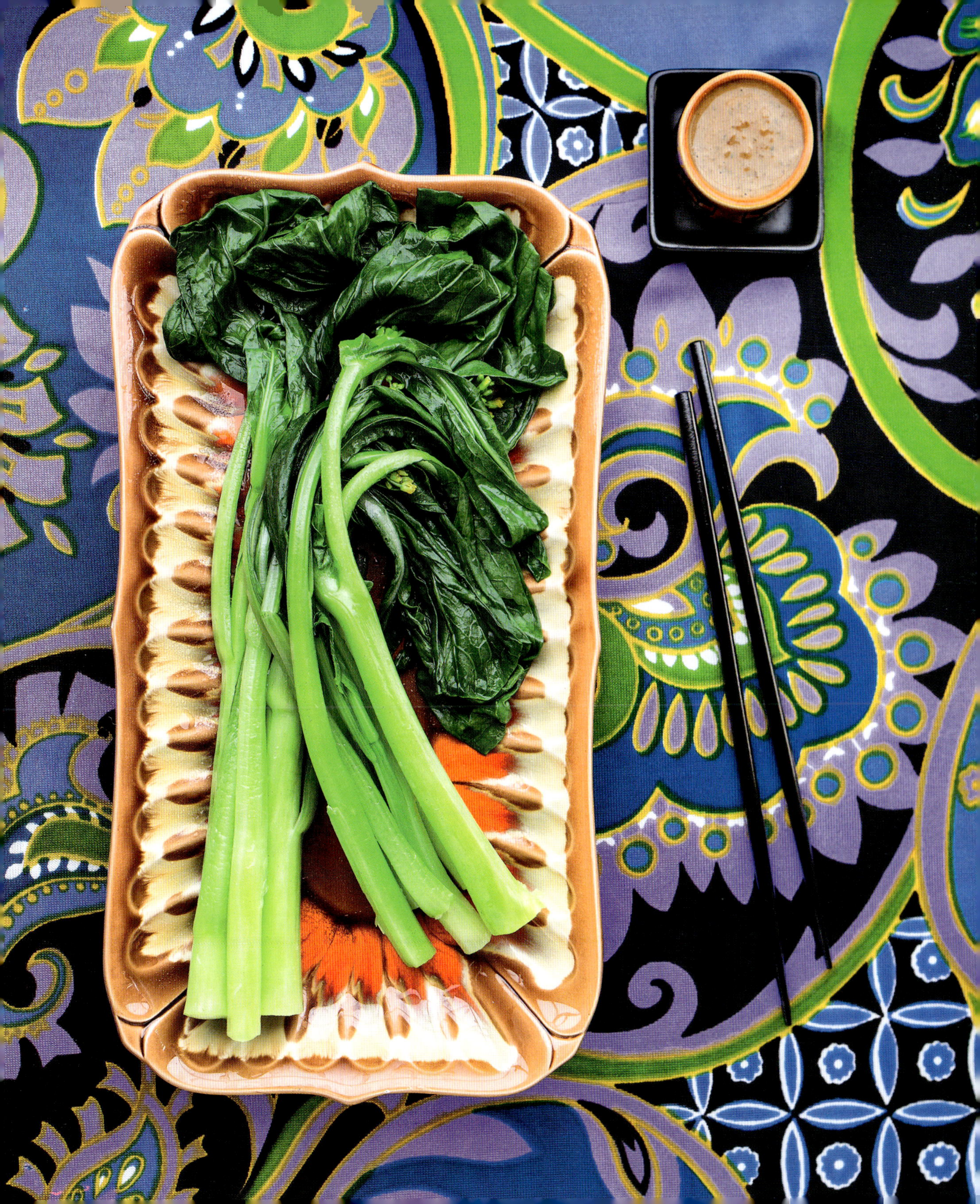

Alan Fong
Perfect Produce

Alan Fong oversees 300 hectares of Chinese vegetables, and supplies many of the best Asian restaurants with his Perfect Produce brand of greens. The farm was established by his father in the 1940s and Alan is a firm believer in finding new ways for Chinese vegetables to slip into our diet. He told me the importance of texture in Chinese cooking. The crunch factor is great for healthy eating, too. If a vege is still crunchy it's likely to still be holding lots of nutrients, so all the better I say!

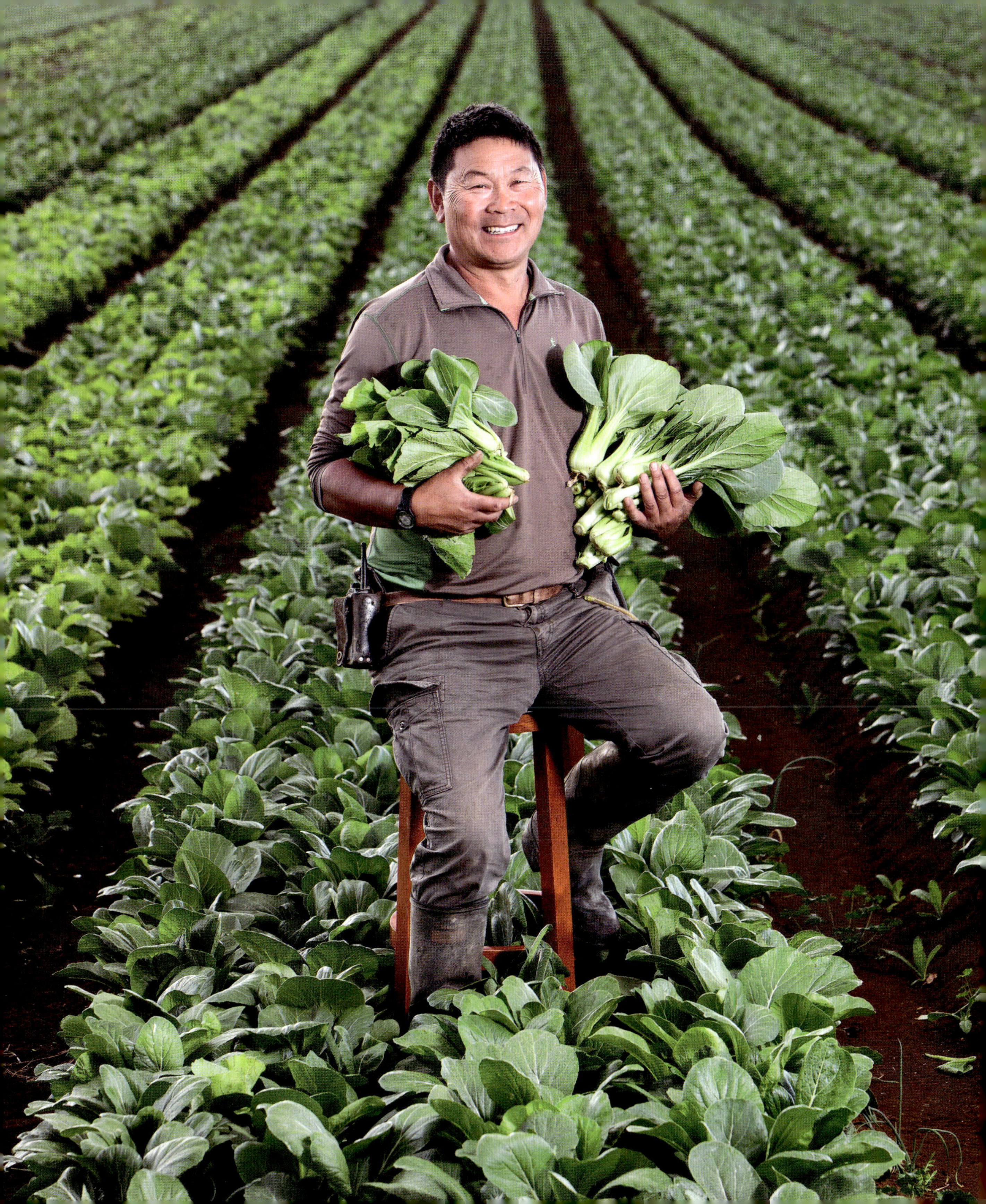

These fish cakes are full of flavour and have a melt-in-the-mouth texture. They will work with any fish, but tarakihi is really special.

Energy KJs	Protein	Total fat
175	5g	.3g

Saturated fat	Carbohydrate	Sodium
0g	5g	472mg

Thai Fish Cakes

Makes 12 fish cakes • Preparation time 40 minutes • Cooking time 10 minutes

POMEGRANATE SWEET CHILLI SAUCE

MAKES: ½ CUP

3 red chillies, deseeded and finely sliced
½ cup red wine vinegar
½ cup pomegranate juice
6 tablespoons coconut sugar
4 tablespoons liquid honey

FISH CAKES

300g white fish fillets, such as tarakihi, cut into chunks
4 tablespoons Thai red curry paste (see recipe page 66)
3 tablespoons fish sauce
2 egg whites, lightly beaten
5 kaffir lime leaves, very finely sliced
½ cup green beans, cut into thin round slices

Asian micro greens or coriander, mint or Thai basil leaves for garnish

FOR THE SAUCE

1. Place all ingredients except honey in a small saucepan and cook over medium heat until reduced by at least half.
2. Add honey and when cool, pour into a jar and place in refrigerator until ready to use. The sauce will keep in the refrigerator for 2 weeks.

FOR THE FISH CAKES

1. Place fish in a food processor and process until fish chunks have broken down. Do not over-process. Add curry paste, fish sauce and egg whites and process until just combined.
2. Transfer to a bowl, add lime leaves and beans and mix together.
3. Divide mixture into 12 and with your hands mould into cakes.
4. Lightly spray a large frying pan with oil spray and cook fish cakes for about 3 minutes, turning once, until golden brown on both sides and just cooked in the centre.
5. To serve, place fish cakes on a serving plate, drizzle with a little sauce and garnish with micro greens or suggested herbs.

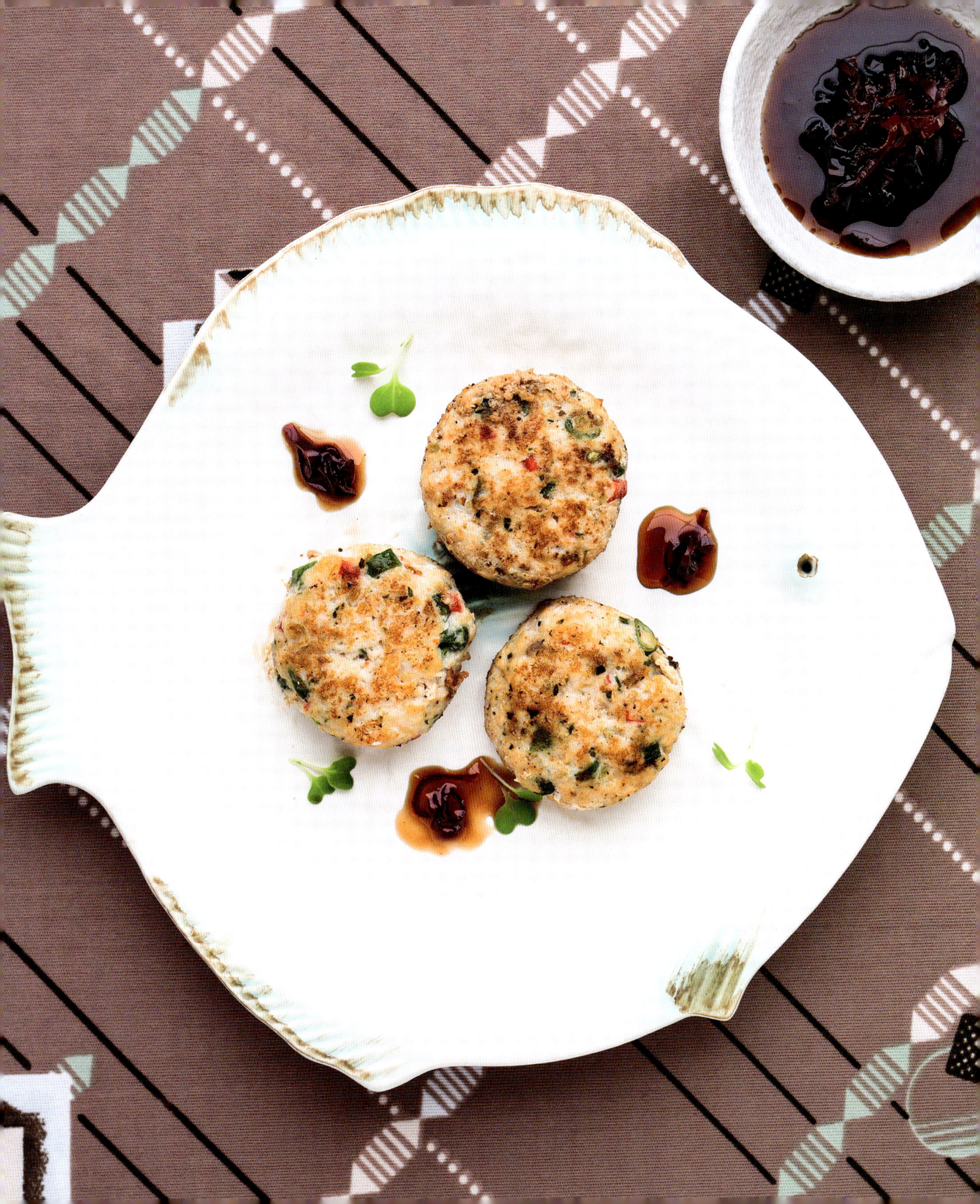

This is a combination of a Pad Thai and a Som Tam. It has the flavours of the crushed peanuts and tofu but with the freshness of a papaya salad. Delicious.

Pad Thai

Serves 2 • Preparation time 1 hour • Cooking time 8-10 minutes

Energy KJs	Protein	Total fat
1204	12g	12g

Saturated fat	Carbohydrate	Sodium
2g	36g	190mg

TAMARIND DRESSING

MAKES: 1 CUP

3 tablespoons tamarind pulp
1 cup hot water
1 small red chilli, deseeded and finely sliced
½ cup vegetable stock
2 tablespoons fish sauce
2 tablespoons honey
pinch white pepper

PAD THAI

200g dried flat rice noodles
1 tablespoon peanut oil
200g firm tofu, cut into small cubes
¼ Savoy cabbage, finely sliced lengthwise
2 baby bok choy, finely sliced lengthwise
4 spring onions, finely sliced lengthwise
½ green papaya, peeled, seeds removed and sliced into long thin strips
1 cup mung bean sprouts
small bunch coriander, roots finely chopped and leaves picked
½ cup dry-roasted cashew nuts, chopped

FOR THE DRESSING

1. Soak tamarind pulp in hot water. When cool, use your hands to mash pulp up. Push pulp through a sieve. Retain purée and discard pulp.
2. Add chilli, vegetable stock, fish sauce, honey and white pepper to tamarind purée. Place in a jar and refrigerate until ready to use. The dressing will keep in the refrigerator for 10 days.

FOR THE PAD THAI

1. Soak rice noodles in warm water for 1 hour or according to directions on packet.
2. Heat peanut oil in a large wok or frying pan over a high heat. Add tofu and cook until golden brown on all sides. Remove from wok and set aside.
3. Add green vegetables to wok and stir-fry until just wilted. Add papaya, drained rice noodles and 3 tablespoons tamarind dressing, and toss.
4. Add mung bean sprouts, chopped coriander roots and most of the coriander leaves and toss well. Return tofu to pan and toss again.
5. To serve, place Pad Thai in serving bowls and top with cashew nuts and remaining coriander leaves.

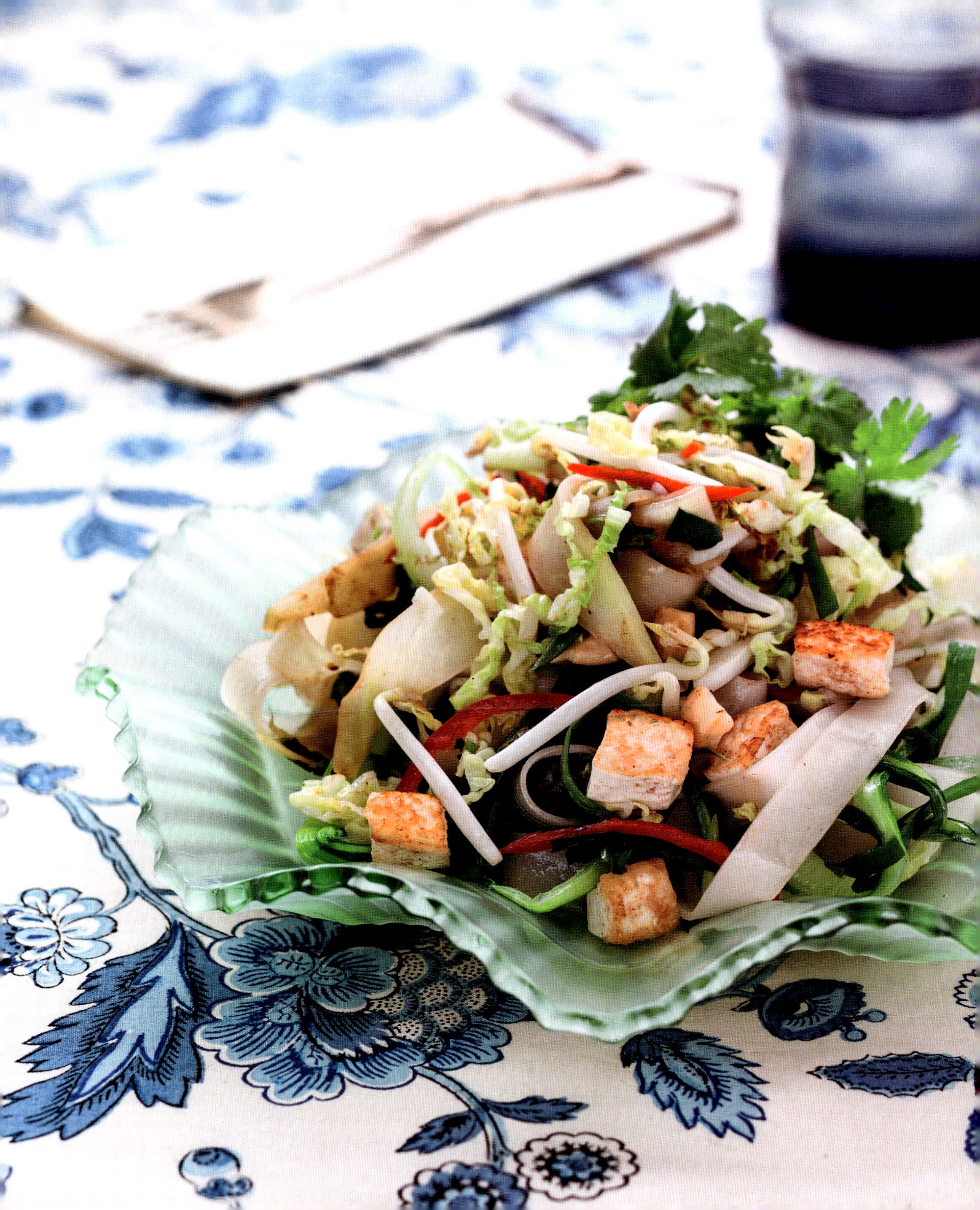

My take on Pad Ka Prao — a popular stir fry with deep-fried basil. I wanted to take the freshness of the basil and bring it to life with heaps of herbs, so it's just a fresh flavour explosion.

Energy KJs	Protein	Total fat
792	26g	4g

Saturated fat	Carbohydrate	Sodium
1.6g	14g	706mg

Braised Beef Salad

Serves 6 • Preparation time 1 hour • Cooking time 1 hour and 20 minutes

THAI RED CURRY PASTE
MAKES: 1½ CUPS

5 red chillies, deseeded and roughly chopped
5 coriander roots, well washed and roughly chopped
4 shallots, roughly chopped
4 cloves garlic, chopped
3 kaffir lime leaves, roughly sliced
1 stalk lemongrass, outer leaves removed and roughly chopped
1 knob galangal, chopped
2 tablespoons dried shrimps
½ teaspoon dry-roasted coriander seeds, crushed
juice of 3 lemons
1 tablespoon fish sauce

600g beef topside

FOR THE CURRY PASTE AND BEEF

1. Preheat oven to 160°C.
2. Place all ingredients except lemon juice, fish sauce and beef in a food processor and process until smooth. Add lemon juice and fish sauce and process to a paste. The paste will keep in the refrigerator for up to a week.
3. Coat beef topside in about ½ cup red curry paste, wrap in aluminium foil. Place in a roasting dish and roast for 1 hour and 20 minutes. Remove from oven and leave to rest for at least 30 minutes before slicing into thin strips.

Recipe continued over page . . .

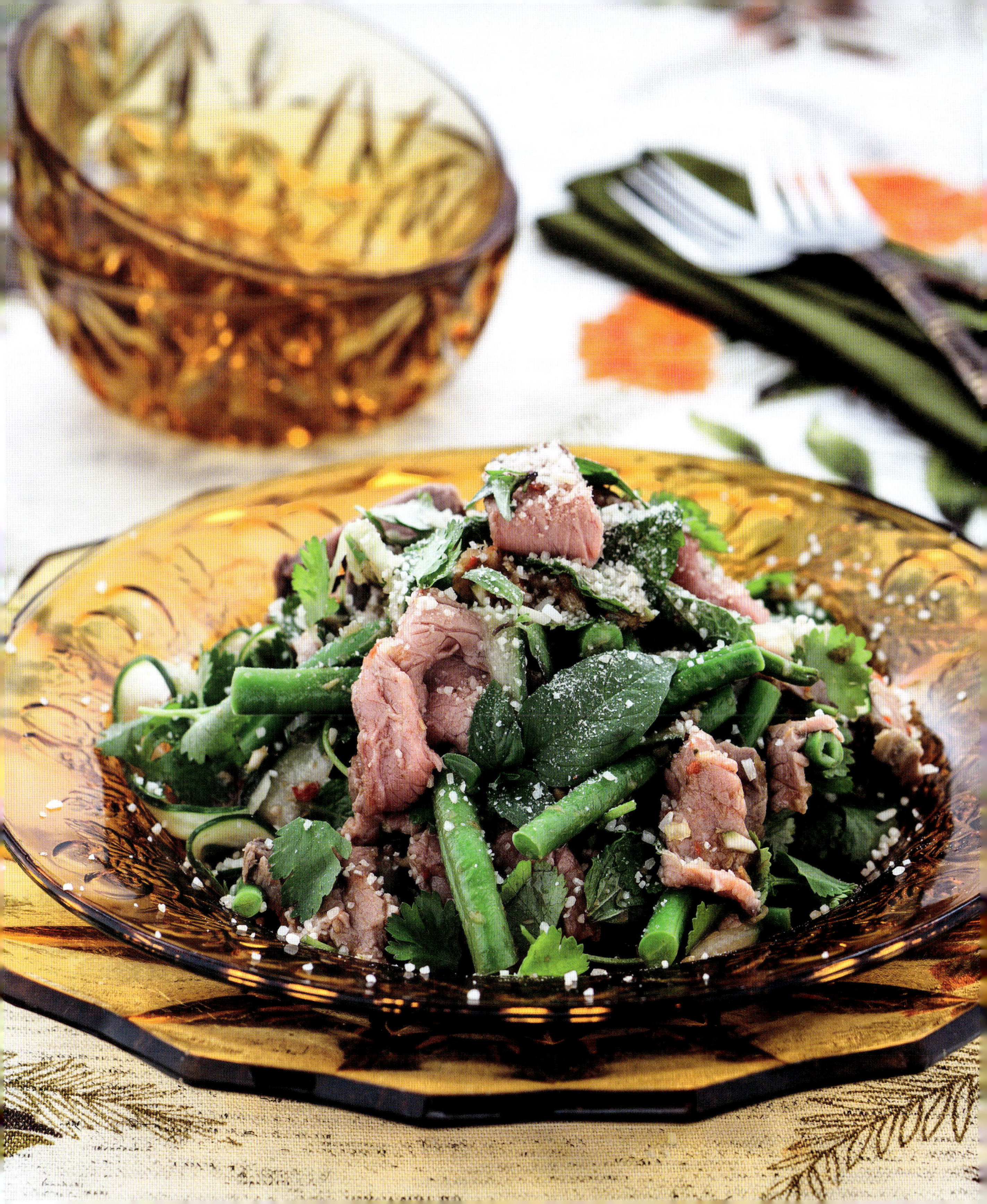

Braised Beef Salad continued . . .

NAM JIM
zest and juice of 2 limes
2 red chillies, deseeded and roughly chopped
2 coriander roots, well washed and roughly chopped
2 shallots, roughly chopped
½ knob galangal, chopped
1 tablespoon fish sauce
2 tablespoons coconut sugar

SALAD
200g snake beans, chopped into small pieces
1 small telegraph cucumber, deseeded
1 cup coriander leaves
1 cup mint leaves
1 cup Thai basil leaves

TOASTED RICE
½ cup brown jasmine rice, soaked in cold water for 5 minutes

FOR THE NAM JIM
1. Place all ingredients in a mortar and pestle and pound into a dressing. Keep in a jar in refrigerator until ready to use.

FOR THE SALAD
1. Cook snake beans in boiling water until bite tender. Drain and, if wished, refresh under cold water. Alternatively, steam or stir-fry snake beans. Set aside to cool.
2. Using a vegetable peeler, cut cucumber into ribbons and place in a large bowl. Add picked herbs, cooled snake beans and toss together.

FOR THE RICE
1. Drain and dry rice well.
2. Place in a dry wok or frying pan and stir-fry over a low heat until rice is fragrant and toasted, about 10 minutes. Allow to cool.
3. Place in a mortar and pestle and pound to a powder. (The powder can be stored in an airtight container for 2 weeks.)

TO ASSEMBLE
1. Add beef to salad and dress with nam jim. Place on a serving platter and sprinkle over some toasted rice.

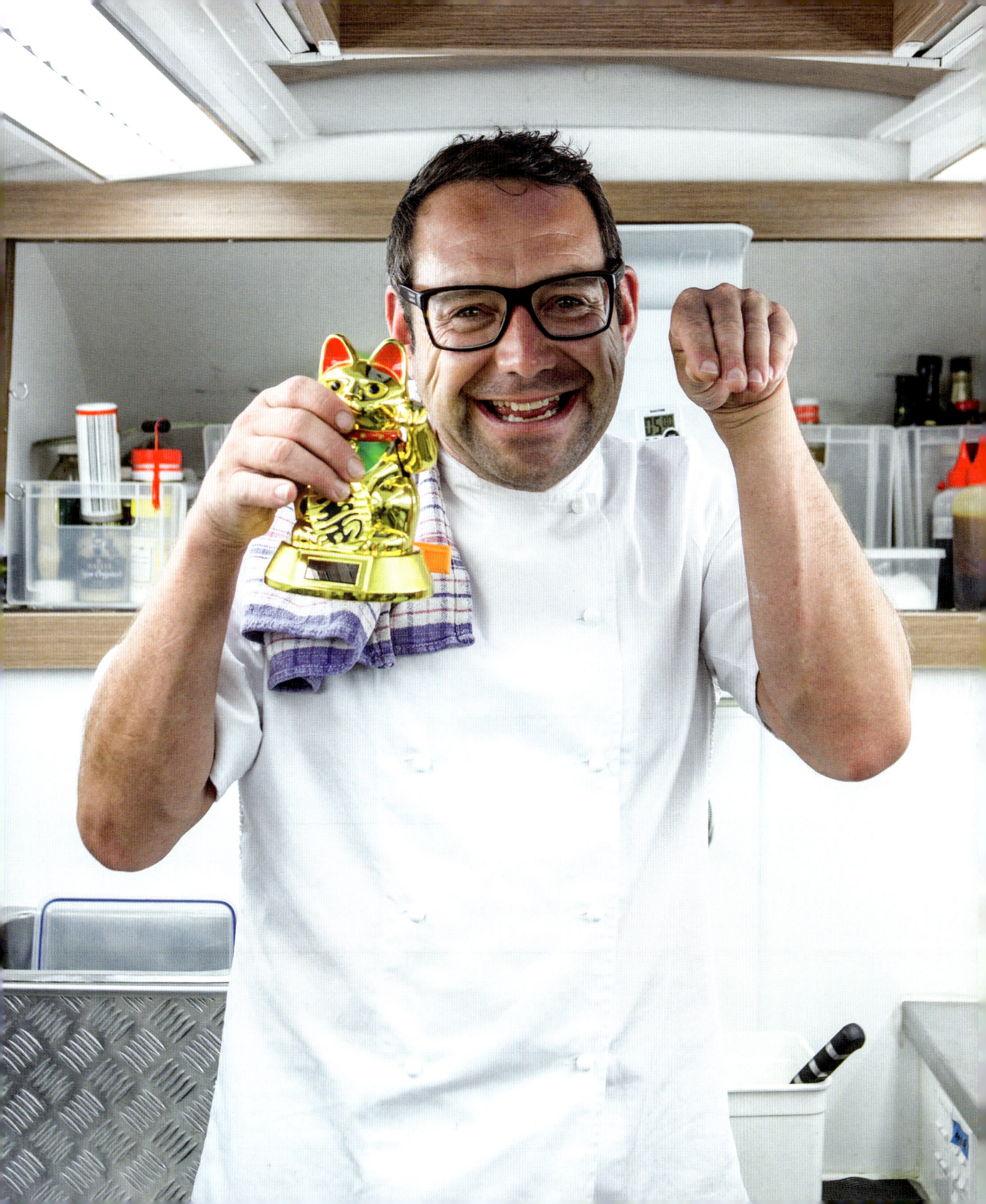

In Thailand drinks are often served in plastic bags on the street. I'm not sure why but I presume it's because bags are so cheap. It's like carrying around a bag of goldfish, except you can drink the liquid!

Energy KJs	Protein	Total fat
255	4g	1.8g

Saturated fat	Carbohydrate	Sodium
1g	7g	61mg

Thai Tea Bag

Makes 6 • Preparation time 20 minutes

TEA SYRUP

MAKES: 3 CUPS

4 green cardamom pods
4 cloves
4 star anise
3 tablespoons black tea leaves
3 cups boiling water
3 teaspoons stevia sugar substitute granules

TEA BAG

6 cups ice
3 cups tea syrup
3 cups low-fat milk
6 plastic lolly bags
a few mint leaves
6 straws

FOR THE SYRUP

1. In a large heatproof jug, place spices and black tea leaves and pour over boiling water. Leave to cool and infuse.
2. Strain through a fine sieve into another jug and stir in stevia.

FOR THE TEA BAGS

1. Put ice, tea syrup and milk into a jug. Stand 6 plastic bags in 6 glasses, and pour in iced tea. Add a few mint leaves and drink with a straw.

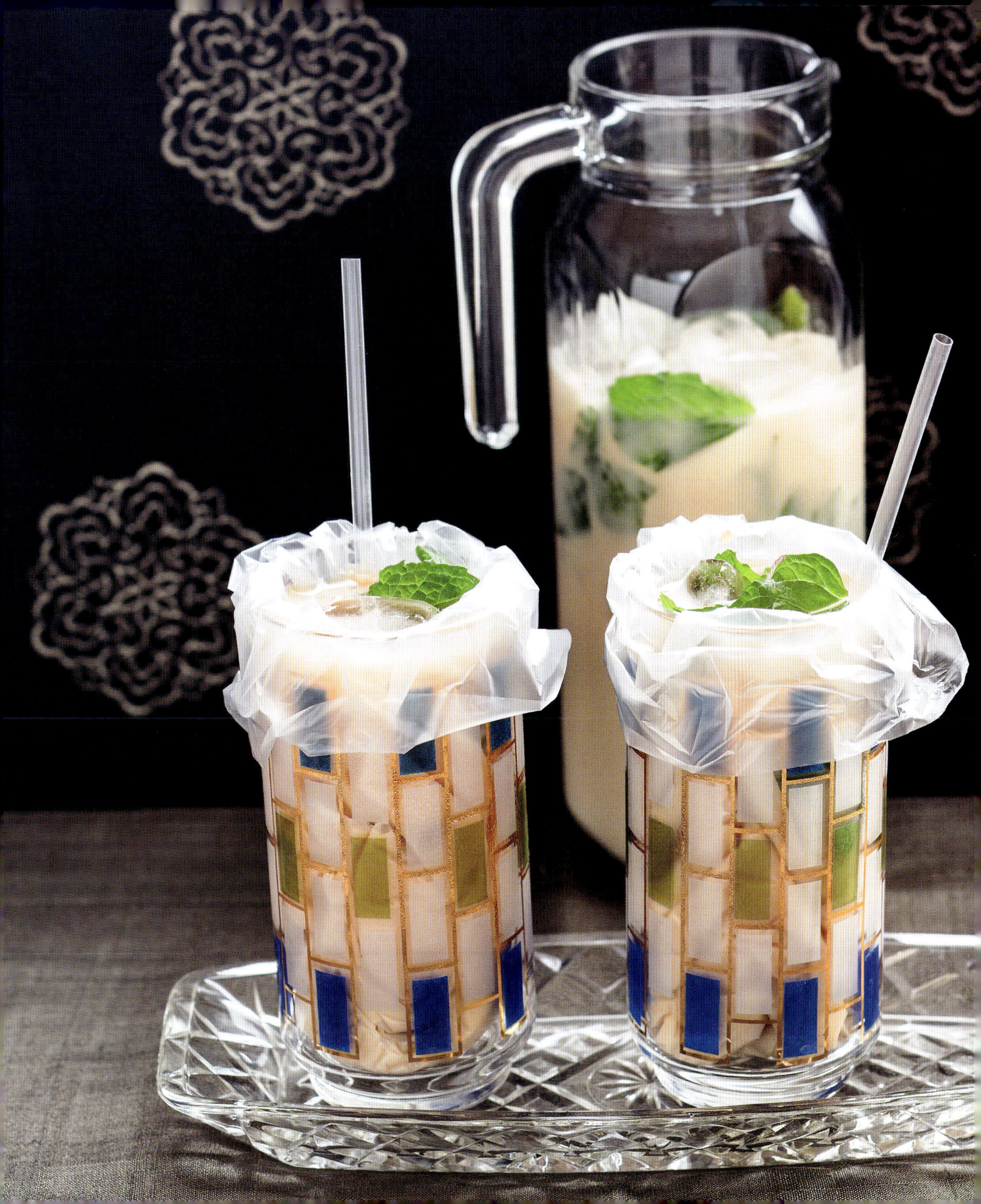

This is a great recipe for teriyaki sauce. Make a batch and keep it in the fridge as its use is not only limited to salmon; try chicken and beef too.

Energy KJs	Protein	Total fat
586	7g	8.4g

Saturated fat	Carbohydrate	Sodium
2g	7g	195mg

Salmon Skewers with Teriyaki Sauce

Makes 6 skewers • Preparation time 20 minutes • Cooking time 2–3 minutes

TERIYAKI SAUCE

4 tablespoons sake
4 tablespoons mirin
2 tablespoons low-salt soy sauce
2 teaspoons ginger juice (see method on page 56)
2 teaspoons honey

SALMON

200g fresh salmon, skinned and boned, cut into small cubes
6 skewers
6 dry-roasted almonds
micro greens to garnish

FOR THE SAUCE

1. Combine all ingredients in a small bowl.

FOR THE SALMON

1. Preheat a barbecue flat plate until hot.
2. Place three pieces of salmon on to each skewer. Brush with a little teriyaki sauce. Place on hot barbecue for 2 minutes, turning once. Cooking time will depend on thickness of your salmon cubes.
3. To serve — place salmon skewers on a serving plate and, using a fine grater, grate over almonds. Finish with micro greens. Serve extra sauce separately.

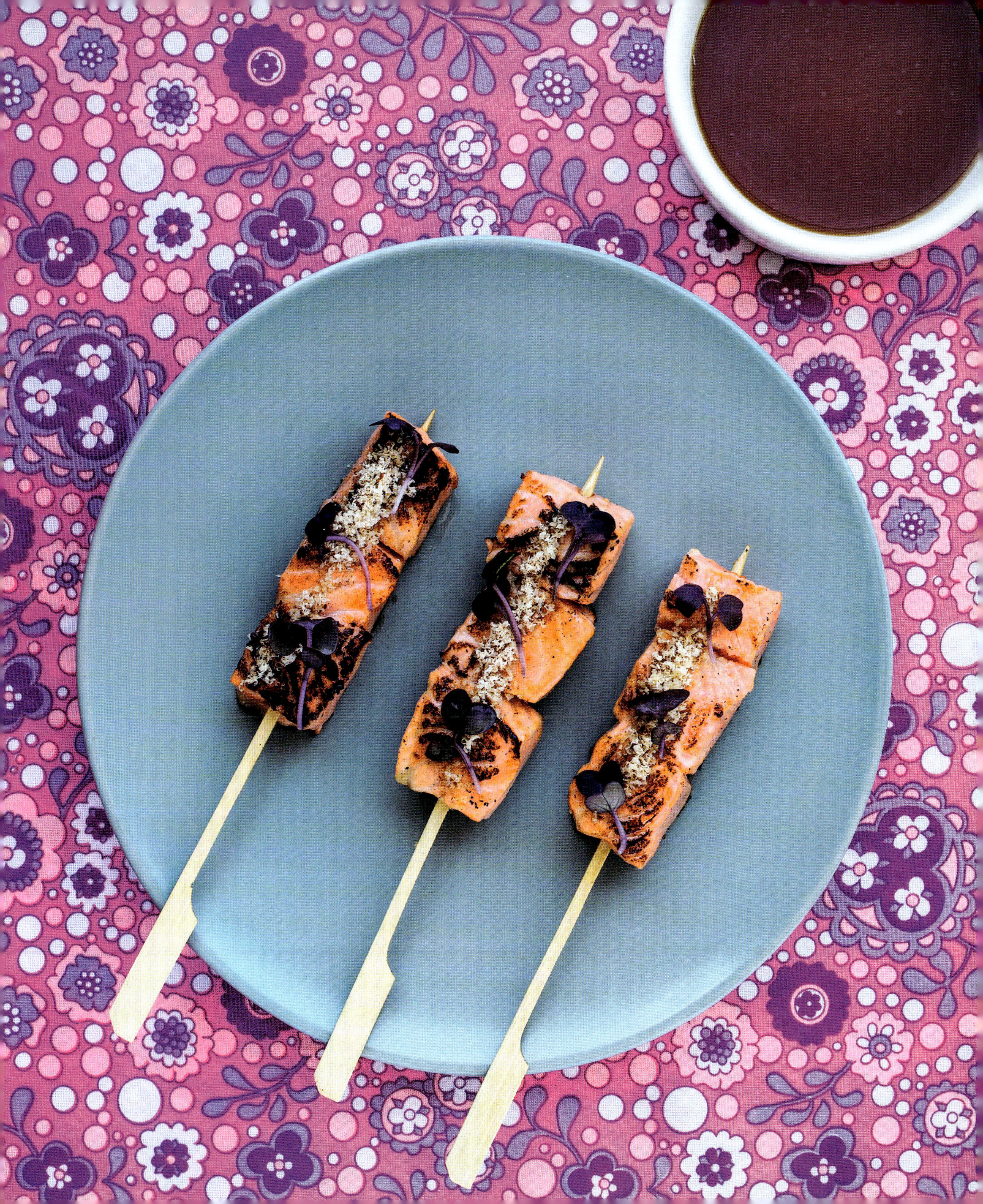

This is a great way to cook salmon as it steams in the banana leaf, keeping it moist. Remember, better to undercook than overcook.

Energy KJs	Protein	Total fat
892	11g	18g

Saturated fat	Carbohydrate	Sodium
4.5g	1g	111mg

Banana Leaf Salmon

Makes 6 parcels • **Preparation time** 15 minutes • **Cooking time** 10 minutes

DRESSING
2 tablespoons sake
2 tablespoons toasted sesame oil
1 teaspoon low-salt soy sauce

SALMON
1 large banana leaf
360g fresh boned salmon, skin on, cut into 60g portions
12 thin slices peeled ginger
6 snow pea shoots, green part only
6 skewers
chilli salt for sprinkling

FOR THE DRESSING
1. Combine all ingredients in a small bowl.

FOR THE SALMON
1. Preheat barbecue flat plate to a medium heat.
2. Cut banana leaf into six squares large enough to wrap around salmon portions. Blanch in boiling water to soften and make pliable. Refresh under cold water.
3. Place each portion of salmon in a banana-leaf square and top with ginger slices and snow pea shoots. Drizzle over a little dressing.
4. Fold each banana leaf to form a parcel and skewer to hold closed.
5. Cook on barbecue flat plate for about 10 minutes, until salmon is just cooked — this will depend on the thickness of your salmon portion. It is best served slightly undercooked.
6. To serve — remove skewers and open parcels, sprinkle with chilli salt and serve.

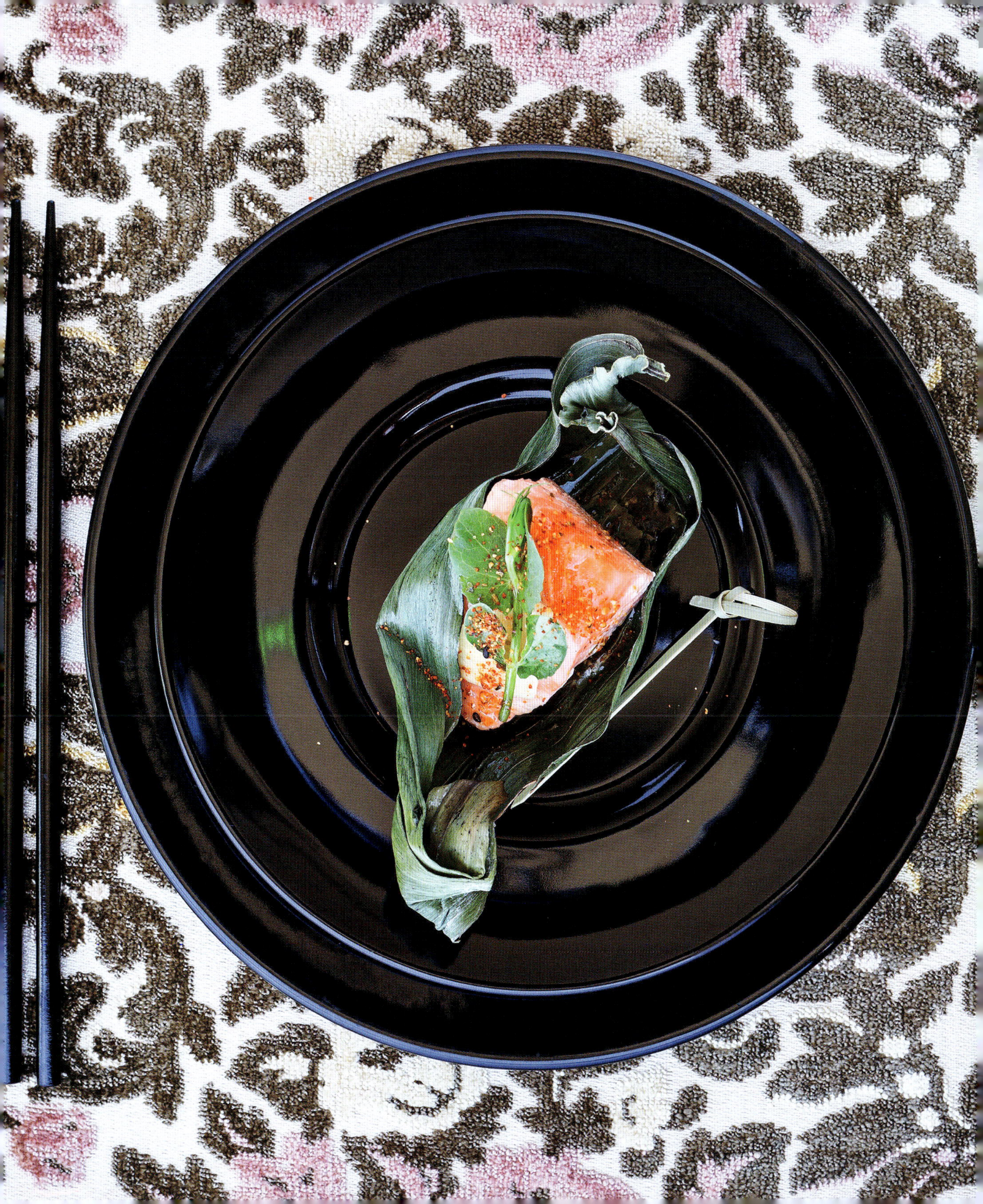

Bonito are fish of the tuna and mackerel family. Katsuobushi, in Japanese cuisine, are flakes of dried, smoked bonito fish. They go brilliantly with simple flavours.

Energy KJs	Protein	Total fat
395	4g	2.3g

Saturated fat	Carbohydrate	Sodium
.3g	14g	98mg

Watermelon and Tofu Skewers

Makes 6 large skewers • Preparation time 30 minutes • Cooking time 15 minutes

GLAZE
4 tablespoons green tea
2 tablespoons honey

WATERMELON AND TOFU SKEWERS
250g firm tofu
1 tablespoon low-salt soy sauce
¼ large watermelon, cut into 18 x 3cm cubes
6 skewers
bonito flakes to garnish
micro greens to garnish

FOR THE GLAZE
1. Combine green tea and honey in a small bowl.

FOR THE SKEWERS
1. Preheat oven to 170°C. Line a baking tray with baking paper.
2. Cut tofu in half horizontally and place on prepared baking tray. Spoon over a little soy sauce and cook for 8–10 minutes until tofu is firm. Remove from oven and leave to cool. Cut into 12 x 3cm cubes.
3. Preheat barbecue chargrill plate until hot.
4. Place three watermelon cubes and two tofu cubes on to each skewer or for smaller skewers, cut watermelon and tofu into smaller cubes and use two watermelon cubes and one tofu cube per skewer. Brush glaze over skewers and grill until skewers are well marked with grill lines.
5. Serve scattered with bonito flakes and micro greens.

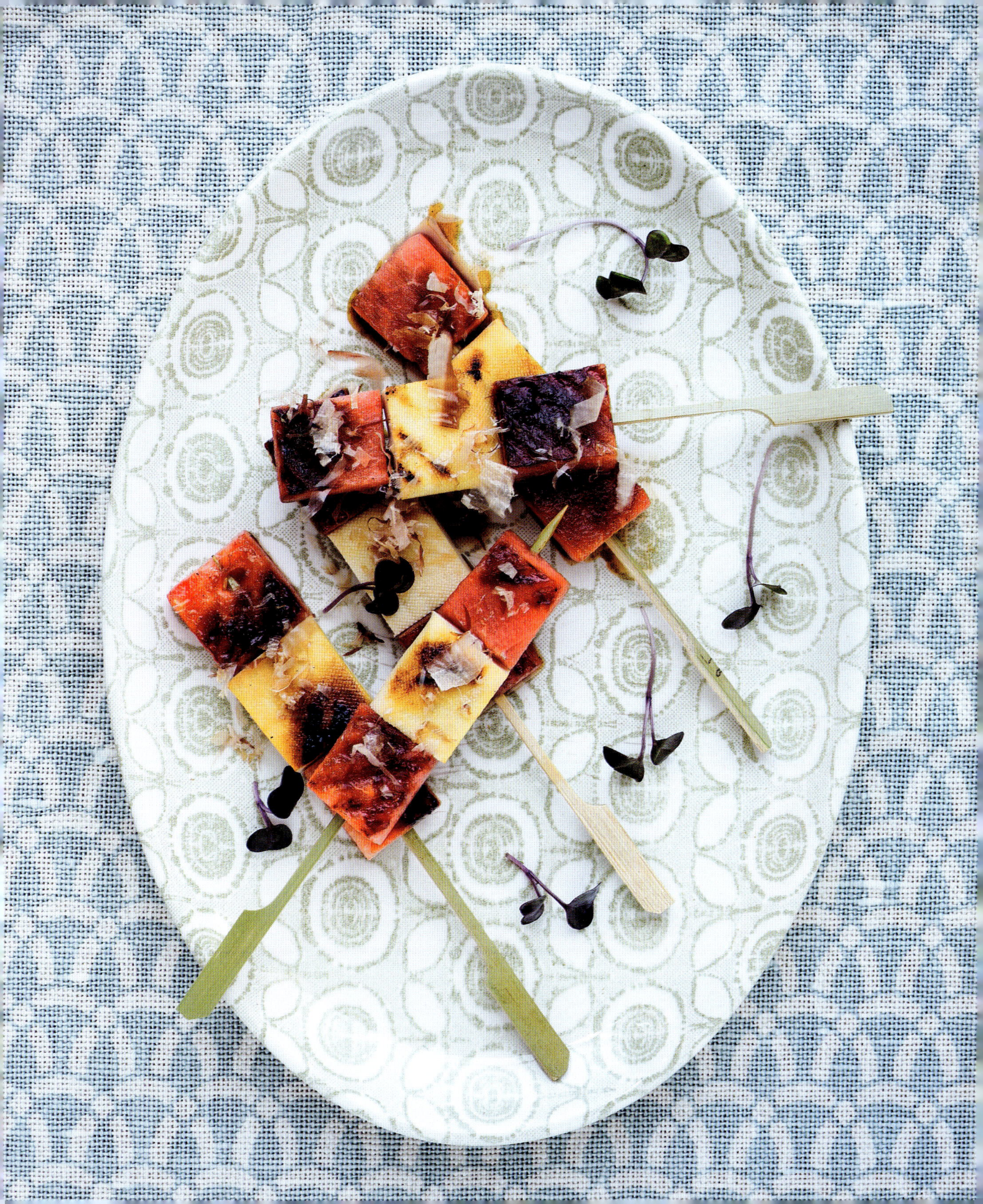

The wasabi mayonnaise is great with both the prawns and the shiitake mushrooms. Other varieties of mushrooms would be fine here too.

Energy KJs	Protein	Total fat
452	8.6g	8g

Saturated fat	Carbohydrate	Sodium
.7g	6g	273mg

Shiitake mushroom and Prawn Skewers *with Wasabi Mayonnaise*

Makes 6 • *Preparation time* 30 minutes • *Cooking time* 2-3 minutes

WASABI MAYONNAISE
MAKES: 1½ CUPS

2 eggs, soft boiled for 5 minutes and peeled
1 teaspoon wasabi powder
6 tablespoons vegetable stock
4 tablespoons grapeseed oil
pinch salt and white pepper

SHIITAKE MUSHROOMS AND PRAWN SKEWERS

6 skewers
12 shitake mushrooms (100g)
12 raw prawn cutlets
peanut oil for brushing
6 soy rice crackers, broken into pieces
micro greens to garnish

FOR THE MAYONNAISE

1. Place eggs, wasabi powder and vegetable stock in a blender and blend until combined. With the motor running, drizzle in grapeseed oil until emulsified. Season with salt and pepper.

FOR THE SKEWERS

1. Preheat barbecue chargrill plate until hot.
2. Place shiitake mushrooms and prawns, alternating as you go, on to six skewers. Brush with peanut oil.
3. Place skewers on the hot grill for 2–3 minutes, turning once, or until prawns turn pink.
4. Serve skewers with wasabi mayonnaise and soy rice crackers. Garnish with micro greens.

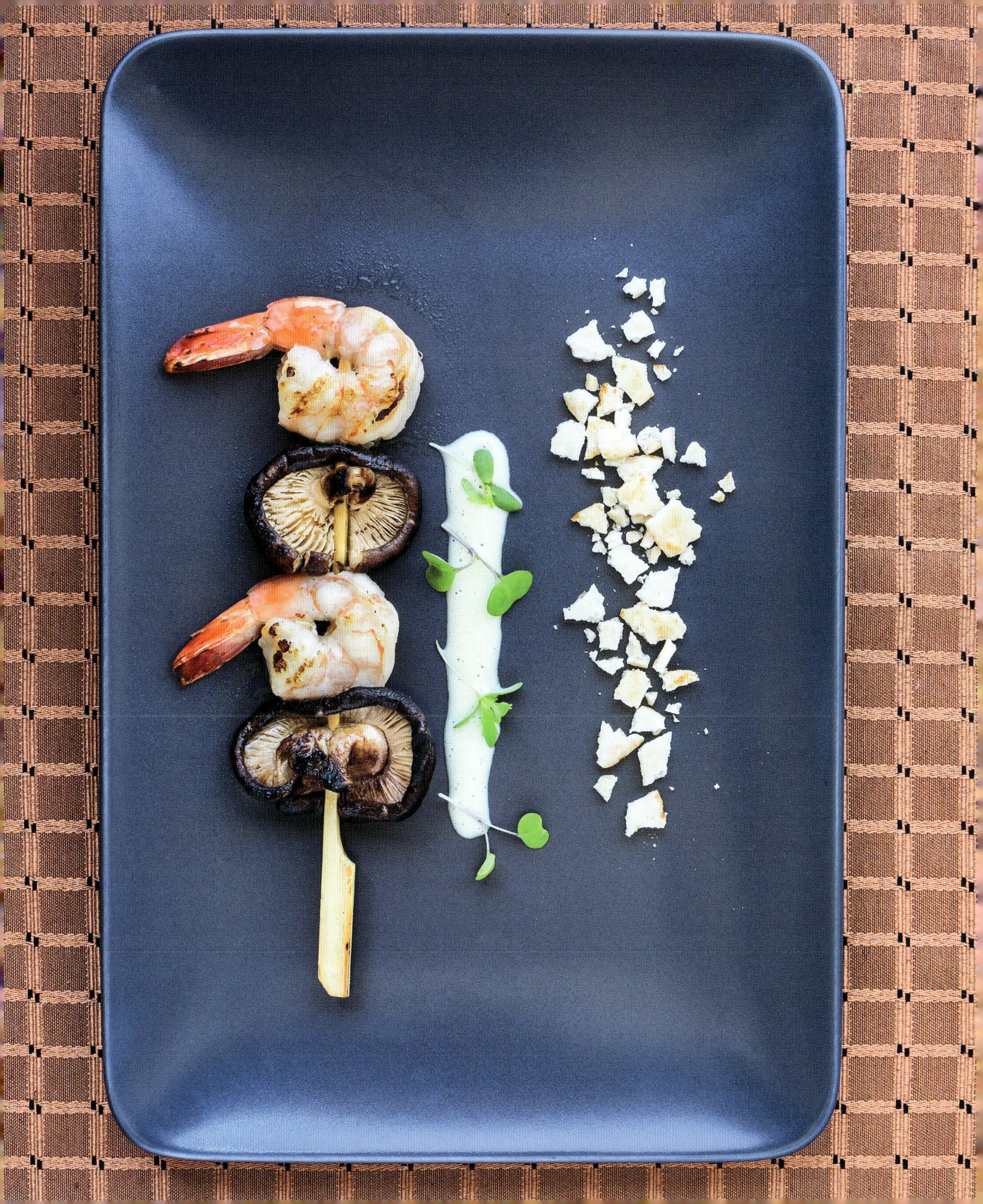

These were a tricky one to make for game day. You have to wrap the noodles really tight and give them enough time to set in the fridge, or you'll have a real mess on your hands!

Energy KJs	Protein	Total fat
240	2.3g	3g

Saturated fat	Carbohy-drate	Sodium
.5g	6g	225mg

Clam and Noodle Skewers
with Eggplant Pickle

Makes 6 • Preparation time 1 hour • Cooking time 20 minutes

EGGPLANT PICKLE

1 tablespoon peanut oil
1 medium-sized eggplant, peeled and cut into 1cm dice
2 spring onions, finely sliced
¼ cup water
2 teaspoons honey
2 teaspoons dark miso
1 teaspoon low-salt soy sauce

CLAM AND NOODLE SKEWERS

36 clams, cockles or tua tua
¼ cup water
6 skewers
60g dried rice noodles, cooked
peanut oil for brushing
1 teaspoon toasted white sesame seeds for sprinkling
1 teaspoon black sesame seeds for sprinkling

FOR THE PICKLE

1. Heat oil in a large frying pan and add diced eggplant. Cook until soft and golden, about 15 minutes, then add spring onion. Cook for a further 2 minutes.
2. Heat water, honey and miso in a small saucepan and stir well to combine. Remove from heat and add soy sauce. Stir in eggplant mixture and set aside.

FOR THE SKEWERS

1. Heat a large saucepan over a high heat, but do not allow to burn. Place in clams, cockles or tua tua along with water. Cover with a lid for a few seconds. Remove from heat — the shellfish should have opened. Remove clams from their shells.
2. Skewer six clams, or other shellfish, on to six skewers.
3. Gather five cooked rice noodles in your hand and wrap around skewer, enclosing clams. Wrap tightly in plastic wrap. Repeat with remaining skewers. Place in refrigerator for 30 minutes.
4. Meanwhile preheat barbecue flat plate until hot.
5. Unwrap skewers and brush noodles with peanut oil. Place on barbecue flat plate and cook until golden on both sides.
6. Sprinkle skewers with sesame seeds and serve hot with eggplant pickle.

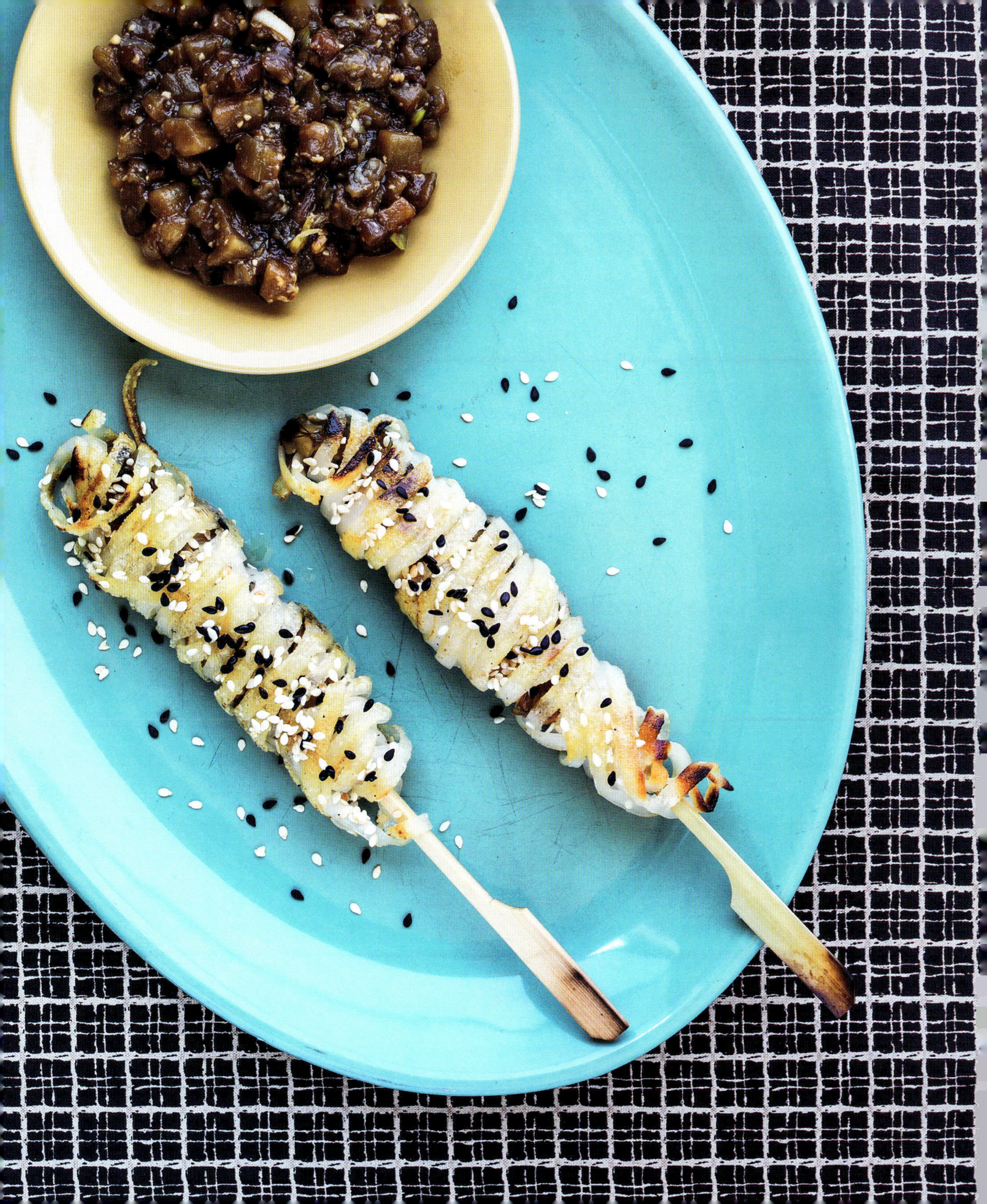

My take on the Japanese classic. Cabbage stimulates the appetite so this is a great starter or side dish for anything Japanese.

Energy KJs	Protein	Total fat
634	1.8g	13g

Saturated fat	Carbohydrate	Sodium
.7g	7g	35mg

Japanese Cabbage Salad

Serves 6 • Preparation time 30 minutes

DRESSING
6 tablespoons grapeseed oil
4 tablespoons rice vinegar
1½ tablespoons lemon juice
1 teaspoon ginger juice (see method on page 56)
1 teaspoon low-salt soy sauce

SALAD
¼ savoy or white cabbage, julienned
2 springs onions, julienned
1 red onion, julienned
1 cup shelled edamame soybeans, cooked

FOR THE DRESSING
1. Combine all ingredients in a small bowl.

FOR THE SALAD
1. Place salad ingredients in a large bowl and spoon over dressing. Toss gently to combine. Serve small portions on small plates.

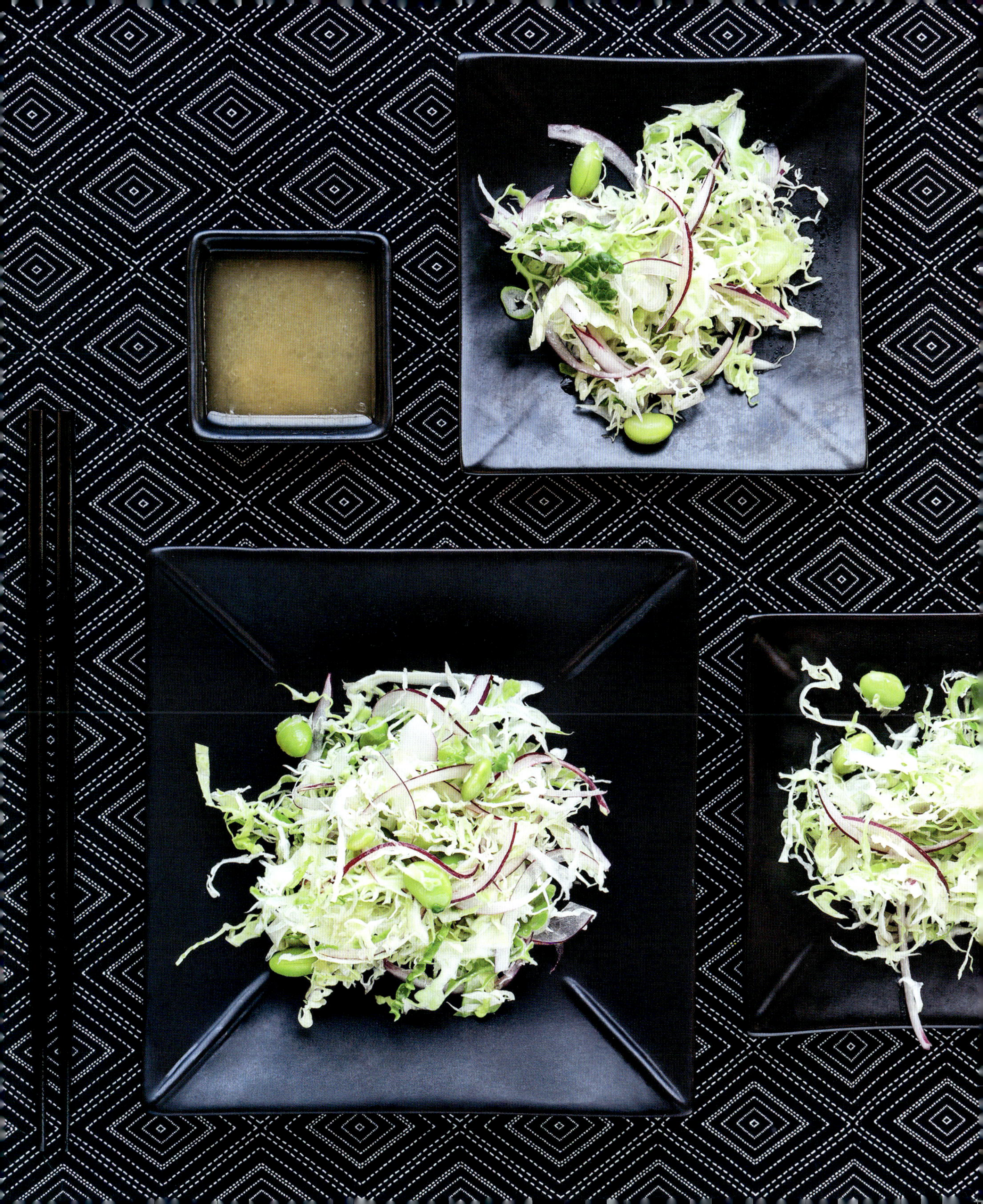

Easy Vietnamese

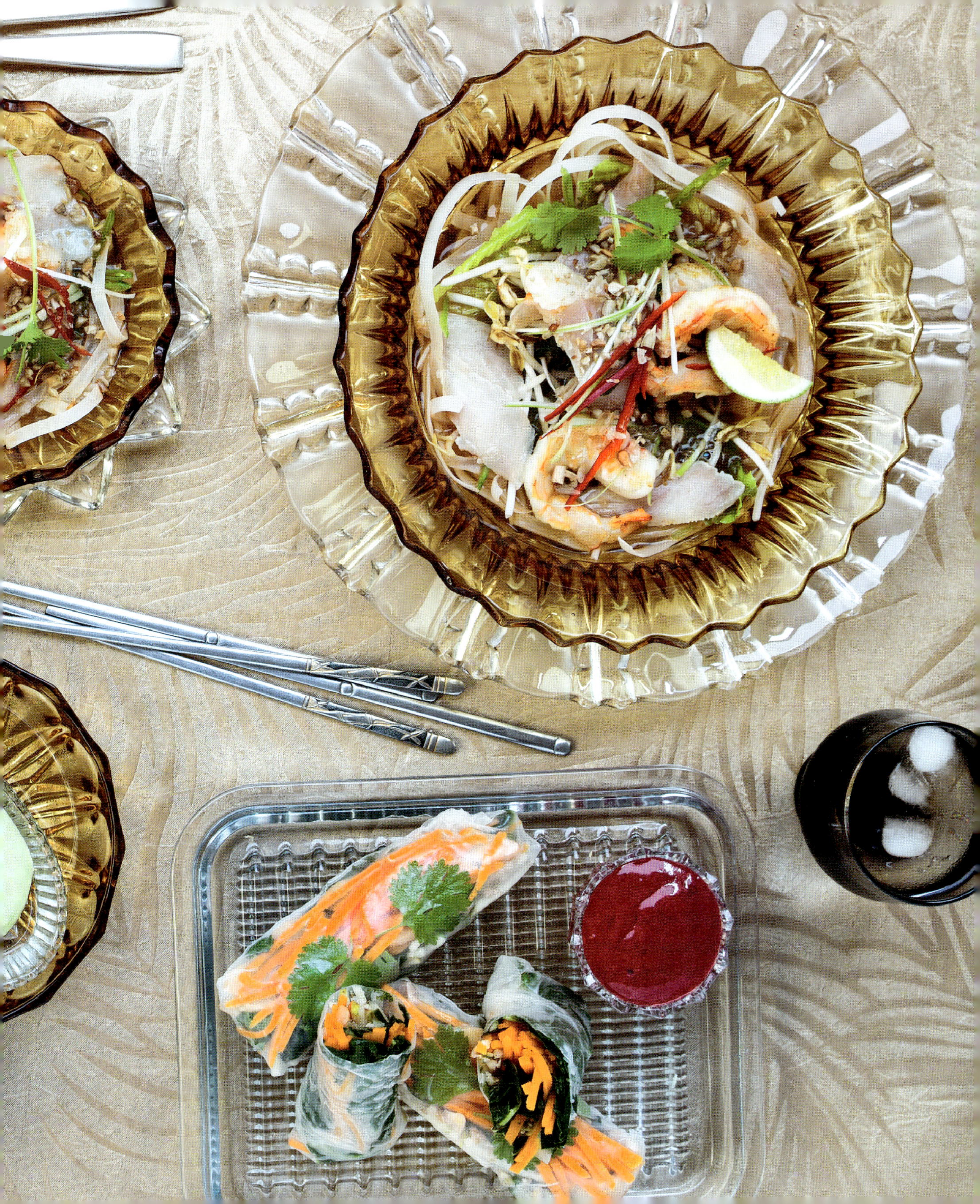

Banh Mi or Vietnamese baguettes were introduced to the Vietnamese people during French colonisation, which lasted nearly 100 years. They are amazingly delicious.

Energy KJs	Protein	Total fat
3445	43g	36g

Saturated fat	Carbohydrate	Sodium
4g	90g	502mg

Banh mi

Serves 8 • *Preparation time* 2 hours • *Cooking time* about 1 hour

VIETNAMESE BAGUETTE

1 teaspoon sugar
⅔ cup warm water
2 tablespoons dried yeast
4 cups high-grade flour, plus extra for dusting
1 cup wholemeal flour
½ teaspoon salt
2 tablespoons grapeseed oil
1 cup warm water
1 egg white, lightly beaten
1 tablespoon black sesame seeds
1 tablespoon rolled oats
spray bottle of water

LEMONGRASS TURKEY OR CHICKEN

3 cloves garlic, very finely chopped
1 shallot, very finely chopped
1 stalk lemongrass, outer leaves removed and very finely chopped

FOR THE BAGUETTE

1. Place sugar and first measure of warm water in a small bowl and sprinkle yeast over. Leave in a warm place to froth, about 5 minutes.
2. Sift white flour into a large bowl, add wholemeal flour, salt and oil. Pour in yeast mixture and second measure of warm water and mix to form a dough.
3. Turn dough out onto a lightly floured bench top and knead until smooth, about 10 minutes. Alternatively, knead dough in an electric mixer fitted with a dough hook.
4. Place in a lightly oiled bowl, cover with a clean tea towel and leave to rise in a warm place until doubled in size, about 1 hour.
5. Preheat oven to 220°C. Line 2 baking trays with baking paper.
6. Turn dough back out onto a lightly floured bench top, divide in half, then cut each half into four equal pieces (about 100g each). Using a rolling pin, roll out one piece to an oval, about 20cm long and 15cm wide. Roll the top down into the middle, then roll the bottom up so they meet. Turn over and form into a cylinder shape. Place baguette on lined baking tray. Repeat with remaining pieces of dough.
7. Brush baguettes with egg white and sprinkle with black sesame seeds and rolled oats. With a sharp knife, make a shallow slash lengthwise down the middle of baguettes.

Recipe continued over page . . .

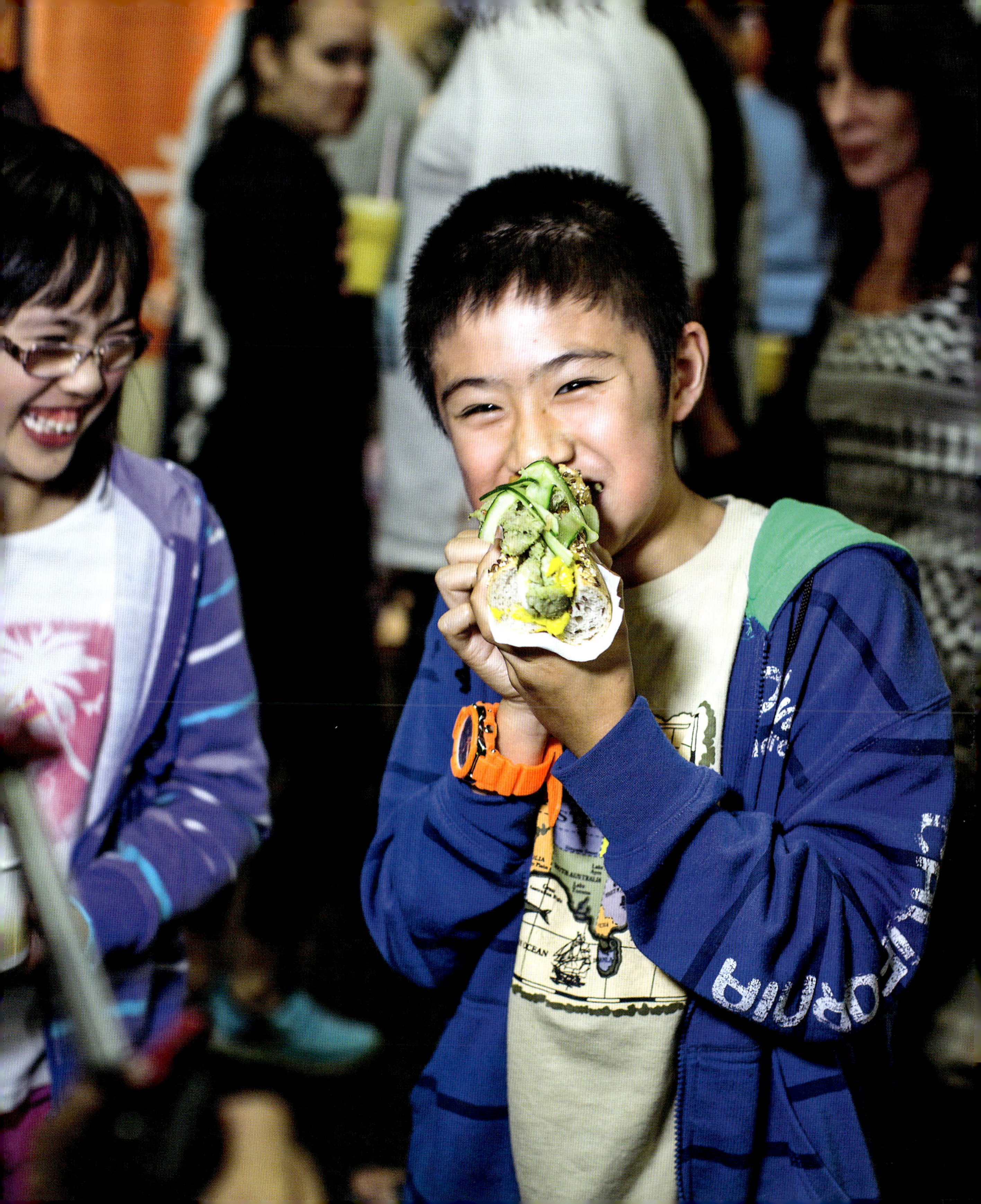

Banh Mi continued . . .

1 tablespoon sesame seeds
1 tablespoon coconut sugar
1 teaspoon fish sauce
1 teaspoon sesame oil
1 teaspoon grapeseed oil, plus 1 tablespoon for pan-frying
pinch salt
¼ teaspoon white pepper
1kg turkey or chicken breast meat, cut into slices

WHITE BEAN PÂTÉ
MAKES: 1¼ CUPS

1 carrot, peeled and finely diced
½ onion, finely diced
3 cloves garlic, crushed
1 x 400g can butter beans, drained
½ cup chopped parsley
1 sprig rosemary, leaves removed and chopped
2 tablespoons lemon juice
pinch salt and white pepper
¼ cup olive oil

8. Place in oven and spray inside oven with water, to help form a good crust. Bake for 10 minutes, then reduce oven temperature to 200°C. Rotate baking trays and bake for a further 10 minutes.
9. Remove from oven and place on a wire rack to cool.

FOR THE TURKEY OR CHICKEN
1. Place all ingredients except turkey or chicken slices in a food processor and process until combined.
2. Place turkey or chicken slices in a non-metallic bowl and spoon marinade over. Cover and refrigerate for at least 1 hour or overnight, if wished.
3. Preheat oven to 160°C.
4. Heat a dash of olive oil in a large frying pan and brown turkey or chicken slices on both sides.
5. Transfer to oven and cook for 6 minutes or until cooked through.

FOR THE PÂTÉ
1. Place carrot, onion and garlic in a saucepan with a dash of olive oil and cook over a low heat until soft, about 10 minutes. Add butter beans, herbs, lemon juice and season with salt and pepper. Stir well to combine, then remove from heat and leave to cool slightly.
2. Place bean mixture in a food processor and process until smooth.
3. Drizzle in olive oil through the feed tube until a smooth pâté forms. Transfer to a bowl, cover and place in the refrigerator until ready to use.

Recipe continued following page . . .

Banh Mi continued . . .

PICKLED CARROTS

½ onion, finely diced
3 cloves garlic, crushed
¼ cup red wine vinegar
¼ cup warm water
2 tablespoons liquid honey
½ teaspoon mustard powder
¼ teaspoon ground allspice
¼ teaspoon ground coriander
pinch salt and freshly ground black pepper
250g baby carrots, scrubbed and cut in half lengthwise

AVOCADO EMULSION

MAKES: 1½ CUPS

1 avocado, halved, stoned and peeled
1 egg, soft boiled for 5 minutes, peeled
6 tablespoons vegetable stock
juice of 1 lemon
100ml grapeseed oil

TO ASSEMBLE

¼ iceberg lettuce or 1 cos lettuce, finely shredded
small telegraph cucumber, cut into ribbons
2 handfuls mint and coriander leaves

FOR THE CARROTS

1. Place onion and garlic in a saucepan with a dash of olive oil and cook over a low heat until soft, about 10 minutes.
2. Add red wine vinegar, warm water, honey, mustard powder, allspice and coriander. Season with salt and pepper.
3. Add baby carrots and cook over medium heat for 5 minutes. Remove from the heat and allow to cool before transferring to a bowl. Cover and refrigerate.

FOR THE EMULSION

1. Place avocado, egg, vegetable stock and lemon juice in a food processor and process until smooth.
2. Drizzle in grapeseed oil through the feed tube until emulsified. Transfer to a bowl, cover and refrigerate.

TO ASSEMBLE

Cut each baguette in half or cut through the top lengthwise. Fill with white bean pâté, shredded lettuce, pickled carrots, turkey or chicken slices, avocado emulsion, cucumber and herbs. Serve with extra avocado emulsion.

Fresh rice paper rolls are great for entertaining. You can make them all before work and have them in the fridge ready to go, or get your guests to make their own.

Autumn Rice Paper Rolls

Makes 12 • *Preparation time* 45 minutes • *Cooking time* 50 minutes

Energy KJs	Protein	Total fat
492	2.7g	2g

Saturated fat	Carbohydrate	Sodium
.2g	24g	47mg

PLUM SAUCE
MAKES: 2 CUPS

500g red plums, halved and stoned
¼ cup red wine vinegar
2 tablespoons maple syrup
5 star anise

RICE PAPER ROLLS

2 quinces, peeled, quartered and cored
1 teaspoon liquid honey
250g pumpkin, peeled and julienned, blanched for 10 seconds
250g butternut, peeled and julienned, blanched for 10 seconds
4 leaves kale, destalked and blanched
4 leaves silverbeet, destalked and blanched
2 fresh pears, skin on, julienned, mixed with juice of 1 lemon
1 small telegraph cucumber, cut into ribbons and julienned
½ cup coriander and mint leaves
¼ cup dry-roasted walnuts, finely chopped
12 (22cm) rice paper rounds

FOR THE SAUCE
1. Place plums, vinegar, maple syrup and star anise in a saucepan. Cover and cook over a low heat for 40 minutes.
2. Remove star anise and place plum mixture in a food processor and process until you have a sauce.

FOR THE ROLLS
1. Preheat oven to 180°C.
2. Place quinces in a roasting dish with honey and a splash of water. Cover and roast for about 50 minutes until soft. Once cooked and cooled, cut into thin slices.
3. Place remaining ingredients except rice paper rounds in a large bowl and stir in 6 tablespoons plum sauce.
4. Have a large bowl of hot water on bench top, drop in 1 rice paper round. Lift out and place on a damp tea towel. Place some mixture in the middle and fold over both sides, then roll up into a cigar shape.
5. Place slightly apart on a tray lined with plastic wrap, cover with plastic wrap and continue making rice paper rolls. If not serving immediately, keep well covered and place in refrigerator. Serve with plum sauce for dipping.

FRESH
TAKEAWAY
FOOD
HEALTHIER
CHEAPER
FASTER!
HEALTHIEST FAST
x2 $5

A must-eat in Vietnam. You have to try a pho sitting on a tiny plastic stool at a sidewalk eatery. It's a beautifully simple broth that you will love.

Energy KJs	Protein	Total fat
2453	60g	19g

Saturated fat	Carbohydrate	Sodium
2.4g	60g	604mg

Prawn and Trevally Pho

Serves 4 • Preparation time 1½ hours • Cooking time 50 minutes

1 x 250g packet dried rice noodles
2 onions, chopped
10cm knob ginger, peeled and chopped
3 cloves garlic, chopped
500g whole raw prawns, heads and shells removed for broth
6 cloves
5 star anise
3 sticks cinnamon
1½ litres vegetable stock
1 tablespoon fish sauce
3 stalks coriander, washed, roughly chopped, leaves reserved
240g sashimi-grade trevally, finely sliced
¼ iceberg or baby cos lettuce, finely shredded
1 cup mung bean sprouts
10 snow peas, finely sliced
2 spring onions, julienned
1 long red chilli, deseeded and julienned
1 cup dry-roasted sunflower seeds, chopped
1 lime, cut into wedges
coriander leaves

1. Soak noodles in warm water for 1 hour or as directed on packet.
2. Place onion, ginger and garlic in a large saucepan with a dash of grapeseed oil and cook over a low heat for 5 minutes. Add prawn shells and heads and allow to just begin to colour.
3. Add cloves, star anise, cinnamon, vegetable stock, fish sauce and coriander stalks. Bring to a boil, reduce heat and simmer for 40 minutes, skimming the surface from time to time.
4. Strain and return broth to saucepan. Bring back up to the boil.
5. Cut shelled prawns in half lengthwise and drop into hot broth.

TO ASSEMBLE

1. Place drained noodles, trevally, shredded lettuce, mung bean sprouts, snow peas, and spring onions into deep serving bowls. Divide prawns between bowls and pour over hot broth.
2. Finish with chilli, sunflower seeds, a small wedge of lime and coriander leaves. Serve at once.

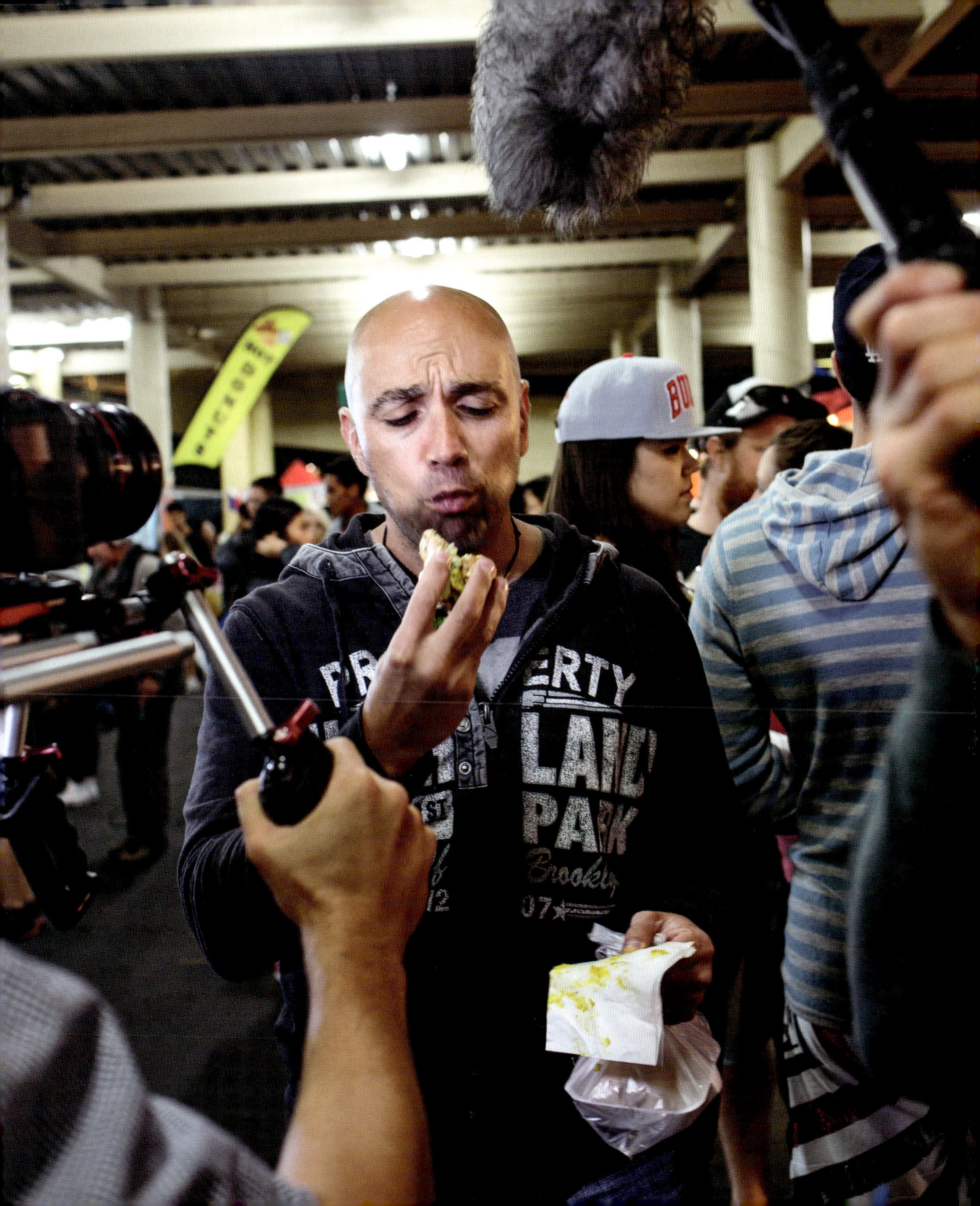

Ma Le
Saigonz

Ma Le's Saigonz caravan is the stuff of legend. She started dishing out amazing Vietnamese food at weekend markets, and over the years developed the family business until they could set up a permanent restaurant in downtown Auckland. Not forgetting her roots, Ma Le returns to the Takapuna markets with her family every weekend to serve up awesome Banh Mi sandwiches, rice paper rolls and more. Their food is super fresh and packed with flavour.

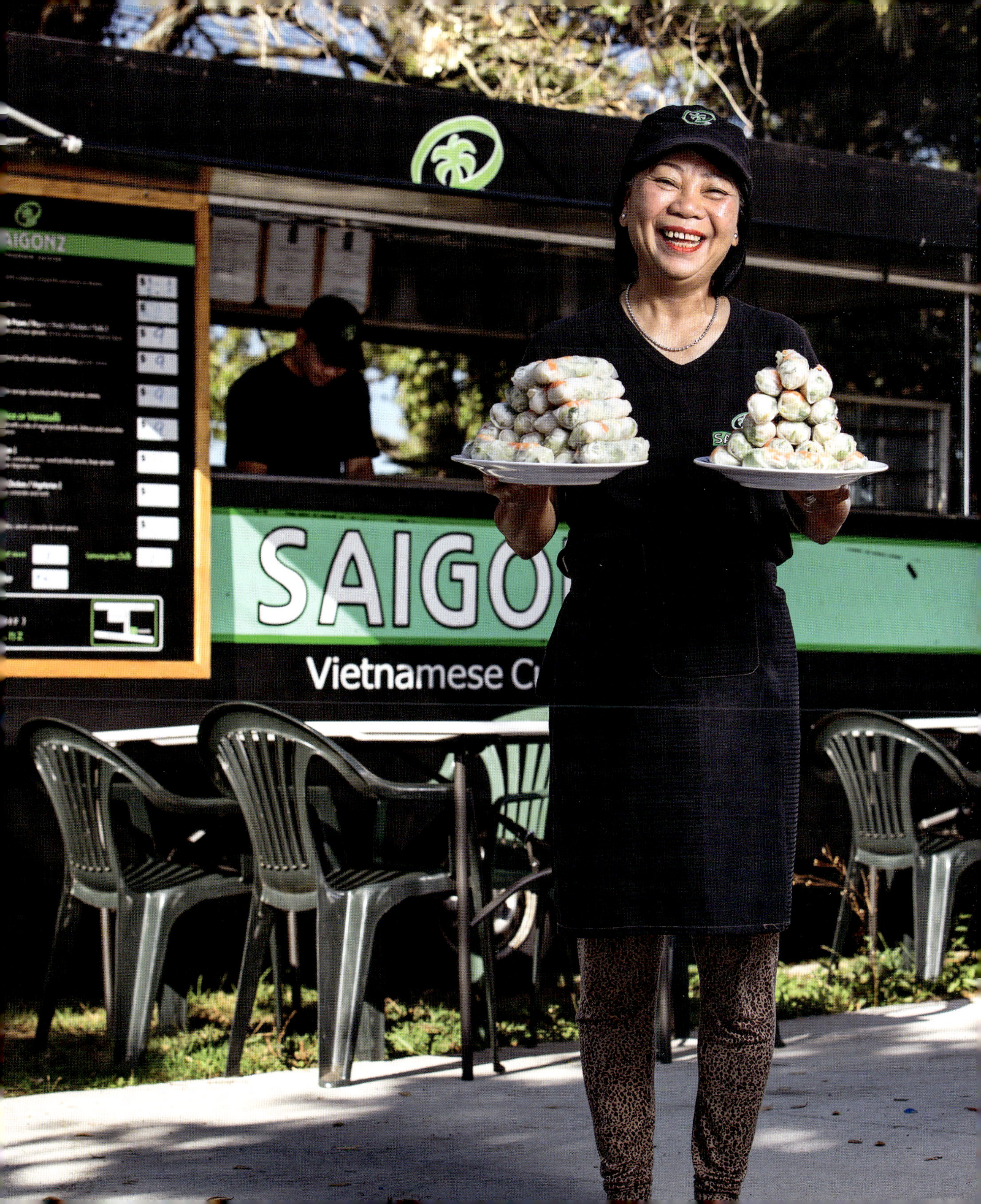
SAIGONZ
SAIGO
Vietnamese C

EUROPE   FRENCH,

ITALIAN AND GERMAN

This hazelnut spread is so simple to make, but make in small batches as it only keeps for about a week.

Energy KJs	Protein	Total fat
1097	11g	18g

Saturated fat	Carbohydrate	Sodium
2g	12g	56mg

Hazelnut Crêpes

Makes 10 crêpes • *Preparation time* 15 minutes • *Cooking time* 15 minutes

CRÊPE BATTER
2 tablespoons plain flour
2 tablespoons tapioca flour
2 tablespoons coconut flour
1½ cups low-fat milk
2 eggs

HAZELNUT FILLING
2 cups raw hazelnuts
1 vanilla bean, split and seeds removed, or 1 teaspoon vanilla bean paste
¼ cup good-quality cocoa powder
½ cup soy milk
2 tablespoons maple syrup

FOR THE BATTER
1. Sift flours into a medium-sized bowl and make a well in the centre.
2. Place milk and eggs in well and whisk to form a smooth batter.
3. Heat a large crêpe pan over a medium heat. Pour in enough batter to coat the base of the pan. Cook for 1 minute or until golden brown. Turn crêpe to cook the other side. Turn out on to a plate and continue cooking remaining batter.

FOR THE FILLING
1. Preheat oven to 150°C.
2. Spread hazelnuts on a baking tray and roast for about 10 minutes. Check and shake tray once or twice during cooking so nuts roast evenly. Remove from oven and place in a coarse textured tea towel or cloth and rub hazelnuts together to remove skins.
3. Place hazelnuts and remaining ingredients in a blender and blend until smooth.

TO ASSEMBLE
1. Spread a little hazelnut filling over each crêpe. Fold in half, then in half again.

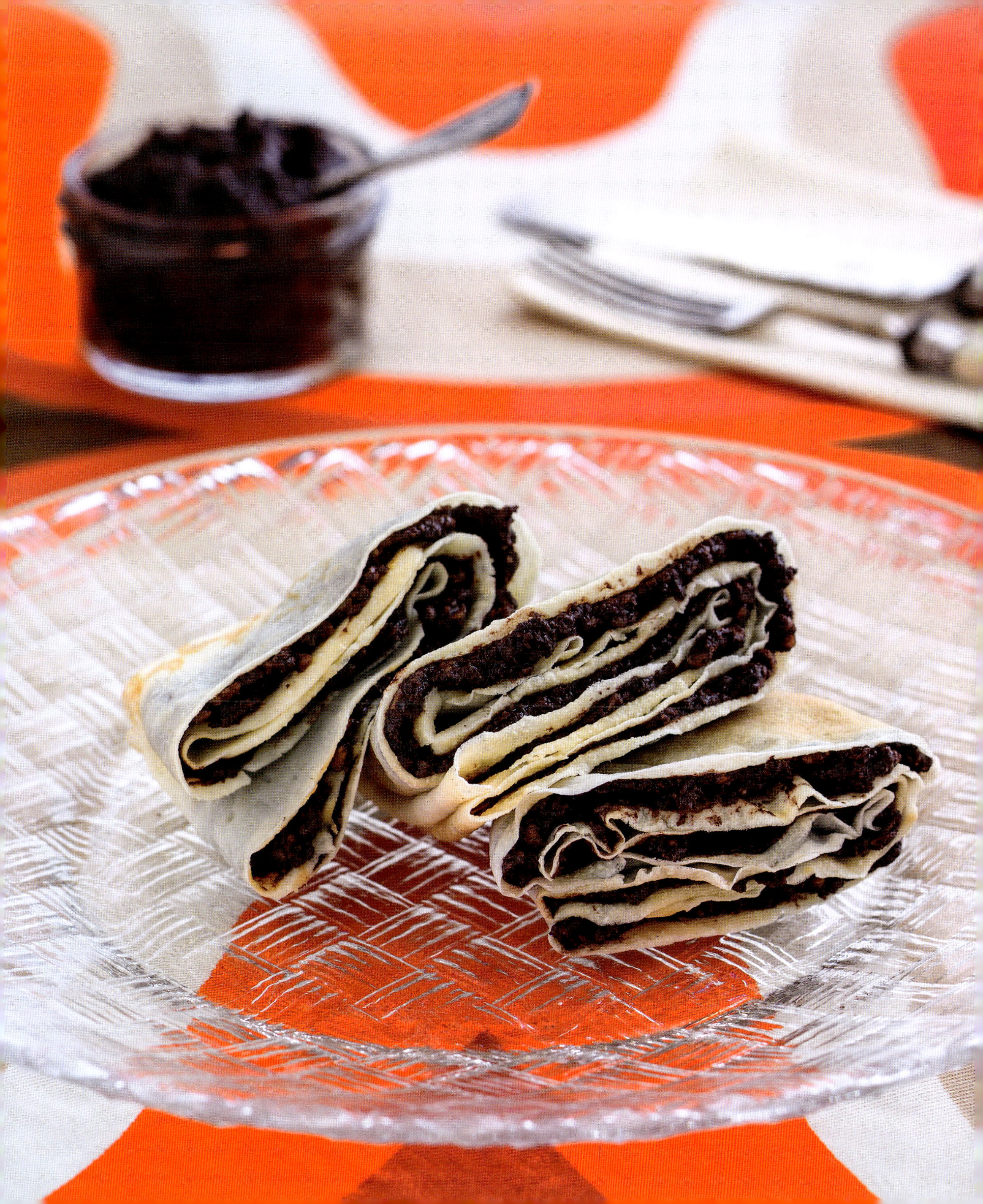

My 'lunch or Sunday night supper' crêpe. Cauliflower makes an exceptionally good white sauce. This is one for your repertoire.

Energy KJs	Protein	Total fat
317	5g	2.6g

Saturated fat	Carbohydrate	Sodium
1g	8g	266mg

Croque monsieur crêpes

Makes 10 crêpes • Preparation time 30 minutes • Cooking time 20 minutes

WHITE SAUCE

1 small head cauliflower, cut into florets
olive oil spray
½ teaspoon smoke salt

TO ASSEMBLE

10 crêpes (see page 98)
10 slices Serrano ham
20 very thin slices Gruyère cheese

FOR THE SAUCE

1. Preheat oven to 150°C.
2. Cook cauliflower in lightly salted boiling water until tender, 3–4 minutes. Drain well, spray lightly with olive oil and sprinkle with smoke salt.
3. Place in a lightly oiled roasting dish and roast until dry and just starting to colour, about 20 minutes. This will concentrate the flavour of the cauliflower.
4. Remove from oven and place roasted cauliflower in a blender and blend until smooth.

TO ASSEMBLE

1. Change the oven setting to grill.
2. Lay your crêpes flat on the bench top, spread each with 'white' sauce, top with half a slice of Serrano ham and finish with a very thin slice of Gruyère cheese.
3. Fold crêpes to enclose filling, place each crêpe on a baking tray, top with a little more white sauce, half a slice of Serrano ham and a slice of Gruyère cheese and place under the hot grill. Grill until golden. Serve hot.

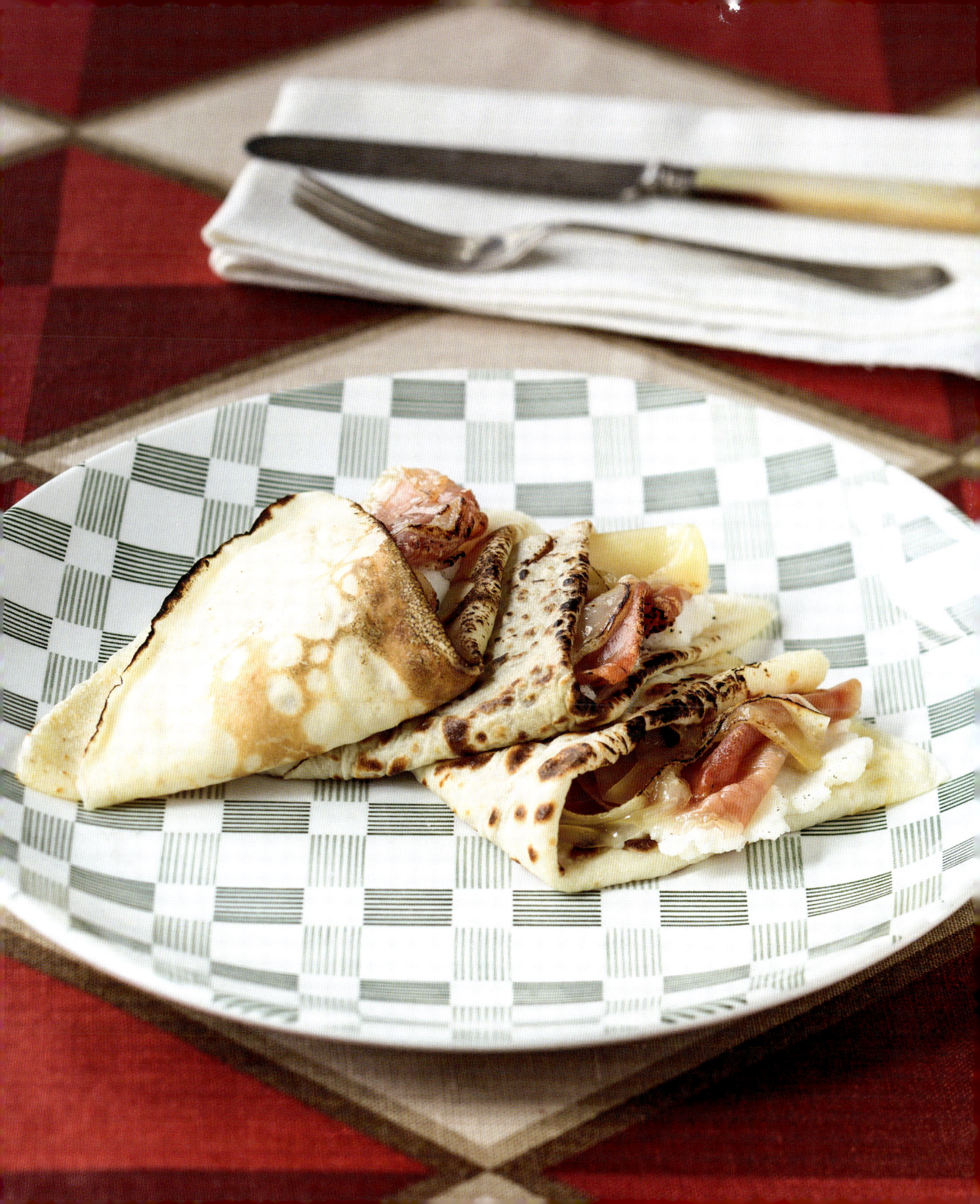

There's a bit of preparation at the beginning for this dish but then you can sit back and relax. These crêpes will impress everyone as cassoulet is a legendary French dish.

Energy KJs	Protein	Total fat
1157	24g	7g

Saturated fat	Carbohydrate	Sodium
1.8g	31g	393mg

Duck Cassoulet Crêpes

Makes 10 crêpes • Preparation time 1 hour and 45 minutes • Cooking time 15 minutes

DUCK CASSOULET

4 duck legs
1 cup diced onion
1 cup diced celery
1 cup diced carrot
1 bay leaf
few sprigs fresh thyme
2 cups vegetable stock
1 cup Puy lentils
3 ripe tomatoes, skinned and diced
1 x 375g can haricot beans, drained and rinsed
½ cup chopped cooked spinach leaves
½ cup chopped parsley

BREADCRUMBS

2 slices wholemeal bread
juice of 1 lemon
1 tablespoon olive oil

TO ASSEMBLE

10 crêpes (see page 98)
breadcrumbs
micro greens to garnish

FOR THE CASSOULET

1. Preheat oven to 170°C.
2. Heat a heavy-based frying pan over a medium heat and place duck legs in. Brown duck legs on both sides, allowing the fat to render down. Discard duck fat!
3. Place duck legs in a casserole dish with diced vegetables and herbs. Pour vegetable stock over, cover and cook in oven for 1 hour.
4. Remove from oven, add lentils and tomatoes and cook for a further 20 minutes.
5. Add haricot beans, spinach and parsley and return to oven and cook for 10 minutes. Using 2 forks, remove duck meat from bones. Discard bones and skin.

FOR THE BREADCRUMBS

1. Preheat grill.
2. Place bread slices on a grill rack and brush with lemon juice and olive oil.
3. Grill (place rack lower in the oven), until dry, turning once. Remove from oven, cool, then pound in a mortar and pestle into fine breadcrumbs. Alternatively, dry bread slices in a low oven (150°C).

TO ASSEMBLE

1. Fill crêpes with duck cassoulet and fold, leaving one end open (as you would a burrito).
2. Sprinkle a few breadcrumbs over each crêpe and top with micro greens.

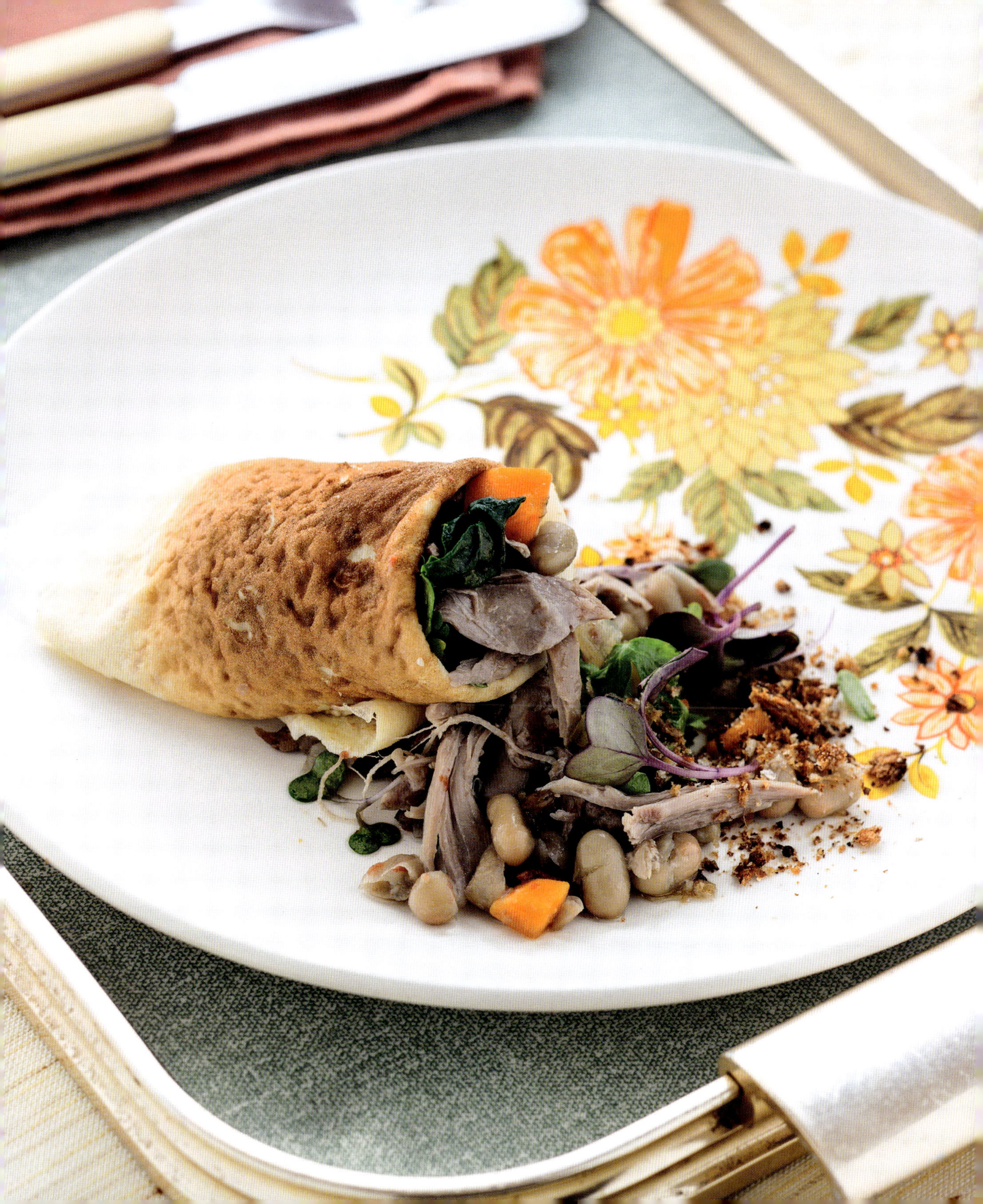

Louis Bouquet
La Tropezienne

Louis Bouquet owns La Tropezienne, a French bakery in Auckland's Browns Bay. He is a passionate Frenchman who is serious about the art of croissant making, using a très très traditionelle method with which to make them. He uses some machines, but the important parts are all done by hand. Until working with Louis I had no idea that one of these delicious little pastries takes nearly two days to make! I was to learn the hard way that it's not easy to make those suckers healthy!

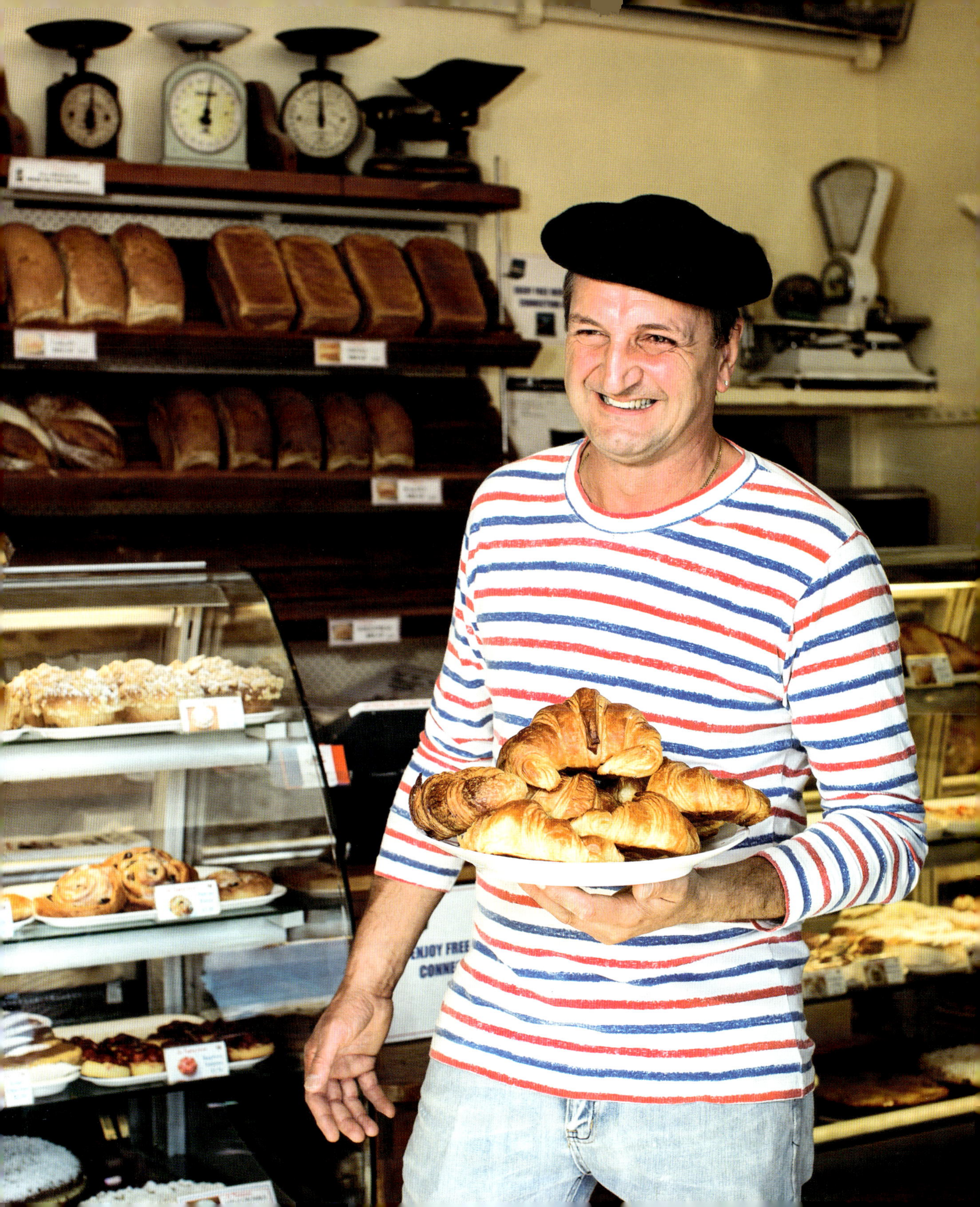

Get the whole family involved in making the pasta — it's fun and terribly satisfying. Putting greens into the mix ups the goodness and looks amazing too.

Energy KJs	Protein	Total fat
2476	20g	30g

Saturated fat	Carbohydrate	Sodium
5g	64g	265mg

Fettuccini and Green Pesto

Serves 6 • *Preparation time* 2 hours • *Cooking time* 4–5 minutes

GREEN PESTO

60g rocket leaves
10 basil leaves
1 clove garlic, crushed
100g shelled pistachio nuts, dry-roasted
80g cottage cheese
1 tablespoon olive oil
juice of ½ lemon
1 teaspoon capers
pinch salt
white pepper

PASTA DOUGH

100g blanched silverbeet leaves, spinach leaves and watercress
450g high-grade or strong flour
4 eggs
2 tablespoons olive oil
extra flour and fine semolina for rolling

FOR THE PESTO

1. Place ingredients in a blender and blend until smooth. Transfer to a bowl, cover well with plastic wrap and place in the refrigerator.

FOR THE DOUGH

1. Squeeze excess moisture from blanched silverbeet, spinach and watercress. Then squeeze again in a clean tea towel until all moisture is removed. Chop very finely.
2. Place silverbeet mixture, flour, eggs and olive oil in an electric mixer fitted with a dough hook. Mix until a soft smooth dough is formed, about 5 minutes. Or knead by hand for 15–20 minutes until smooth.
3. Wrap dough in plastic wrap and refrigerate for 30 minutes. Remove from refrigerator and cut dough in half. Keep dough covered to prevent it from drying out.
4. Set pasta machine at widest setting and put dough through (one half at a time), then fold and turn. Do this five to six times. Dust with extra flour and semolina to prevent sticking. Continue to put dough through each setting three times until you reach the second to last setting.
5. Set pasta machine on fettuccini cutter, cut dough into even lengths, then feed through the fettuccine cutter. Hang fettuccine to dry for 1 hour (or less if it is a hot day). Continue with remaining piece of dough.

Recipe continued over page . . .

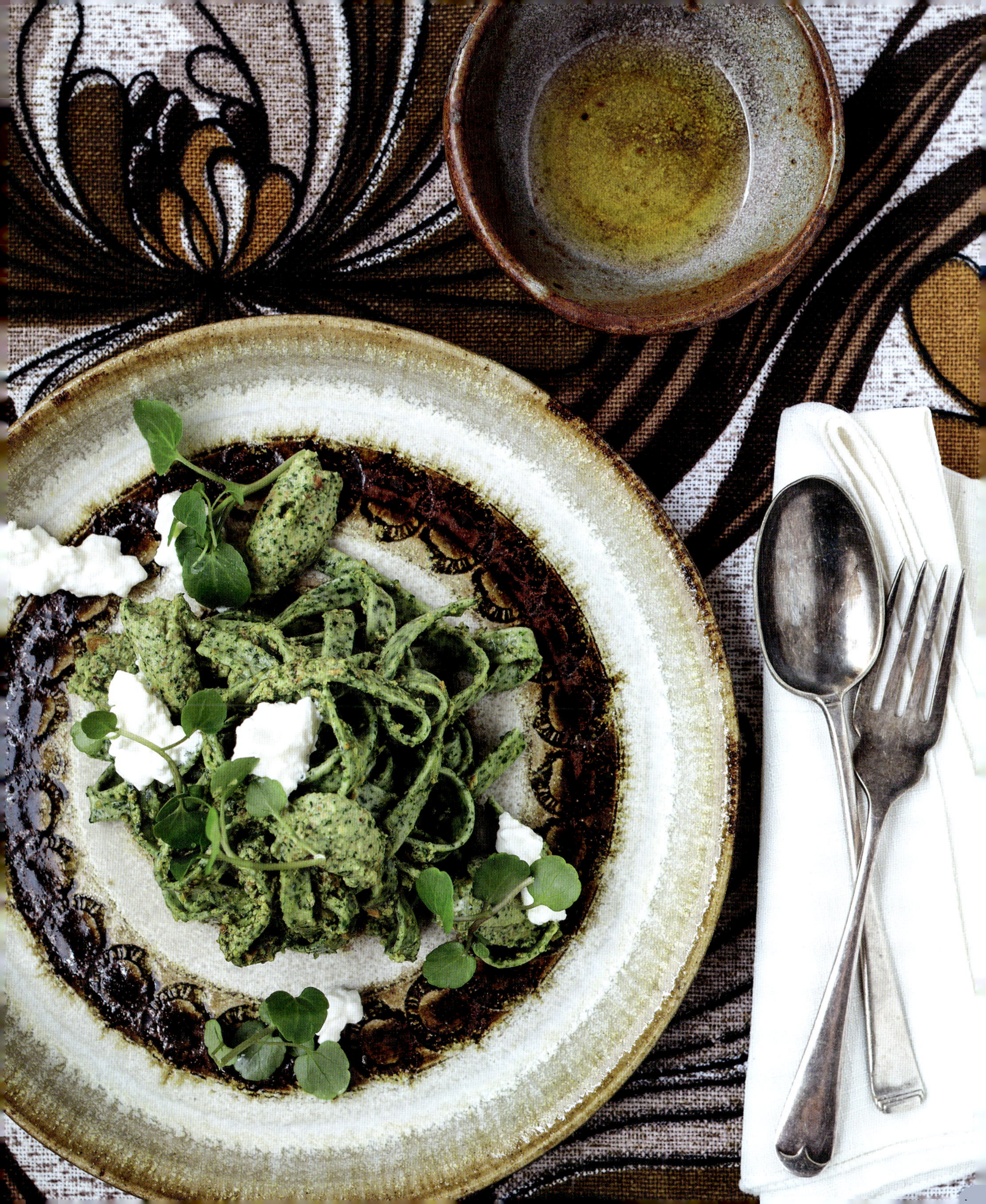

Fettuccini and Green Pesto continued . . .

LEMON OIL

½ lemon
6 tablespoons olive oil

TO SERVE

⅓ cup cottage cheese
extra watercress to garnish

6. Fill a large saucepan with water and lightly salt. Bring to the boil, place in pasta and cook for 1–2 minutes or until al dente. Drain well, reserving pasta water for serving.

FOR THE OIL

1. Crush lemon with the blade of a large sharp knife and place in a small saucepan with the oil.
2. Bring to a simmer, then immediately take off heat, otherwise oil will turn bitter.

TO SERVE

1. Heat a dash of oil in a large hot frying pan, toss in fettuccini with 6 tablespoons green pesto and 1 cup reserved pasta water. Cook until hot (you don't want to overcook fettuccini). Tip into serving bowls, sprinkle 1 teaspoon cottage cheese over each serving of fettuccini and top with watercress. Drizzle over a little lemon oil.

Tip: Cook in batches if your frying pan is not large enough.

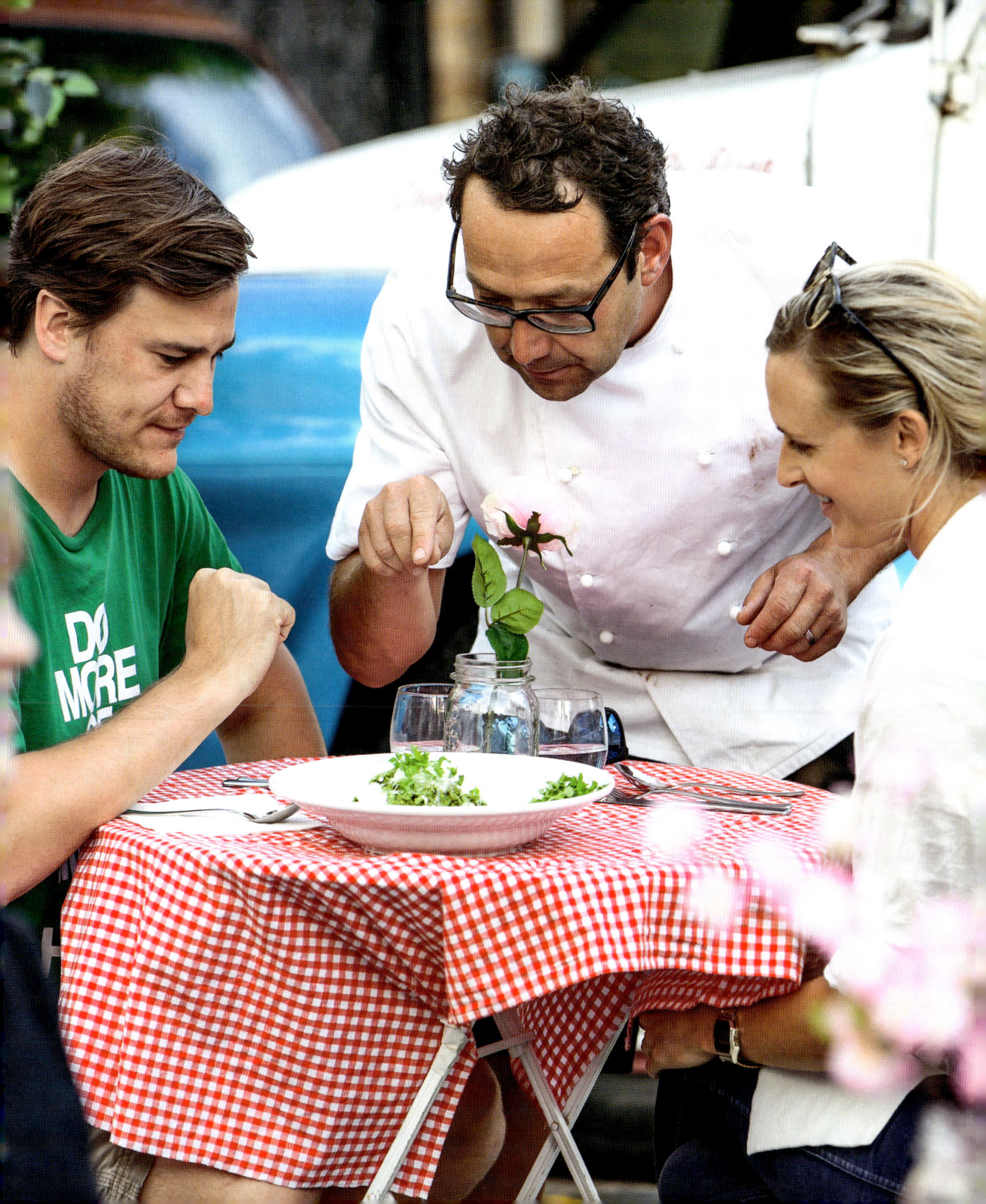
DO MORE

The Bolognese sauce makes more than you will need, so serve it with other ravioli, freeze for later use, or make half the quantity.

Energy KJs	Protein	Total fat
3264	34g	22g

Saturated fat	Carbohydrate	Sodium
5g	105g	497mg

Ravioli Bolognese

Serves 4 • *Makes* 16 x 10cm ravioli • *Preparation time* 2 hours • *Cooking time* 24 minutes

BOLOGNESE SAUCE

350g premium beef mince
olive oil for cooking
1 onion, chopped
1 clove garlic, crushed
½ teaspoon chopped thyme
½ teaspoon chopped oregano
2 x 400g cans chopped tomatoes
1 tablespoon honey
pinch salt and freshly ground black pepper
½ cup chopped Italian parsley leaves
4 flat mushrooms, roasted and finely chopped
2 carrots, finely chopped
½ cup green lentils, cooked
¼ cup bulghur wheat, cooked (see method on page 179)

FOR THE SAUCE

1. Brown mince in a little oil in a wide heavy-based frying pan, transfer to a plate and set aside.
2. Soften onion and garlic in a dash of olive oil in the same pan, about 5 minutes.
3. Add thyme, oregano, chopped tomatoes, honey, salt and pepper. Bring to the boil, then remove from heat.
4. Stir through chopped parsley, mushrooms, carrots, lentils, bulghur wheat and beef mince. Taste for seasoning and set aside to cool.

FOR THE PASTE

1. Place all ingredients in a blender and blend until smooth. Transfer to a bowl, cover with plastic wrap and set aside.

FOR THE DOUGH

1. Place flour, eggs, olive oil and 6 tablespoons red paste in an electric mixer fitted with a dough hook. Mix until a soft smooth dough is formed, about 5 minutes. If dough is sticky add more flour, or knead by hand for 15–20 minutes until smooth.
2. Wrap dough in plastic wrap and refrigerate for 30 minutes. Remove from refrigerator and cut dough in half. Keep dough covered to prevent it from drying out.

Recipe continued over page . . .

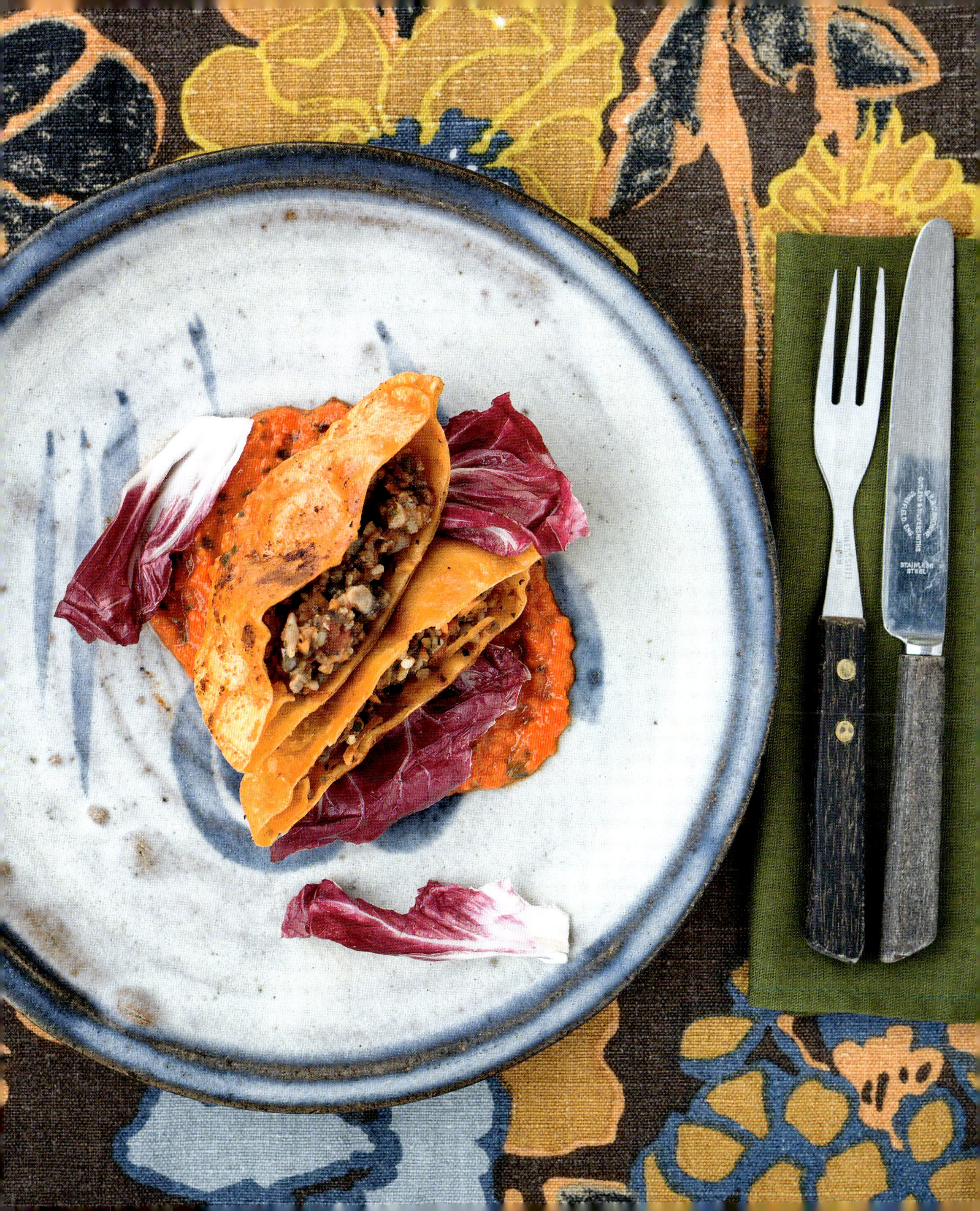

Ravioli Bolognese continued . . .

RED PASTE

MAKES 1 CUP

¼ cup semi-dried tomatoes
2 tablespoons paprika
2 tablespoons tomato paste
1 tablespoon olive oil

PASTA DOUGH

450g high-grade or strong flour
4 eggs
2 tablespoons olive oil
extra flour and fine semolina for rolling

PEPPERANATO PURÉE

1 tablespoon olive oil
3 onions, finely sliced
2 cloves garlic, crushed
500g Roma tomatoes, skinned and cut into quarters
4 red peppers, chargrilled, skinned, deseeded and sliced (see method on page 36)
1 handful fresh basil leaves
pinch salt
freshly ground black pepper

radicchio leaves for serving

3. Set pasta machine at widest setting and put dough through (one half at a time), then fold and turn. Do this five to six times. Dust with extra flour and semolina to prevent sticking. Continue to put dough through each setting three times until you reach the last setting.
4. Cut rolled dough into 10cm rounds. Spoon 2 tablespoons Bolognese sauce on to one round, brush edges with a little cold water, then place another round on top and press down. Continue with remaining rounds of dough.
5. Fill a large saucepan with water and lightly salt. Bring to the boil and, in batches, blanch ravioli in boiling water for 8 minutes, then plunge into iced water. Remove ravioli once cold and place on a tray lined with plastic wrap, slightly apart, until ready to pan-fry.

FOR THE PURÉE

1. Heat olive oil in a heavy-based saucepan. Add onions and garlic and cook until soft.
2. Add tomato quarters, sliced peppers and cook for 2–3 minutes or until most of the liquid has evaporated.
3. Add basil and purée with a stick blender or in a food processor. Season with salt and pepper.

TO ASSEMBLE

1. Preheat oven to 180°C. Line a shallow baking tray with baking paper.
2. Place ravioli in a frying pan with a dash of oil and pan-fry until golden on both sides. You will need to do this in batches.
3. Place ravioli in prepared baking tray and cook for 10 minutes.
4. Serve ravioli with pepperanato purée and radicchio leaves.

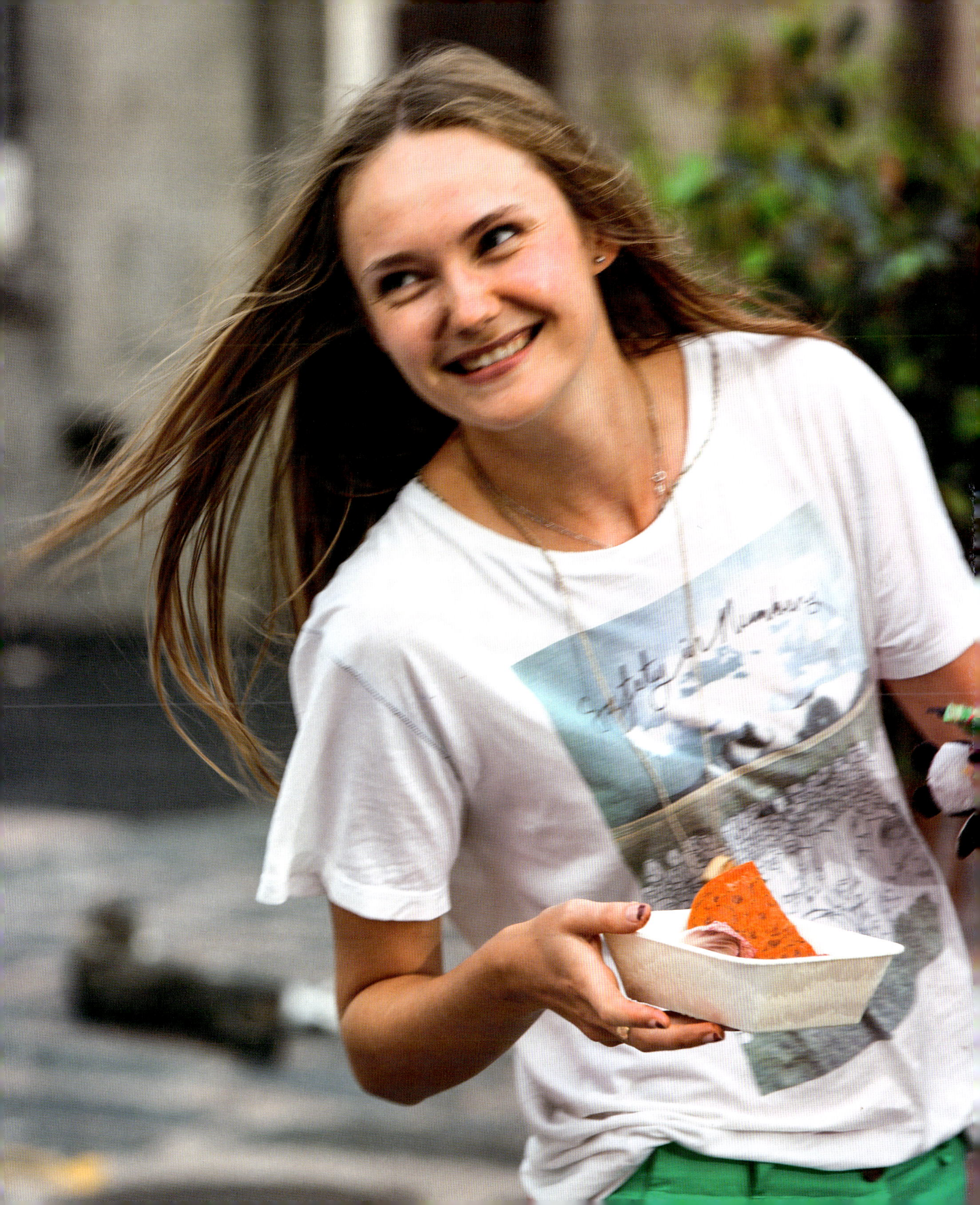

These are a great combo of two well-known Italian desserts. They're a fantastic end to a meal.

Energy KJs	Protein	Total fat
796	5g	10g

Saturated fat	Carbohydrate	Sodium
8g	20g	40mg

Tiramisu Profiteroles

Makes 12 • **Preparation time** *Soak fruit overnight* • **Cooking time** *35 minutes*

RAISIN AND FIG PASTE
1 cup raisins
8 dried figs
100ml Marsala wine
2 tablespoons honey

CHOUX PASTRY
50ml coconut oil
50ml lite olive oil
1½ cups plain flour
3 eggs
30ml espresso coffee
1 teaspoon brown sugar

FILLING
200g ricotta cheese
1 teaspoon vanilla bean paste
2 tablespoons raisin and fig paste

GLAZE
60ml espresso coffee
2 tablespoons honey
good-quality cocoa powder for dipping

FOR THE PASTE
1. Place raisins and figs in a small bowl, pour over Marsala wine, cover and leave to soak overnight.
2. Place soaked fruit and honey in a blender and blend until smooth. Transfer to a bowl and set aside.

FOR THE PASTRY
1. Preheat oven to 170°C. Line a baking tray with baking paper.
2. Place coconut and olive oils in a medium-sized saucepan and allow to melt. Stir in flour and cook for about 5 minutes.
3. Beat in eggs, one at a time until mixture is smooth and glossy. Beat in espresso and brown sugar.
4. Spoon or pipe choux pastry onto lined baking tray, making about 12 buns. Place in oven and bake for 25 minutes, then lower oven temperature to 120°C and bake for a further 10 minutes.
5. Remove profiteroles from oven and pierce on one side with a small sharp knife to allow steam to escape.

FOR THE FILLING
1. Mix ingredients together in a bowl. Using a piping bag fitted with a small plain nozzle, pipe mixture into profiteroles. Alternatively, cut a slightly larger hole in profiteroles and spoon in filling.

FOR THE GLAZE
1. Mix together coffee and honey. Dip filled profiteroles in glaze, then dip in cocoa powder.

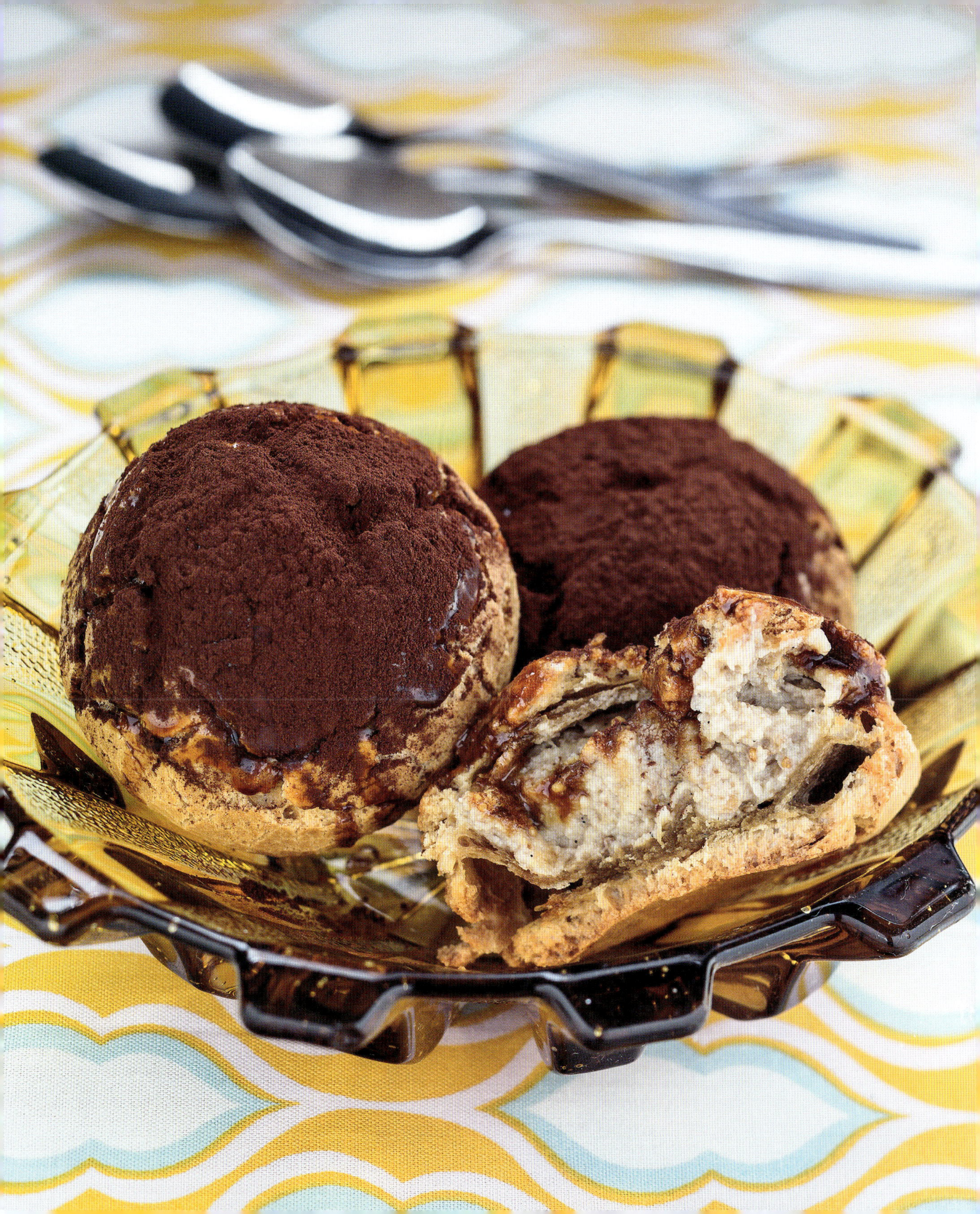

Tito Cucciniello
Pane & Vino

Tito is the owner of Pane & Vino restaurant, a quaint little eatery in Auckland's Grey Lynn. Tito is like a walking Italian cartoon character, talking, yelling and screaming with his hands. He's so full of passion, so full of life, he's amazing! I could have happily listened to him talk about food until my eardrums bled. It's debatable whether the level of his voice would have done it first though!

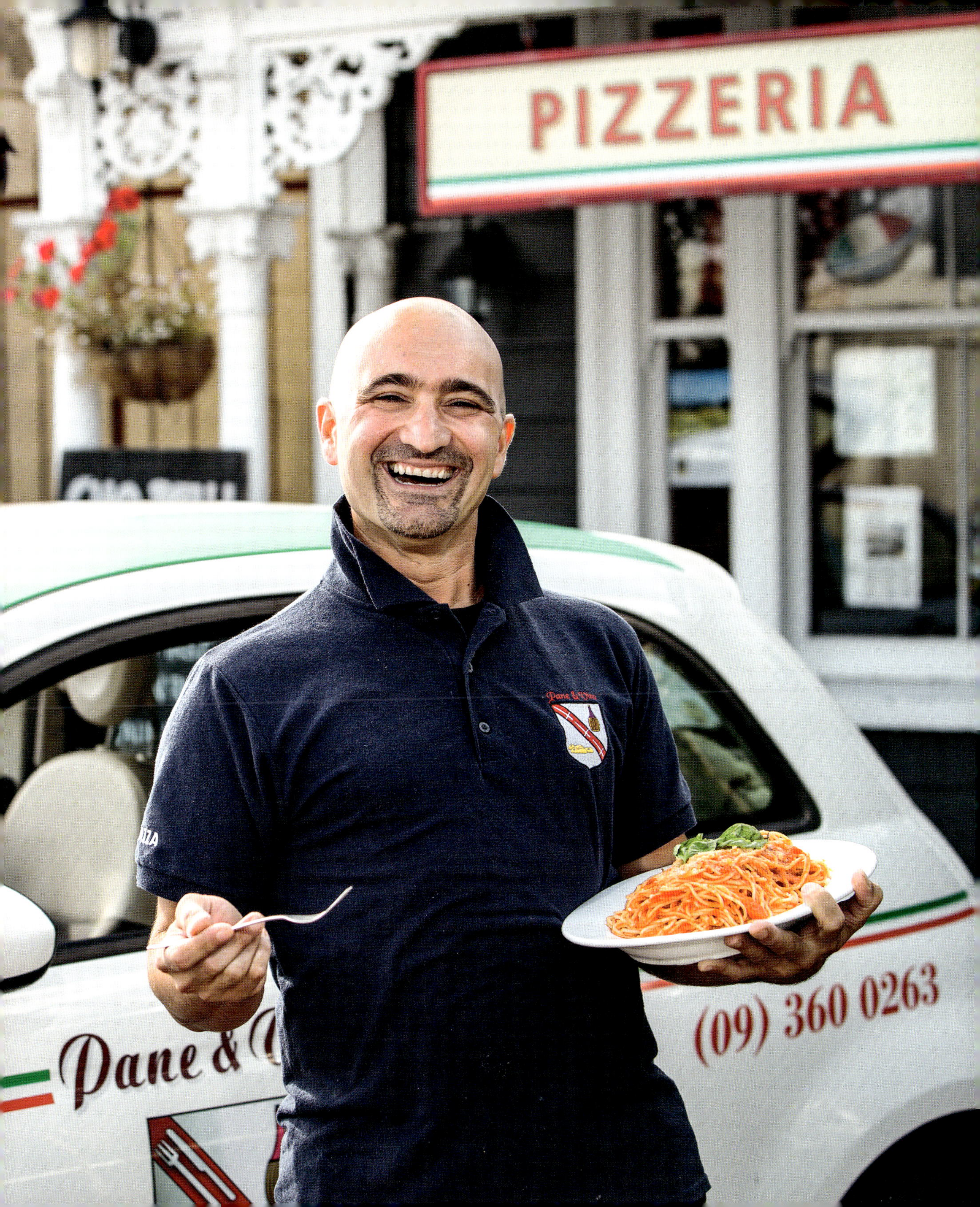
PIZZERIA
(09) 360 0263
Pane &

If you saw the German episode you'll know these didn't work out so well. This recipe has been changed to make a softer pretzel, so you won't *need* a beer to wash them down, though it would only help.

Energy KJs	Protein	Total fat
661	5g	4.3g

Saturated fat	Carbohydrate	Sodium
.6g	27g	85mg

Pretzels

Makes 12 • Preparation time 1½ hours • Cooking time 12–15 minutes

2 tablespoons sugar
1 cup warm water
7g dried yeast
2 cups wholemeal flour
1 cup plain flour, plus extra for kneading
½ teaspoon salt
⅓ cup flax meal
1 tablespoon olive oil
1–2 teaspoons chopped fresh thyme leaves
1 egg yolk mixed with 2 tablespoons water
2 teaspoons poppy seeds
2 teaspoons sesame seeds

1. Place 1 tablespoon of sugar and the warm water in a small bowl and sprinkle over yeast. Leave in a warm place to froth, about 5 minutes.
2. In a large mixing bowl combine flours, salt, flax meal and remaining sugar. Add oil, thyme and yeast mixture and mix to form a dough.
3. Place dough onto a lightly floured bench top and knead for about 10 minutes until dough is smooth and no longer sticky. Use a little extra flour as needed. Alternatively, kneading can be done in an electric mixer with a dough hook.
4. Place dough back in lightly oiled bowl, cover with a tea towel and leave in a warm place to rise until doubled in size, about 1 hour.
5. Preheat oven to 190°C. Line a large baking tray with baking paper.
6. Knock back dough and divide into 12 even-sized pieces. Roll 1 piece into a 40cm long rope and shape into a pretzel (bow). Place on baking tray and repeat with remaining pieces.
7. Brush pretzels with egg wash and sprinkle with poppy and sesame seeds.
8. Place in oven and bake for 12–15 minutes until well browned. Serve warm.

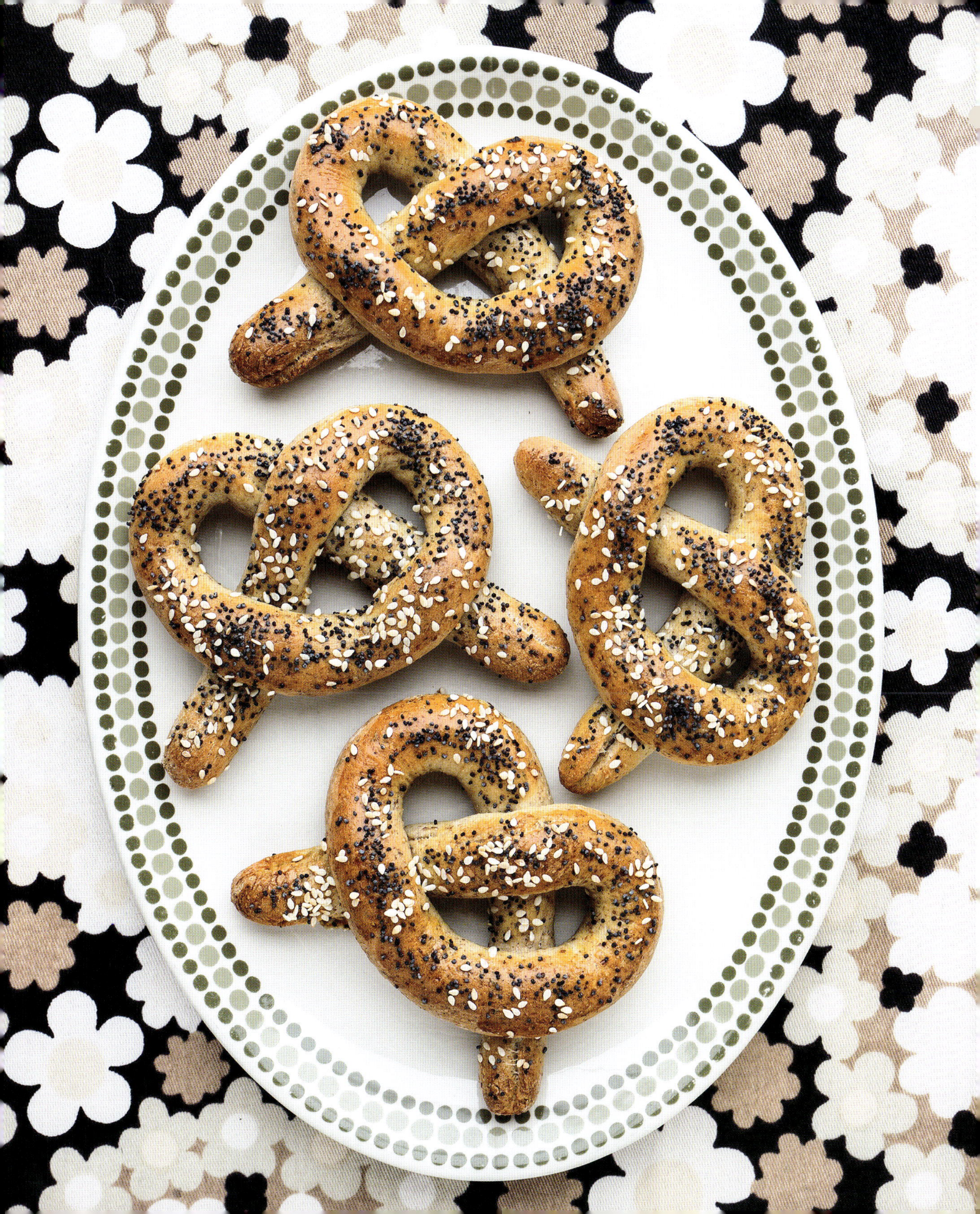

This crumb is sensational. Make a batch and keep in your freezer to pull out at short notice. Put it on your next baked fish 'n' chips.

Energy KJs	Protein	Total fat
1276	30g	10g

Saturated fat	Carbohydrate	Sodium
1.8g	25g	373mg

Almond-Crusted Pork Schnitzel

Serves 6 • *Preparation time* 20 minutes • *Cooking time* about 4 minutes

2 cups dried wholemeal sourdough breadcrumbs
½ cup dry-roasted almonds, finely chopped
4 tablespoons ground LSA (linseed, sunflower, almond)
2 tablespoons toasted sesame seeds
1–2 tablespoons mustard powder
2 tablespoons chopped parsley
zest of 1 lemon
pinch salt
¼ teaspoon ground black pepper
6 pork schnitzel (about 100g each), cut into strips
2 egg whites, lightly beaten

1. Preheat fan oven grill to high. Lightly oil a shallow roasting dish.
2. In a large shallow bowl, combine breadcrumbs, almonds, LSA, sesame seeds, mustard powder, parsley, lemon zest, salt and pepper.
3. Dip pork schnitzel strips into egg white, then coat evenly in crumb mixture. Place in roasting dish and place under grill, turning once and cooking until golden brown and crisp.
4. Serve straight away with sauerkraut aïoli (see page 122).

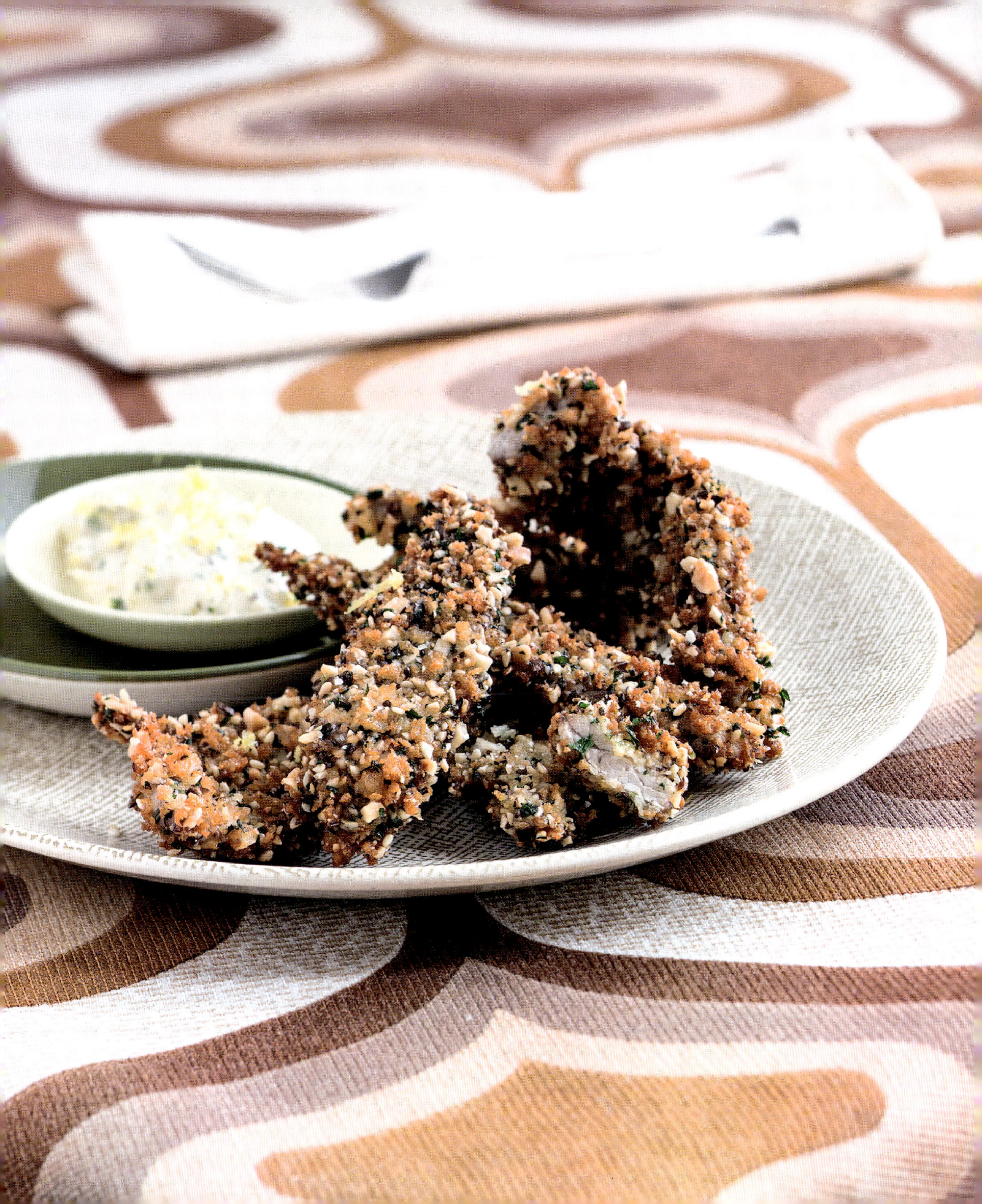

You can enjoy the sauerkraut and aïoli on their own, or combine to make a sauce that's perfect with the almond-crusted pork schnitzel.

Energy KJs	Protein	Total fat
850	2g	19g

Saturated fat	Carbohydrate	Sodium
1.4g	8g	236mg

Sauerkraut Aïoli

Makes 2 cups • Preparation time 30 minutes • Cooking time 35 minutes

SAUERKRAUT

1 tablespoon grapeseed oil
½ onion, finely sliced
1 tablespoon crushed garlic
¼ savoy cabbage, very finely sliced
½ teaspoon caraway seeds
½ teaspoon Himalayan fine-ground salt
¾ cup cider vinegar
¼ cup apple cider
¼ cup water

SAUERKRAUT AÏOLI

2 egg yolks
2 tablespoons water
1 cup cooked and mashed potato (use 1 large peeled potato)
100ml grapeseed oil
pinch salt and white pepper

FOR THE SAUERKRAUT

1. Heat oil in a frying pan, add onion and garlic and cook over a low heat until soft but not coloured.
2. Add cabbage, caraway seeds, salt, vinegar, cider and water. Simmer for 30 minutes until all liquid has been absorbed. Leave to cool.

FOR THE AÏOLI

1. Place cooled sauerkraut in a food processor and blend until smooth.
2. Add egg yolks, water and mashed potato and process until combined. Drizzle oil through feed tube until mixture is emulsified, then season with salt and white pepper. If sauerkraut aïoli is too thick, add a little extra water to thin. The aïoli will keep in the refrigerator for 2–3 days.
3. Serve with almond-crusted pork schnitzel.

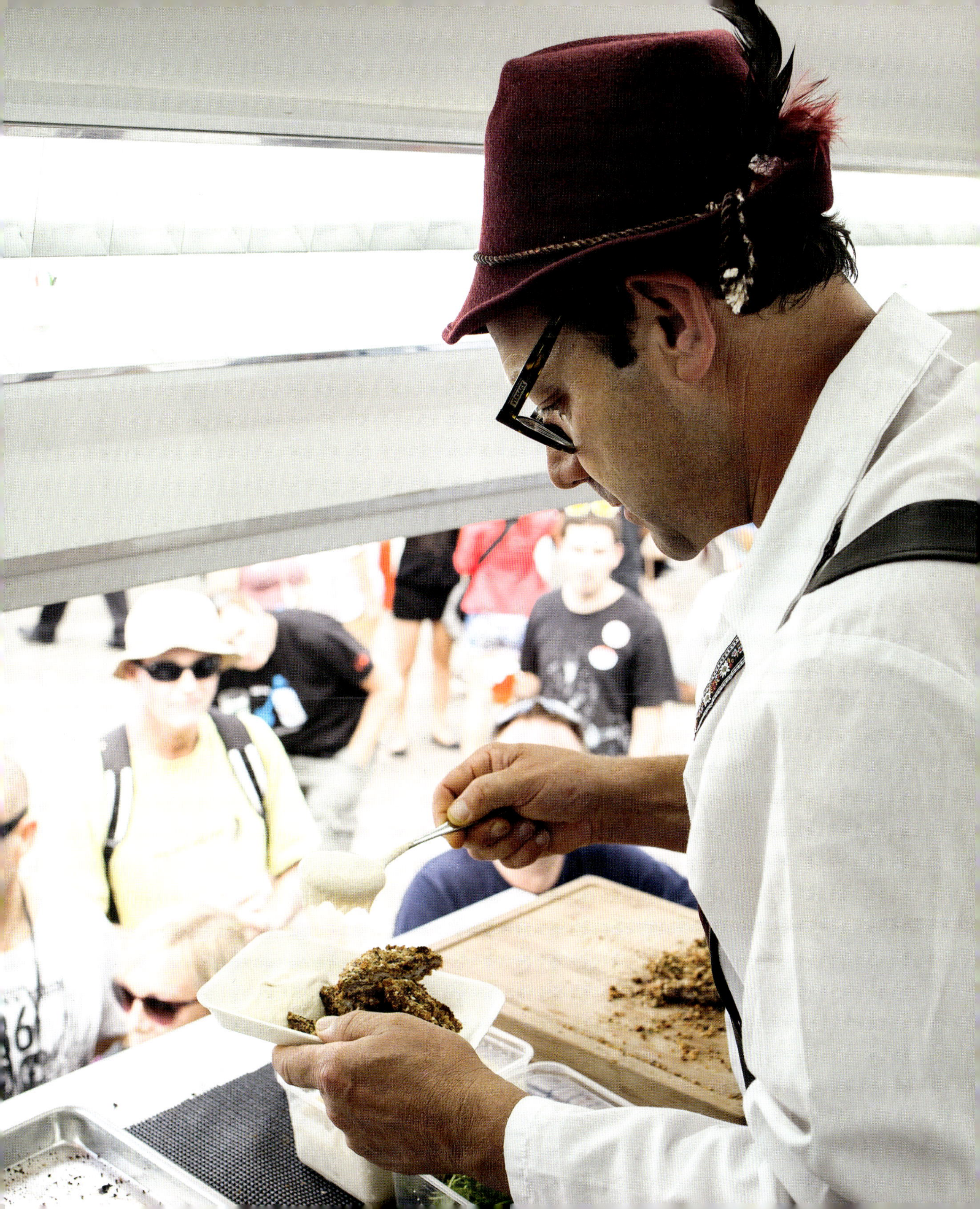

The skinless sausage! When I sold this at the New Zealand Beer Festival, it was a slow seller because I called it 'Currywurst'! When I changed it to 'Currywurst Sausage' it flew out the door!

Energy KJs	Protein	Total fat
2133	51g	16g

Saturated fat	Carbohydrate	Sodium
5g	42g	893mg

Bratwurst with Curry Sauce

Serves 4 • Preparation time 1 hour, plus chilling time for bratwurst • Cooking time 50–55 minutes

CURRY SAUCE

MAKES: 2 CUPS

1 tablespoon grapeseed oil
1 onion, chopped
2 cloves garlic, chopped
1 tablespoon curry powder
2 cooking apples, peeled, cored and chopped
1 green kiwifruit, peeled and chopped
1 x 400g can chopped tomatoes
1 tablespoon tomato paste
1 tablespoon liquid honey
pinch salt
½ teaspoon white pepper

FOR THE SAUCE

1. Heat oil in a medium-sized saucepan, add onion and garlic and cook over a low heat until soft, about 10 minutes. Stir in curry powder and cook for 1 minute.
2. Add apple, kiwifruit, tomatoes, tomato paste, honey, salt and pepper. Cook for 20–25 minutes. Allow to cool a little before puréeing in a food processor or blender. Set aside until ready to reheat.

Recipe continued over page . . .

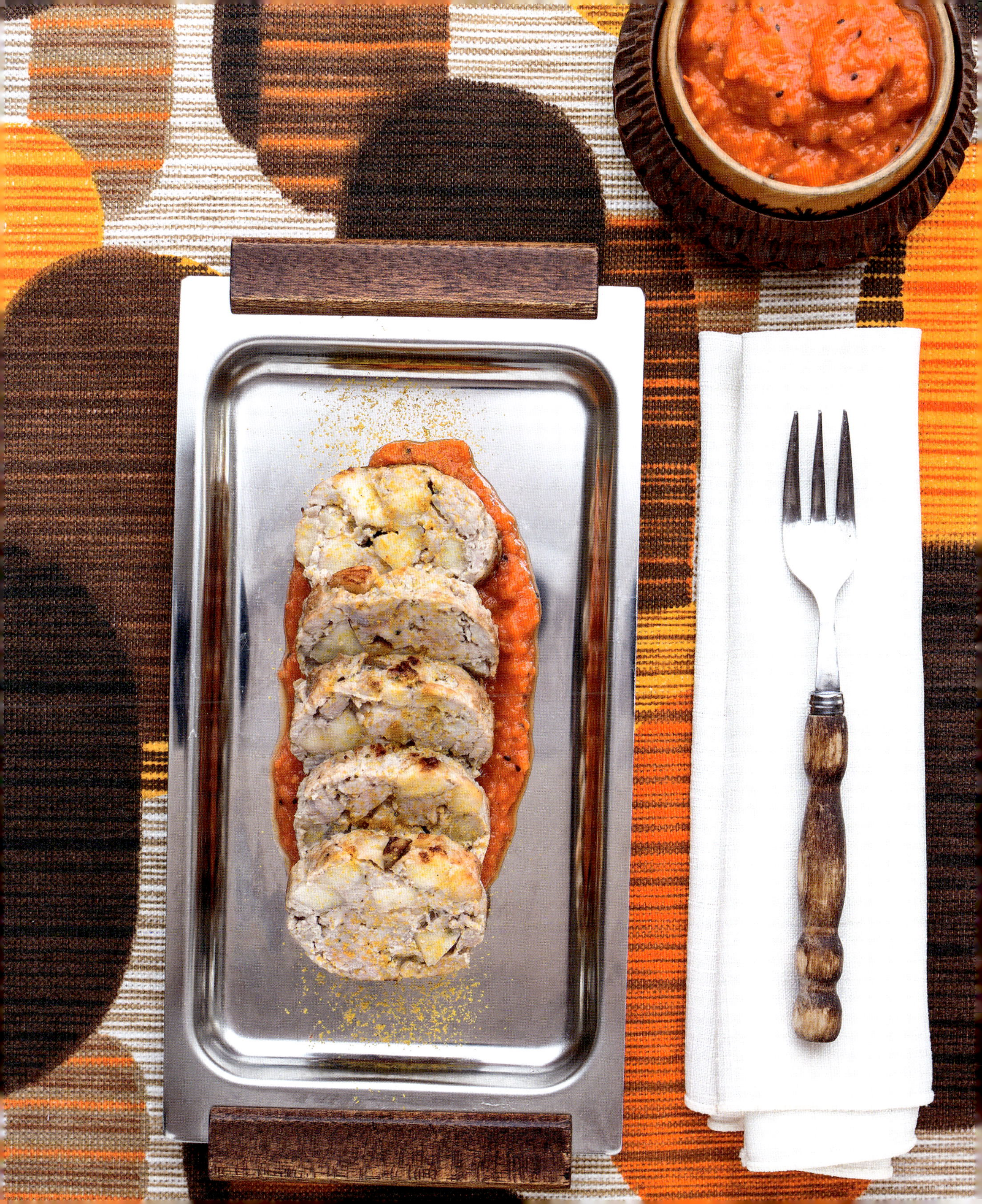

Bratwurst with Curry Sauce continued . . .

BRATWURST

1kg pork shoulder, minced
1 teaspoon Himalayan fine-ground salt
½ teaspoon ground black pepper
1 teaspoon sugar
¾ teaspoon dried marjoram
¾ teaspoon ground coriander
¾ teaspoon ground ginger
¾ teaspoon ground nutmeg
½ teaspoon mustard powder
½ cup dried apple, chopped
1 cup iced water

2 sheets greaseproof paper, cut into A4 size
plastic wrap and string

FOR THE BRATWURST

1. Combine all ingredients except iced water in the bowl of an electric mixer with a paddle attachment. Beat in iced water until well combined. Alternatively, you can use a large metal spoon to mix ingredients. (At this stage I like to fry a little piece off to check the seasoning).
2. Lay 2 sheets of greaseproof paper on bench top and place half of mixture on each piece of paper.
3. Roll up tightly to form a cigar shape, then roll each in plastic wrap, twice. Twist both ends and tie tightly with string.
4. Fill a large frying pan with water and bring to boil. Reduce heat to a simmer and place in bratwurst. Poach for 12 minutes. Remove bratwurst from water, and leave to cool before placing in refrigerator to firm up.
5. Heat a dash of oil in a large frying pan. Remove plastic wrap and greaseproof paper from bratwurst and pan-fry bratwurst until golden brown on all sides and hot in the centre.
6. Slice bratwurst and serve with curry sauce.

PORK CURRYWURST SAUSAGE $5

PORK w/ SAU

EALTHIER

SERVING NEW

Jono Walker
Soggy Bottom

When I turned up at Jono's farm in Ngaruawahia I was greeted with a freshly baked pork pie. How awesome is that! This guy is serious about pigs. He has his own butchery (or man cave, as he calls it) on the farm so that he can control the quality from whoa to go. He says his pigs taste so good because they are hugely affectionate and intelligent. It probably also has something to do with the fact they run free-range and have access to everything a pig would love: shelter, shade, wallows, and heaps of mozzarella cheese!

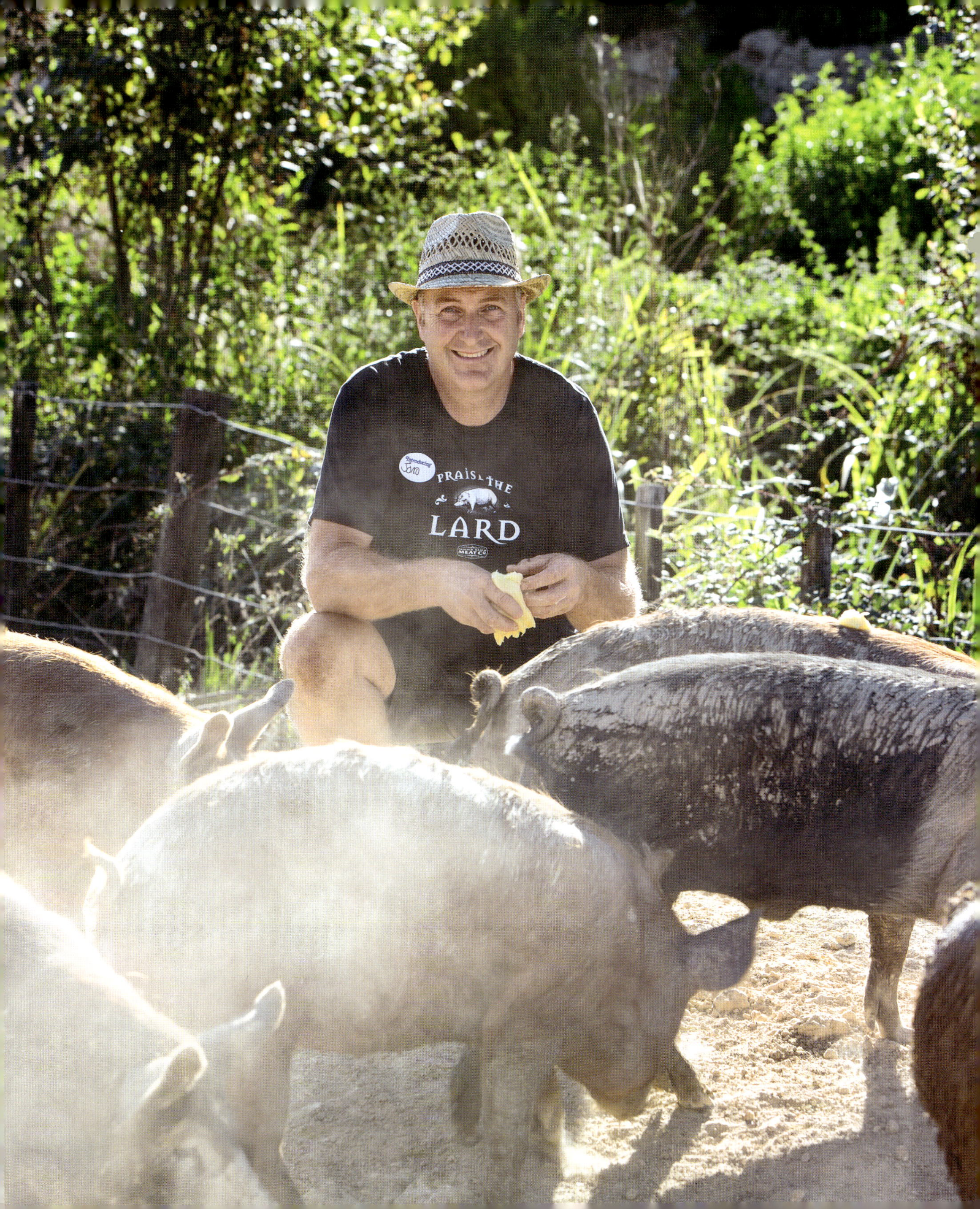
PRAISE THE
LARD

HOME FAVOURITES

BURGERS, PIZZAS, PIES AND MORE

Goat is a super lean meat that's a great alternative to beef or lamb. It may seem exotic here, but it's actually the world's most widely eaten meat. Who woulda thought?!

Energy KJs	Protein	Total fat
518	7g	2.6g

Saturated fat	Carbohydrate	Sodium
.5g	18g	163mg

Cajun-spiced Goat Sliders
served with Home-made Mustard, Tomato Sauce and Roasted Garlic Aïoli

Makes 12 sliders – serve 3 per person • *Preparation time* Soak mustard seeds overnight • *Cooking time* 1 minute

HOME-MADE MUSTARD
MAKES ABOUT 1 CUP

½ cup yellow mustard seeds
½ cup black mustard seeds
½ cup cider vinegar, or to cover
2 tablespoons honey
pinch salt
grapeseed oil to thin, if needed

CAJUN SPICE MIX

1 tablespoon freeze-dried ground garlic
1 tablespoon freeze-dried ground onion
1 tablespoon dried oregano
1 tablespoon dried thyme
1 tablespoon cayenne pepper

GOAT PATTIES
300g goat mince
½ onion, minced
1 tablespoon Cajun spice mix

FOR THE MUSTARD

1. Soak mustard seeds in cider vinegar overnight.
2. The following day, place soaked mustard seeds in a blender with honey and a pinch of salt and blend until smooth. Add a little grapeseed oil to thin, if necessary.

FOR THE SPICE MIX AND PATTIES

1. Mix all Cajun spice mix ingredients together in a bowl.
2. Mix all patty ingredients together. Form into 12 small flat patties.
3. Heat a large heavy-based frying pan over a high heat, add a dash of oil. Place goat patties in and cook quickly for 1 minute, turning once.

Recipe continued over page . . .

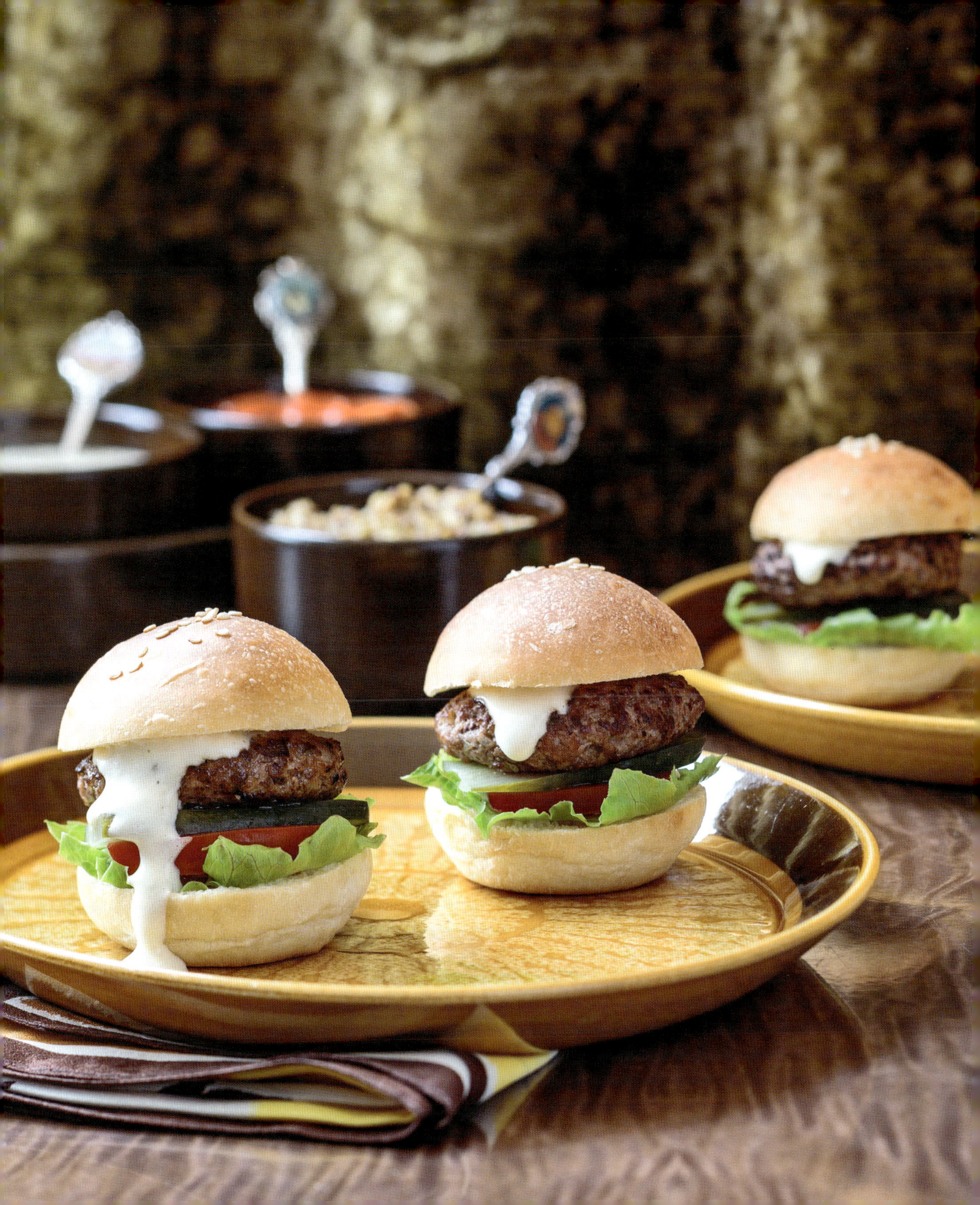

Cajun-spiced Goat Sliders continued . . .

TOMATO SAUCE

300g beefsteak tomatoes, cut in half horizontally
5 cloves garlic, peeled
6 sprigs thyme
4 stalks rosemary
pinch salt
1 tablespoon olive oil
1 handful each fresh basil and parsley

PICKLED DILL CUCUMBERS

½ onion, finely diced
3 cloves garlic, crushed
¼ cup red wine vinegar
¼ cup warm water
2 tablespoons liquid honey
½ teaspoon mustard powder
¼ teaspoon ground allspice
¼ teaspoon dill seed
¼ teaspoon ground coriander
250g small pickling cucumbers, well washed
1 tablespoon chopped fresh dill
pinch salt and freshly ground black pepper

ROASTED GARLIC AÏOLI

2 eggs, soft boiled for 5 minutes and peeled
½ cup plus 2 tablespoons vegetable stock
1 tablespoon olive oil
1 cup cooked potato (about 1 large potato)
5 cloves roasted garlic, peeled
2 tablespoons grapeseed oil

TO ASSEMBLE

tomato sauce
12 slider buns, cut in half
2 large iceberg lettuce leaves, torn
12 cherry tomatoes, cut in half
4 pickled dill cucumbers, sliced
roasted garlic aïoli
home-made mustard

FOR THE SAUCE

1. Preheat oven to 100°C. Spray an oven tray with oil. Arrange tomato halves on oven tray. Sprinkle over garlic, thyme, rosemary and a pinch of salt. Place in oven and leave to dry for 8 hours. Remove herbs. Transfer tomatoes to a blender, add olive oil and fresh basil and parsley, and purée.

FOR THE CUCUMBERS

1. Place onion and garlic in a heavy-based saucepan with a dash of oil and cook over a low heat until soft, about 10 minutes.
2. Add vinegar, water, honey, mustard powder, allspice, dill seed, coriander and pickling cucumbers and cook for 5 minutes. Toss through fresh dill and season with salt and pepper.

FOR THE AÏOLI

1. Place all ingredients except grapeseed oil in a blender and blend until combined.
2. With the motor running, drizzle in grapeseed oil until emulsified. Thin with extra stock or water, if necessary.

TO ASSEMBLE

1. Spread a little tomato sauce on the base of each slider bun, top with lettuce, cherry tomatoes and pickled cucumbers. Place on a patty, spoon over a little roasted garlic aïoli and finish with slider bun tops.
2. Serve with home-made mustard, extra tomato sauce and roasted garlic aïoli.

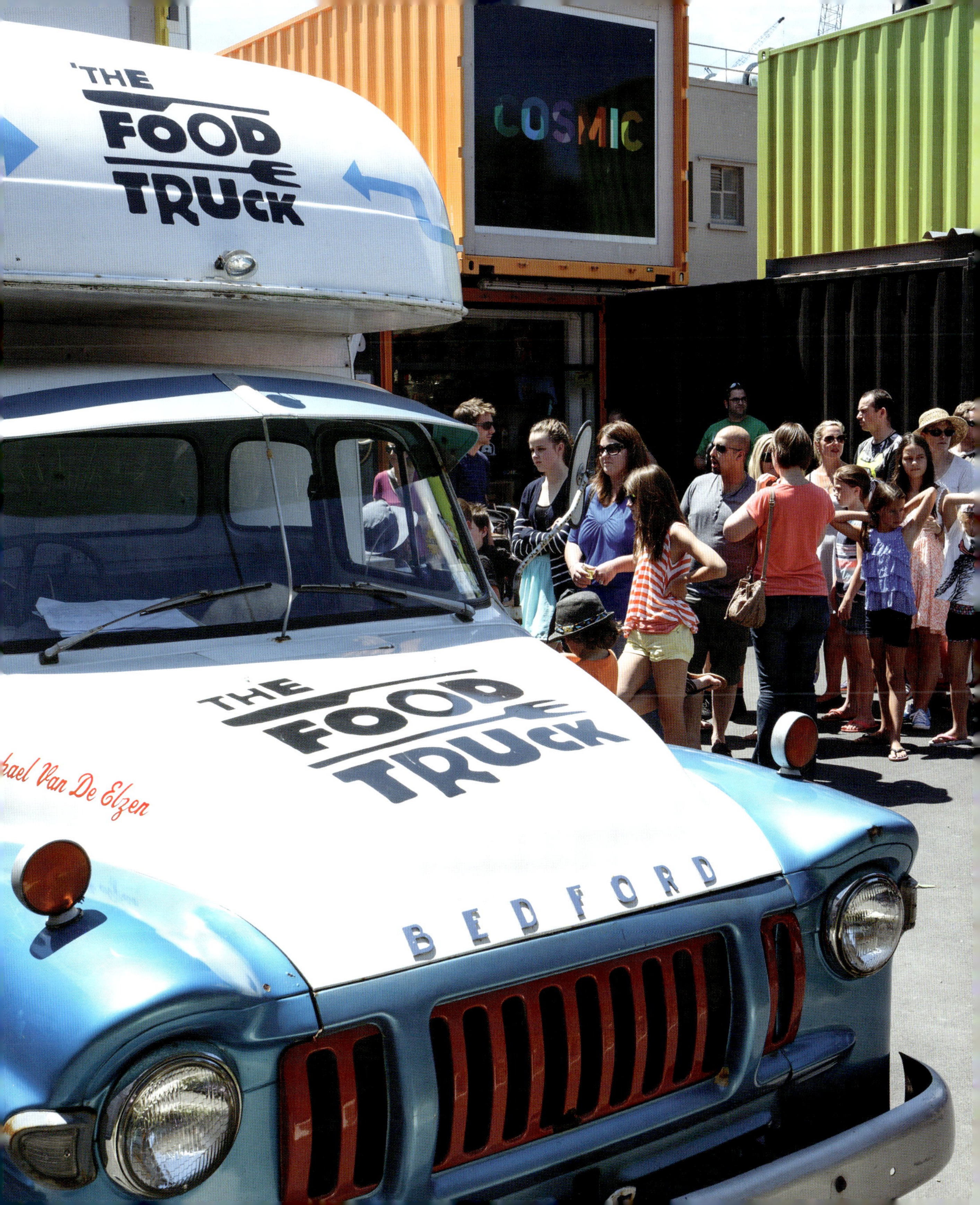
THE FOOD TRUCK
COSMIC
THE FOOD TRUCK
BEDFORD

This is a new spin on the 'Big Mike' from the last book. It's great for a BBQ with the chimichurri salad and lamb chops.

Energy KJs	Protein	Total fat
2247	40g	24g

Saturated fat	Carbohydrate	Sodium
6g	44g	548mg

Spicy Beef Burgers

Serves 4 • Preparation time 1½ hours • Cooking time 10 minutes

PATTIES
500g premium lean beef mince
1 onion, finely diced
1 courgette, grated
½ beetroot, grated
1 teaspoon Dijon mustard
½ teaspoon smoked paprika
3 egg whites

RED SALSA
4 tomatoes, skinned, deseeded and chopped
½ onion, chopped
2 cloves garlic, roughly chopped
10 red chillies, halved and deseeded
pinch salt
1 avocado, diced or sliced

TO ASSEMBLE
4 wholemeal buns
1 cup chimichurri salad and dressing (see page 36)
1–2 heads baby cos lettuce, shredded

FOR THE PATTIES
1. Preheat oven to 180°C.
2. Mix all ingredients together in a bowl. Form into 8 patties.
3. Heat a heavy-based frying pan until hot and brown patties on both sides. Place on a shallow baking tray and place in oven.
4. Cook for 4–5 minutes.

FOR THE SALSA
1. Heat a heavy-based frying pan over a medium heat. Add tomatoes, onion and garlic and cook until just beginning to colour. Transfer to a food processor.
2. Lightly brown chillies in the same frying pan and add to tomato mixture with a pinch of salt.
3. Process until mixture is well blended. Transfer to a bowl and gently fold through avocado.

TO ASSEMBLE
1. Slice buns into three pieces. Add red salsa, patty, chimichurri salad and lettuce on each bun base. Repeat with a second patty on each bun middle. Finish with bun tops.

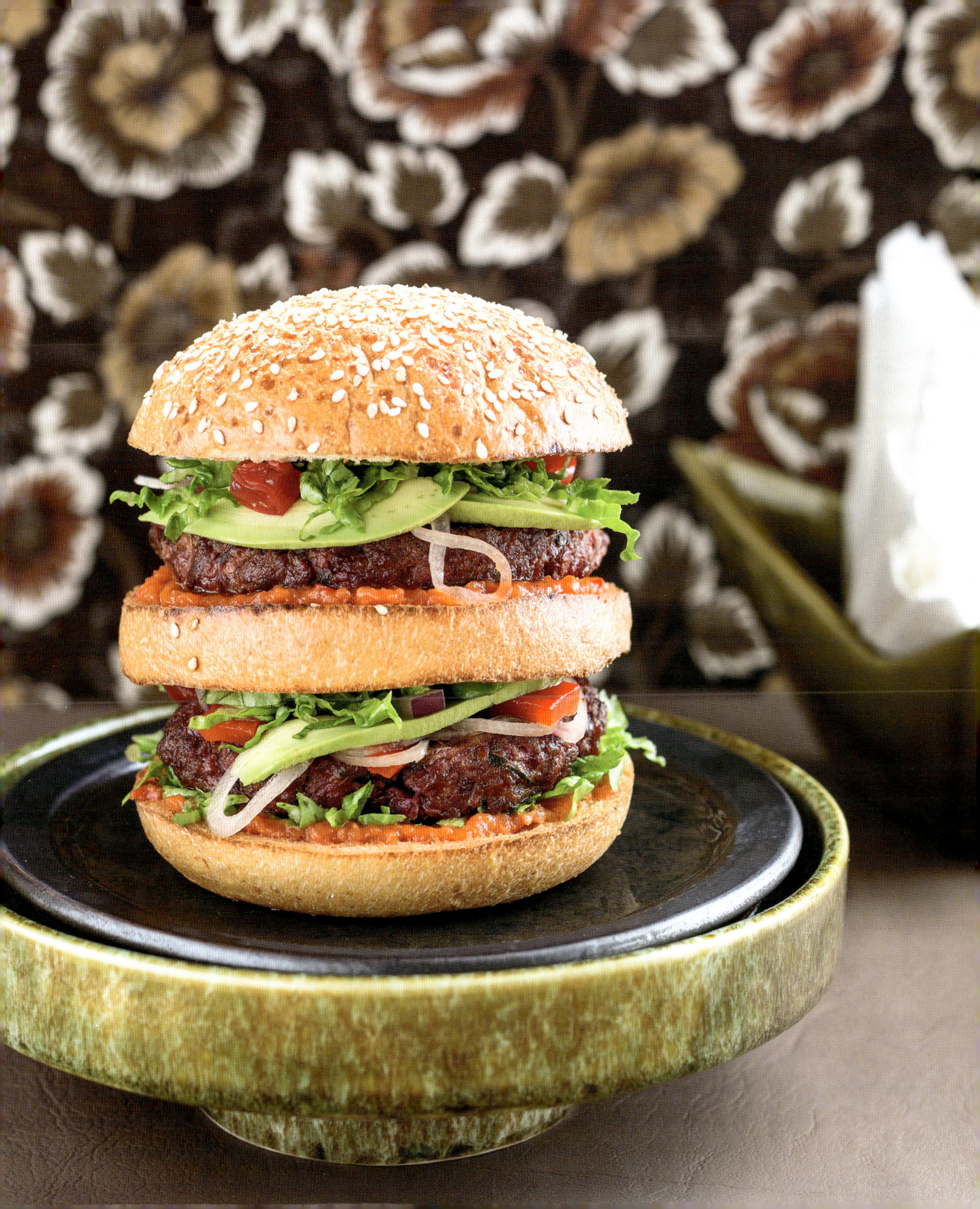

Grilling courgettes enhances their flavour, making them team well with the tomato sauce. The crumble is a clever little finish.

Energy KJs	Protein	Total fat
2735	19g	30g

Saturated fat	Carbohydrate	Sodium
4g	85g	283mg

Grilled Courgette and Tomato Crumble Pizza

Serves 4 *Makes* 2 bases • *Preparation time* 2 hours • *Cooking time* about 30 minutes

CRUMBLE

70g wholemeal flour
70g plain flour
50ml vegetable oil
2 tablespoons coconut sugar
50g prunes, pitted and chopped
50g walnuts, chopped

COURGETTES

5 courgettes, sliced in half lengthwise
2 tablespoons olive oil
pinch salt and pepper

TO ASSEMBLE

2 wholemeal pizza bases, rolled and cooked (see page 140)
6 tablespoons tomato sauce, heated (see page 134)
3 tablespoons pecorino cheese, grated or shaved

FOR THE CRUMBLE

1. Preheat oven to 200°C.
2. Place flours and vegetable oil in a food processor and process until fine breadcrumb stage. Add sugar and process for 10 seconds.
3. Spread out to 1cm thick in a large baking dish and place in oven. Cook until golden. Check crumble and toss after 5 minutes.
4. When golden, add prunes and walnuts and cook for a further 5 minutes, but watch carefully so crumble doesn't burn.

FOR THE COURGETTES

1. Place courgettes in a bowl, add olive oil, salt and pepper, and toss.
2. Heat a barbecue grill plate or chargrill. Grill courgettes until coloured and bite tender.

TO ASSEMBLE

1. Spoon hot tomato sauce over each pizza base, stack courgettes randomly on top and sprinkle generously with crumble and pecorino cheese.

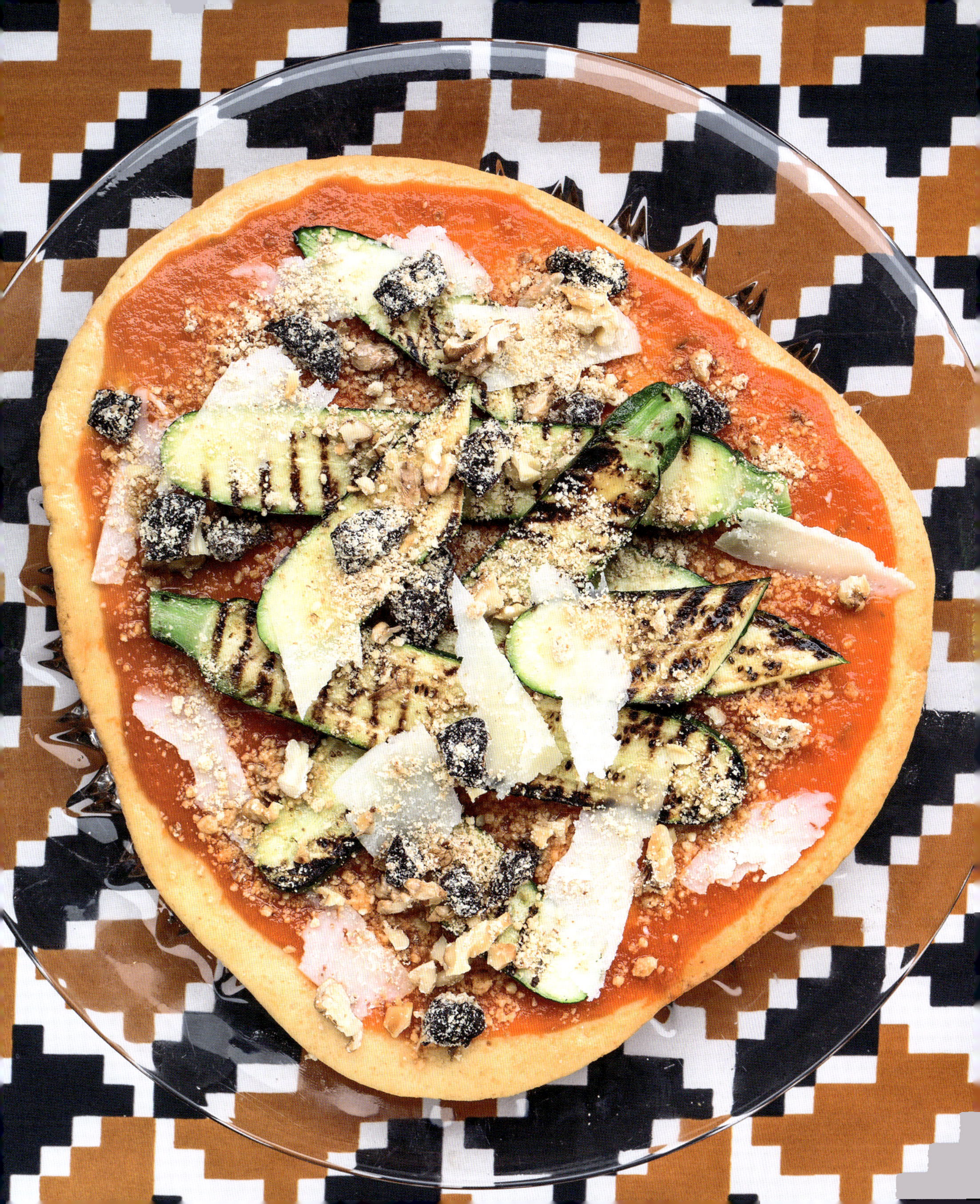

This thin crisp pizza base is covered in sliced potato and finished with a piquant mixture of pickled fennel and tart apple. Leave the apple skin on if you prefer.

Energy KJs	Protein	Total fat
1833	11g	8g

Saturated fat	Carbohydrate	Sodium
3g	89g	427mg

Potato Pizza with Pickled Fennel, Green Apple, Sheep's Feta and Rocket

Serves 4 *Makes* 2 bases • *Preparation time* 2 hours • *Cooking time* 20 minutes

WHOLEMEAL PIZZA DOUGH

150g high-grade or white flour
50g wholemeal flour
pinch salt
60ml low-fat milk
60ml water
7g dried yeast
¼ teaspoon sugar

POTATO TOPPING

10 baby potatoes, cooked to al dente and cooled
2 cloves garlic, crushed
1 tablespoon extra virgin olive oil
½ tablespoon rosemary leaves
pinch salt and freshly ground black pepper

FOR THE DOUGH

1. Sift white flour into a bowl, add wholemeal flour and salt and leave in a warm place.
2. Gently heat milk and water to blood temperature, add yeast and sugar. Leave in a warm place for yeast to froth, about 5 minutes.
3. Add liquid ingredients to dry and mix to form a dough. Turn out onto a lightly floured bench top and knead until smooth, about 10 minutes. Alternatively, knead using an electric mixer fitted with a dough hook.
4. Place dough back in lightly oiled bowl, cover with a clean tea towel and leave in a warm place until double in size, about 1 hour.
5. Knock back dough and leave to rise again, covered, for 20 minutes before using.
6. Divide dough in half and roll out as thinly as possible into 2 pizza bases.

Recipe continued over page . . .

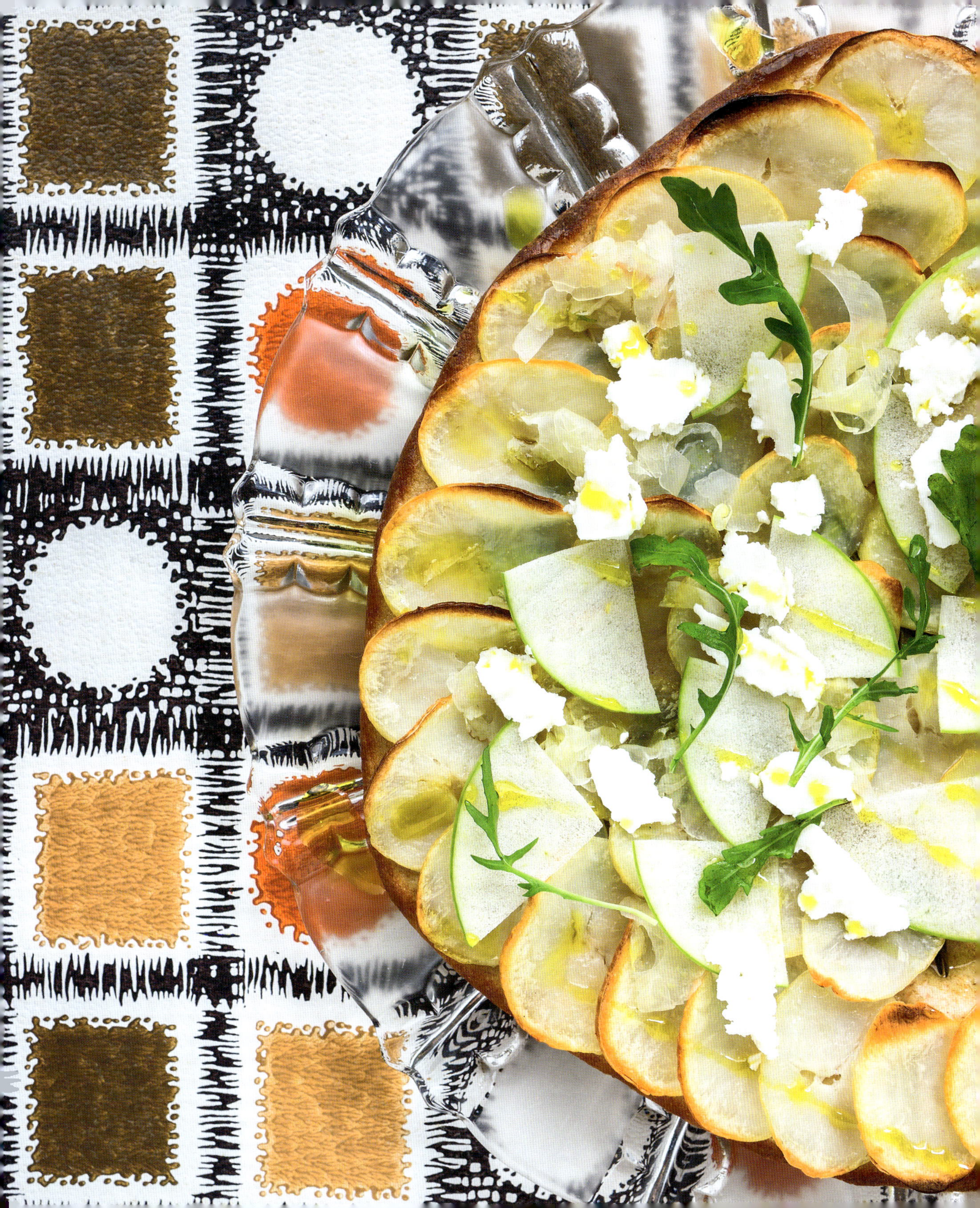

Potato Pizza continued . . .

PICKLED FENNEL

1½ cups white wine vinegar
½ cup sugar
1 star anise
1 bulb fennel, finely sliced using a mandolin

TO ASSEMBLE

2 Granny Smith apples, very thinly sliced
pickled fennel
60g sheep's feta, crumbled
1 handful rocket leaves

FOR THE TOPPING

1. Preheat oven to 190°C. Place 2 baking trays in the oven to heat.
2. Slice potatoes 2mm thick and arrange in a wheel on top of pizza bases. Mix together garlic and oil and brush potato slices, brushing the garlic under the potatoes so it doesn't burn. Sprinkle with rosemary leaves and season with salt and pepper.
3. Carefully transfer pizzas to hot baking trays. Cook for 20 minutes until golden, rotating trays halfway through cooking. Alternatively, place pizza bases on hot baking trays and work very quickly to place on topping.

FOR THE FENNEL

1. Bring vinegar, sugar and star anise to the boil in a saucepan. Remove from heat, add fennel and allow to cool in liquid.

TO ASSEMBLE

1. Toss apples through pickled fennel and arrange on top of cooked pizzas. Dot with sheep's feta and finish with rocket.

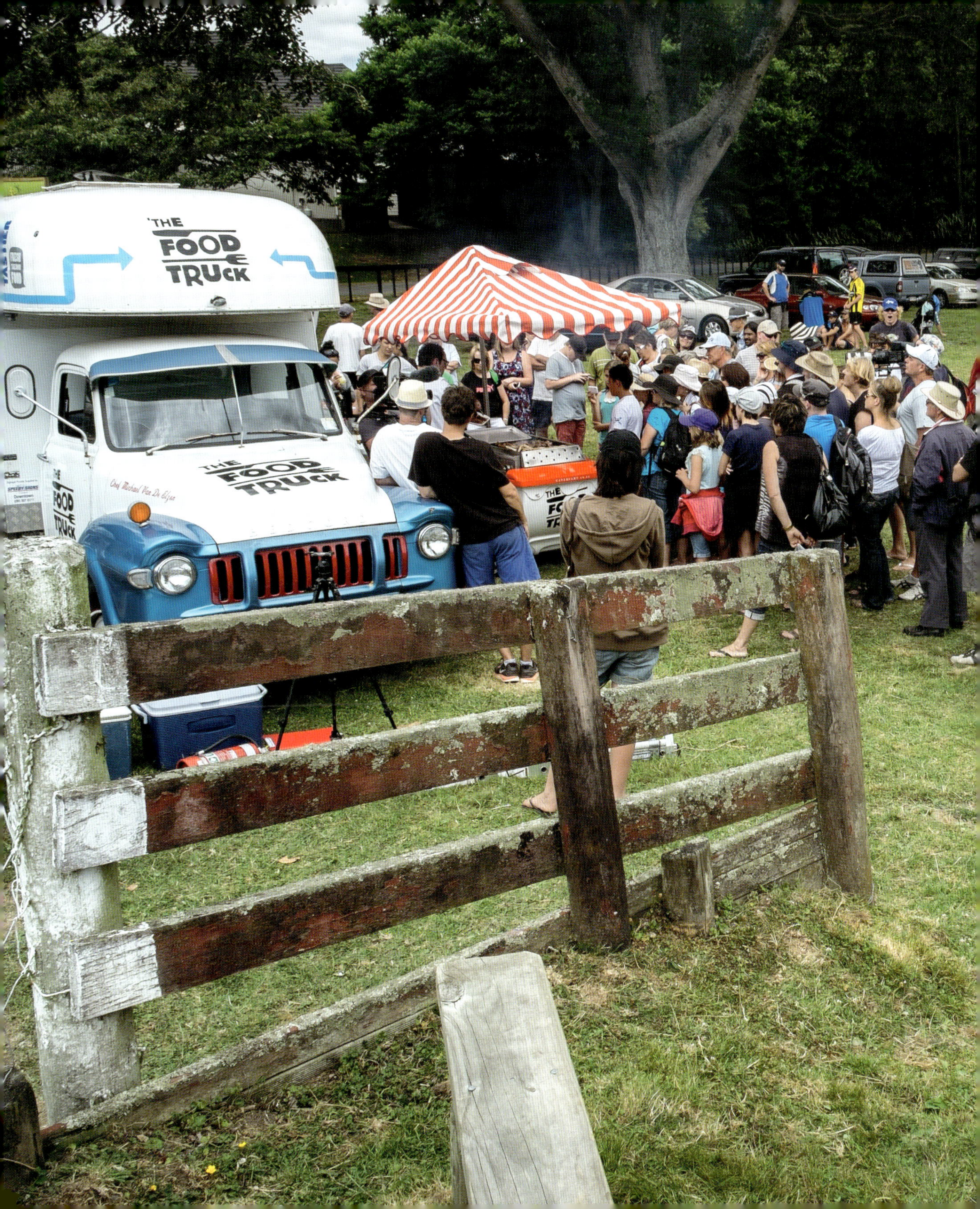
THE FOOD TRUCK
THE FOOD TRUCK

I really wanted to make another pie but couldn't find an episode to sneak this in. So here it is. Who doesn't love a chicken pie?

Energy KJs	Protein	Total fat
1293	27g	8g

Saturated fat	Carbohydrate	Sodium
1.7g	37g	308mg

Chicken Pie

Makes 8 • Preparation time 1 hour and 30 minutes • Cooking time 15-20 minutes

WHOLEMEAL DOUGH

130ml warm water
1 teaspoon sugar
1 teaspoon dried yeast
200g wholemeal flour
100g white flour, sifted
pinch salt
1 tablespoon olive oil

POACHED CHICKEN FILLING

4 skinless, boneless chicken breasts
1½ litres vegetable stock
1 large leek, white part only, finely sliced
2 cloves garlic, crushed
2 cups frozen peas
2 teaspoons cornflour
2 teaspoons Dijon mustard
white pepper to taste

FOR THE DOUGH

1. Place warm water (blood temperature) and sugar in a small bowl and sprinkle over yeast. Leave to froth, about 5 minutes.
2. Place wholemeal flour, white flour, salt and olive oil in a warm bowl. Pour in yeast mixture and mix to form a dough. Add a little more warm water if dough is too dry.
3. Turn out onto a bench top and knead for 10 minutes until dough is smooth. Place dough in a lightly oiled bowl, turning over to coat completely. Cover with plastic wrap and leave to rise in a warm place until doubled in size, about 1 hour.
4. Knock back dough, roll into a ball and cover.

FOR THE FILLING

1. Meanwhile, prepare filling.
2. Place chicken breasts in a suitably sized saucepan with the vegetable stock and place over a medium heat. Bring nearly to a boil, reduce heat to low and poach chicken for about 30 minutes or until the juices run clear.
3. Preheat oven to 180°C.
4. Place a medium-sized saucepan over a low heat with a dash of olive oil. Add leek and garlic and cook until very soft, at least 10 minutes. Add 1 cup chicken poaching liquid (leave remainder to cool, then freeze for another use). Add peas and cook for 2–3 minutes.

Recipe continued over page . . .

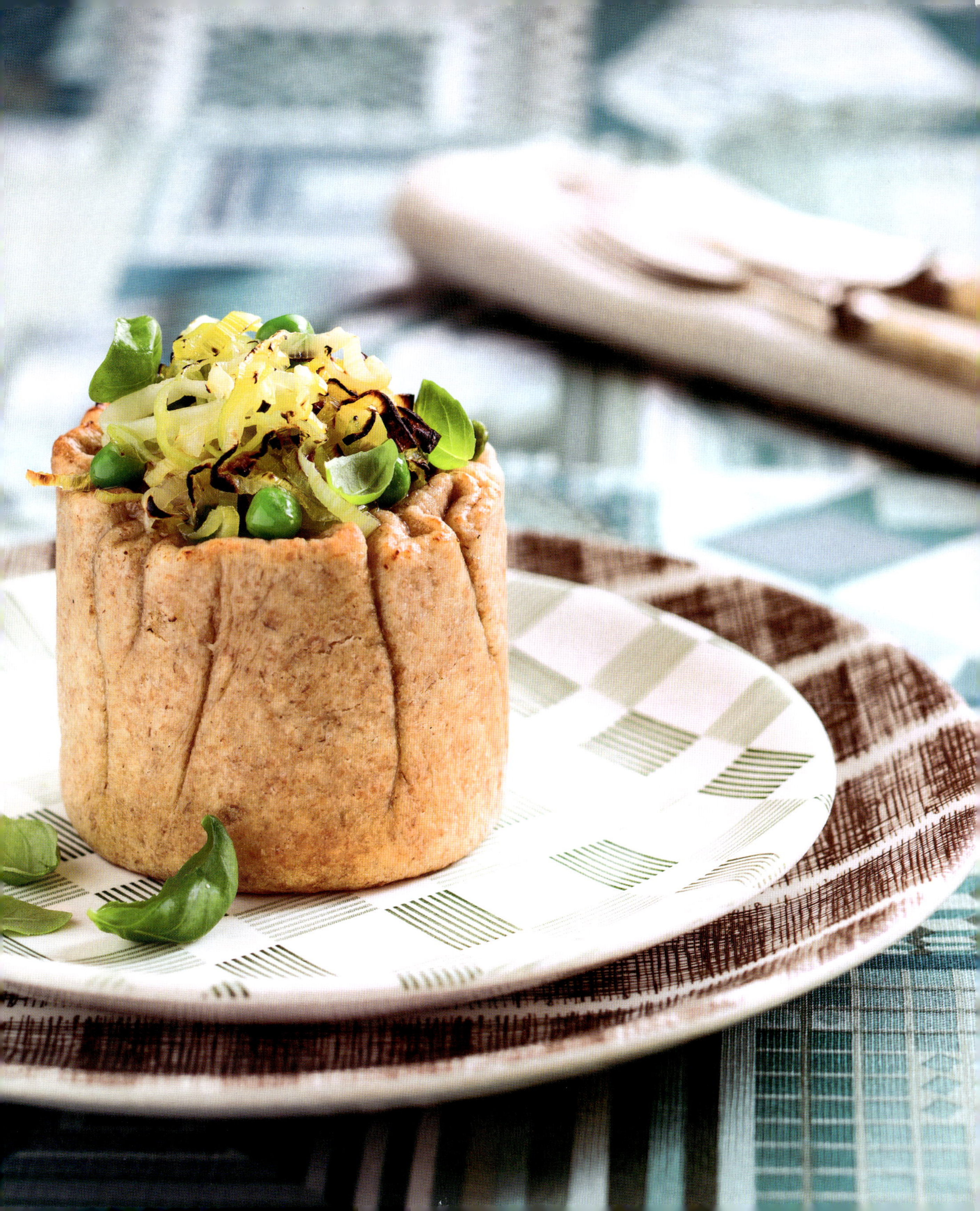

Chicken Pie continued . . .

SALSA VERDE

MAKES ABOUT ½ CUP

½ cup basil leaves, chopped
½ cup Italian parsley leaves, chopped
1 tablespoon baby capers, drained and chopped
1 clove garlic, crushed
zest and juice of 1 lemon
2 tablespoons olive oil
2 tablespoons finely grated Parmesan
2 tablespoons avocado oil
pinch salt and freshly ground black pepper to taste

small basil leaves or watercress to garnish if wished

5. Mix cornflour with a little water and add to mixture. Cook until thickened. Set aside.
6. Remove chicken meat from carcass and shred. Add to sauce with mustard and season with white pepper.
7. Cut dough into 8 even-sized pieces and roll each piece into a round large enough to fit into 8 large muffin tin holes or use small individual pie dishes or pastry rings.
8. Spoon chicken mixture into each pastry case. Place in oven for 15–20 minutes until case is golden brown and the filling is hot and bubbling.

FOR THE SALSA

1. Place basil, parsley, capers, garlic and lemon zest into a bowl. Add enough olive oil to make the mixture wet. Add Parmesan, remaining olive oil, avocado oil and lemon juice to taste. Season with salt and pepper.
2. To serve — remove chicken pies from oven and top with a little salsa. If wished, garnish with small basil leaves or watercress.

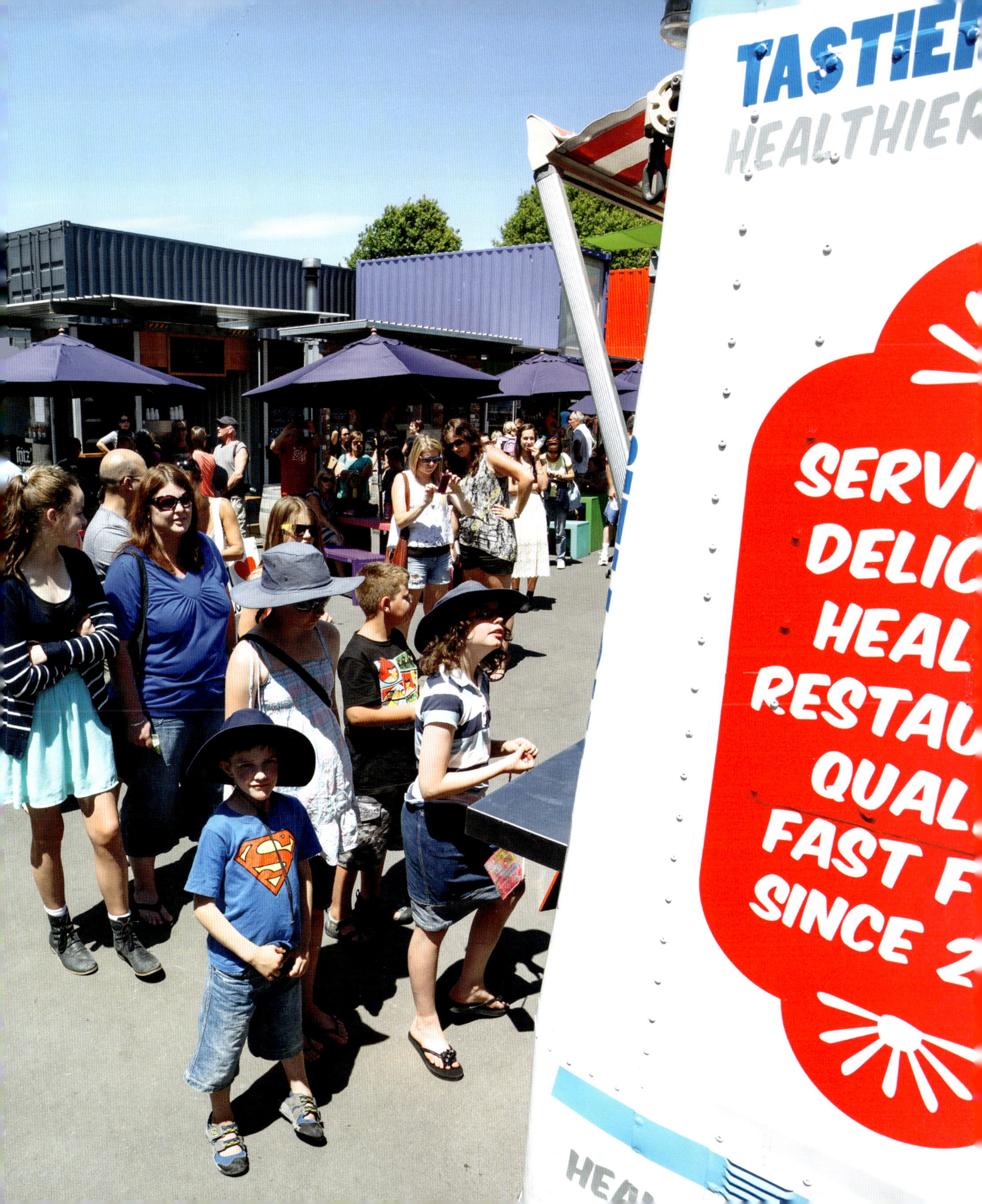
TASTIE
HEALTHIER
SERV
DELIC
HEAL
RESTAU
QUAL
FAST F
SINCE 2

Panzanella has to be one of my favourite salads. Teaming it up with smoked fish and a salsa verde makes for a healthy lunch dish.

Energy KJs	Protein	Total fat
1589	27g	21g

Saturated fat	Carbohydrate	Sodium
3.6g	24g	1503mg

Smoked Fish with Tomato and Cucumber Panzanella and Salsa Verde

Serves 4 • Preparation time 30-40 minutes

PANZANELLA
4 slices day-old wholemeal sourdough bread
¼ cup olive oil
3 tablespoons red wine vinegar
1 teaspoon soft brown sugar
pinch salt and freshly ground black pepper
4 large vine-ripened tomatoes, diced
1 small telegraph cucumber, deseeded and diced
1 red onion, finely sliced

TO ASSEMBLE
500g smoked fish, such as kahawai or trevally, bones removed and flaked
2 tablespoons salsa verde (see page 146)
2 handfuls rocket leaves

FOR THE PANZANELLA
1. Tear wholemeal sourdough into chunks and place in a bowl.
2. Mix together oil, vinegar, sugar, salt and pepper and sprinkle over sourdough chunks.
3. Add tomatoes, cucumber and red onion and toss to combine.

TO ASSEMBLE
1. Spoon panzanella onto a large serving plate. Place smoked fish on top and drizzle with salsa verde. Finish with rocket leaves.

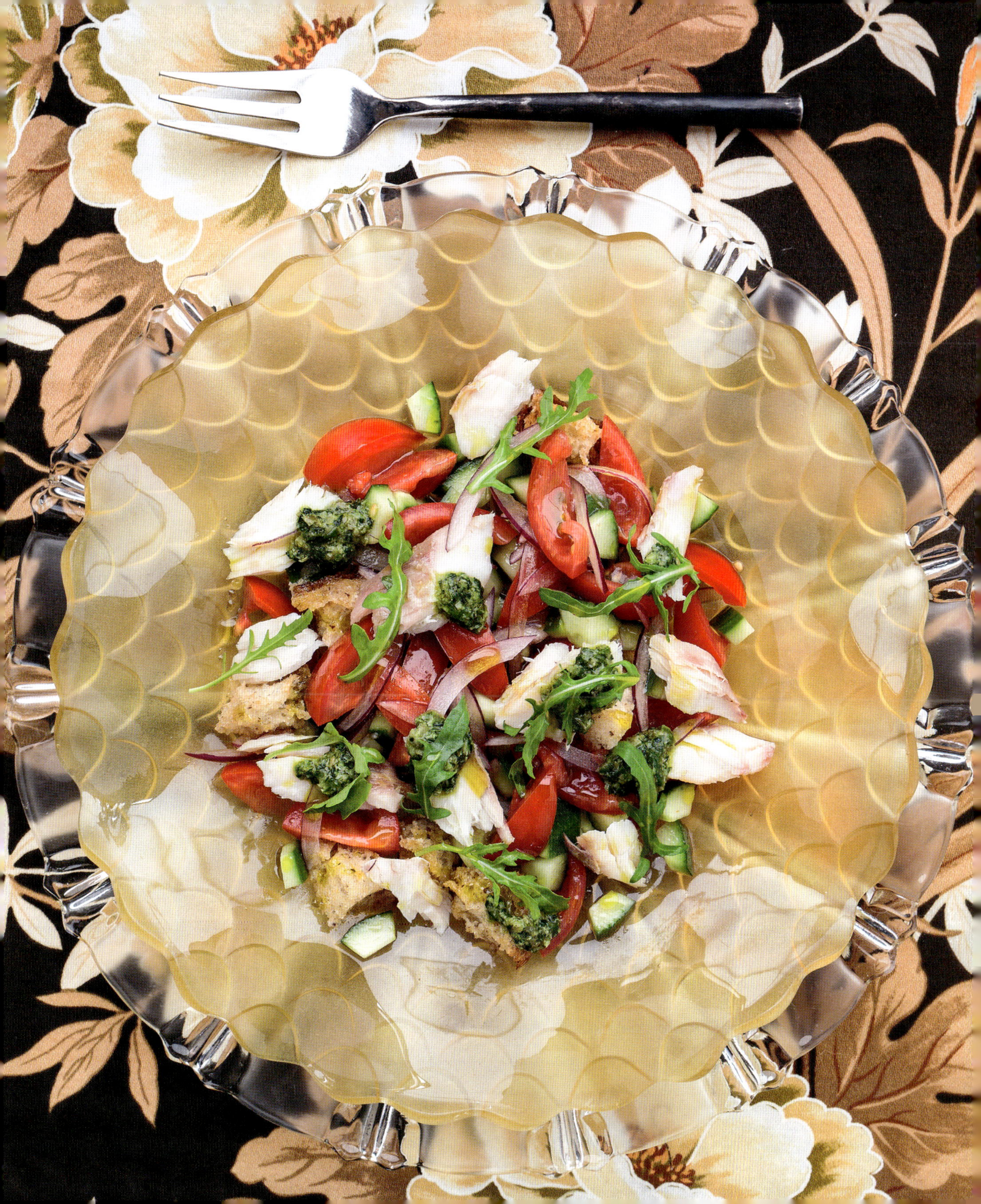

Broccoli may not be one of *your* old favourites, but made like this it soon will be! Dipping sweet stem broccoli or broccolini in the blue cheese emulsion with chopped fruit and nuts ups the flavour stakes, not to mention the chance of it being eaten!

Energy KJs	Protein	Total fat
996	6.7g	19g

Saturated fat	Carbohydrate	Sodium
4g	11.7g	305mg

Sweet Stem Broccoli Crunch

Serves 4 • *Preparation time* 20 minutes • *Cooking time* 7–8 minutes

BLUE CHEESE EMULSION

MAKES: 1¼ CUPS

2 eggs, soft boiled for 5 minutes, peeled
2 teaspoons white wine vinegar
6 tablespoons vegetable stock
6 tablespoons grapeseed oil
100g soft blue cheese, crumbled
pinch salt and white pepper

SWEET STEM BROCCOLI

12 stems sweet stem broccoli
1 tablespoon extra virgin olive oil
pinch salt and freshly ground black pepper
6 tablespoons mixed dried fruit, such as raisins, sultanas and craisins, chopped
3 tablespoons roughly chopped dry-roasted hazelnuts

FOR THE EMULSION

1. Place eggs, vinegar and stock in a food processor or blender and process until combined.
2. Drizzle oil in through the feed tube with the motor running, add cheese and season with salt and pepper.

FOR THE BROCCOLI

1. Boil or steam broccoli until bite tender. Drain if necessary and toss with olive oil, salt and pepper.
2. Mix together dried fruit and hazelnuts.
3. Dip each stem of broccoli into blue cheese emulsion, then dip into nut and dried fruit mixture. Serve at once.

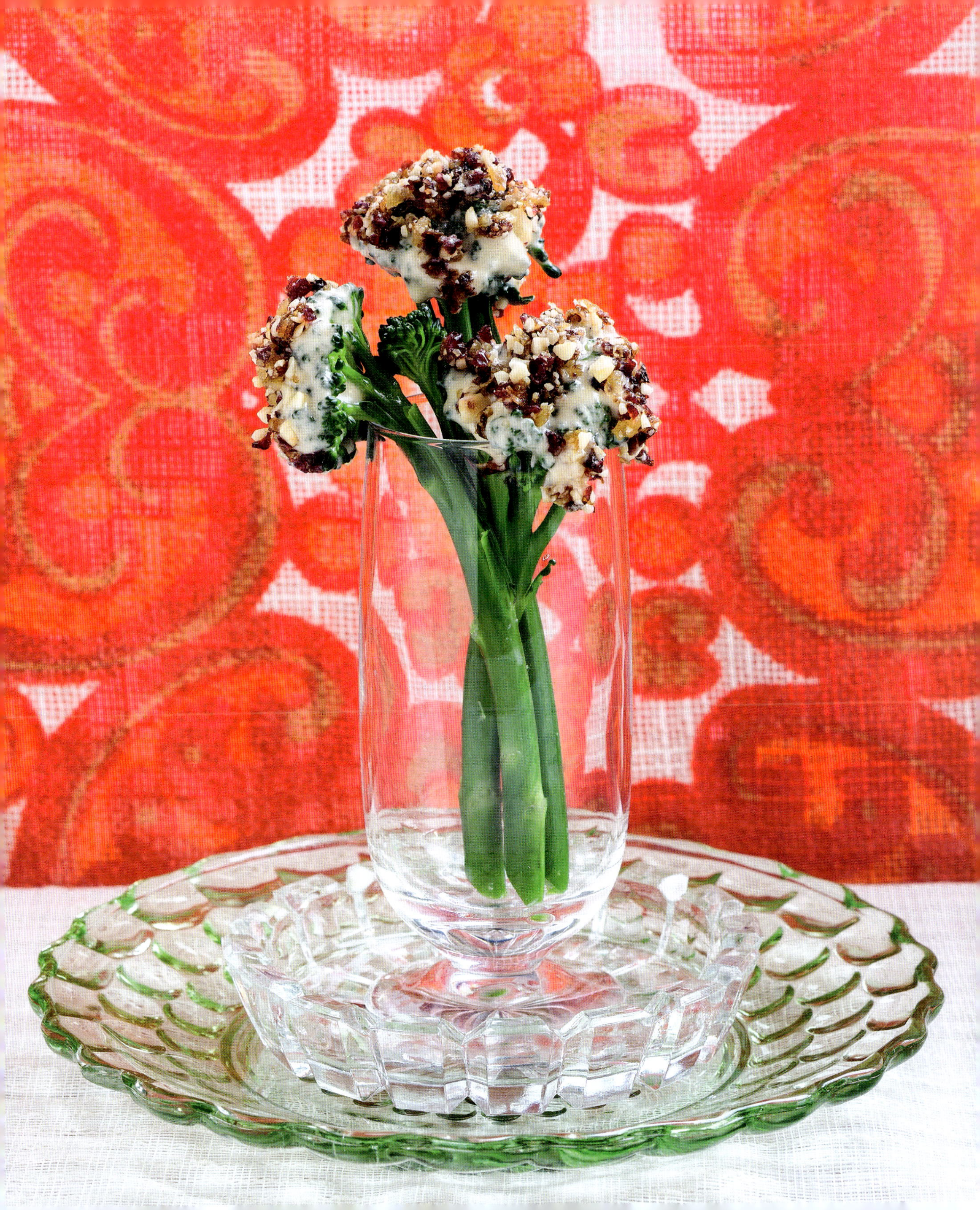

I made these for the annual Polyfest music festival. Taro certainly isn't the easiest vegetable to cook with. In fact, it's damn hard. But these chips are quick and easy and the egg-white and coconut pulp coating gives them a really great crunch.

Energy KJs	Protein	Total fat
1352	5g	20g

Saturated fat	Carbohydrate	Sodium
7.9g	33g	52mg

Taro Chips with Mango Sauce

Serves 4 • Preparation time 30 minutes • Cooking time 12 minutes

MANGO SAUCE

MAKES ¾–1 CUP

½ ripe mango, peeled and sliced
1 egg, soft boiled for 5 minutes and peeled
3 tablespoons vegetable stock
50ml grapeseed oil

TARO CHIPS

1 large taro, peeled
½ cup desiccated coconut
¼ teaspoon white pepper
1–2 egg whites, lightly beaten

FOR THE SAUCE

1. Place mango slices, soft-boiled eggs and vegetable stock in a food processor and process until smooth.
2. Drizzle in grapeseed oil through feed tube until emulsified. Transfer to a bowl, cover and refrigerate for up to 2–3 days, until ready to use.

FOR THE CHIPS

1. Preheat oven to 160°C. Line a large baking tray with baking paper.
2. Cut taro into even-sized chips, about 5cm long by 2cm wide. Blanch in boiling water for 20 seconds, drain and drop into a bowl of cold water.
3. Place desiccated coconut in a mortar and pestle and pound until coconut has a finer texture. Season with white pepper.
4. Drain and dry taro chips well, using a clean tea towel.
5. Dip in egg white, then coconut and place on baking tray. Bake for 12 minutes or until tender.
6. Serve taro chips hot from the oven with mango sauce.

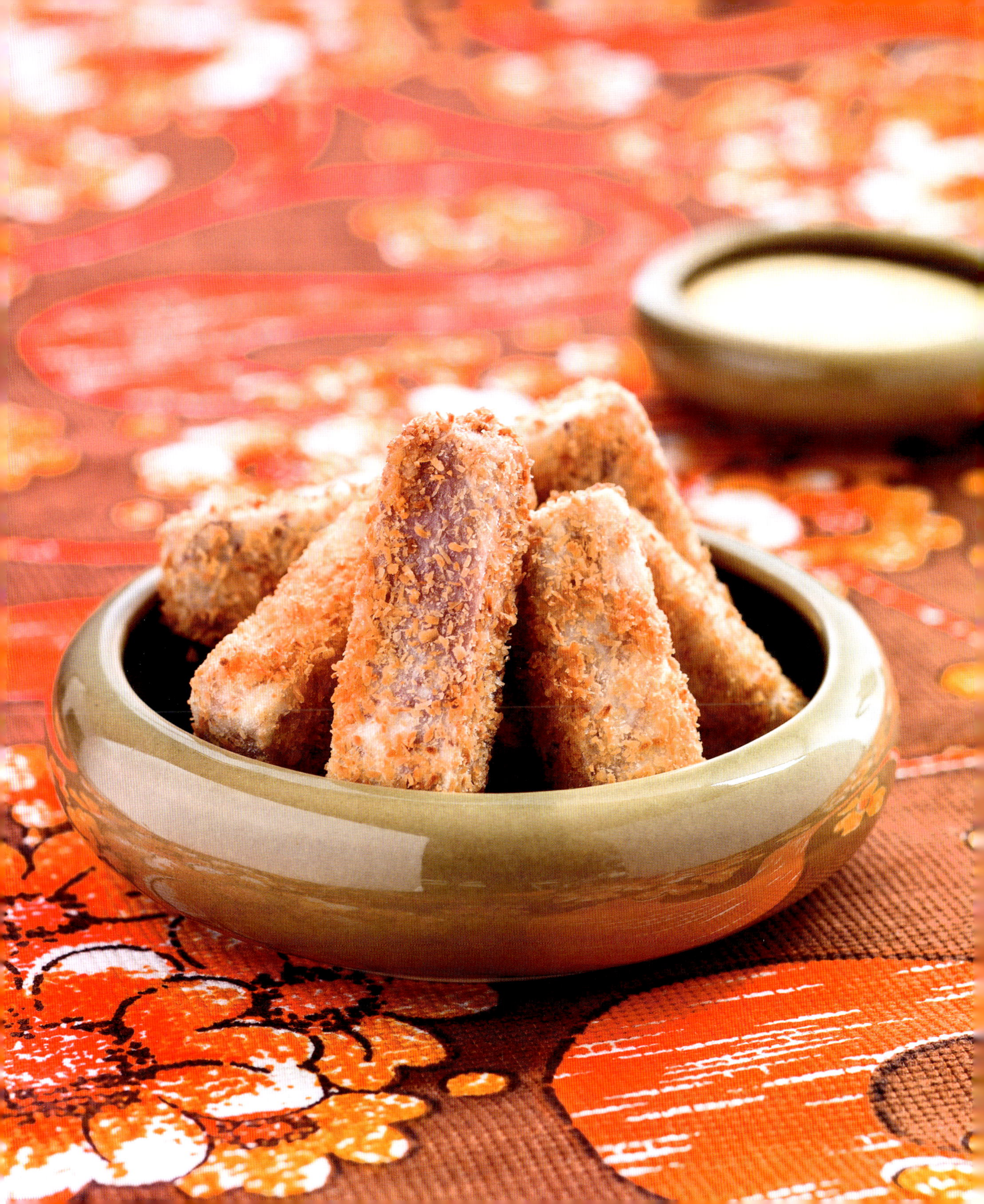

The amount of fat and oil in traditional chop suey (a dish that shows the Chinese influence on Samoan cooking) is shocking. This recipe is packed with goodness. I've snuck in vegetables disguised as noodles!

Energy KJs	Protein	Total fat
1768	35g	18g

Saturated fat	Carbohydrate	Sodium
5.6g	34g	570mg

Chop Suey (or Sapasui)

Serves 4 • Preparation time 40 minutes • Cooking time 2 hours

LAMB SHANKS
1 tablespoon grapeseed oil
1 carrot, chopped
1 onion, chopped
1 leek, white part only, sliced
1.2kg lamb shanks (2 large or 4 small shanks)
4 cloves garlic
1 sprig rosemary and thyme
1½ cups vegetable stock, hot
pinch salt and freshly ground black pepper

VEGETABLES
125g vermicelli, soaked until translucent and soft
¼ pumpkin, peeled, sliced and julienned
1 red kumara, peeled, sliced and julienned
1 carrot, peeled, sliced and julienned
1 parsnip, peeled, sliced and julienned
1 tablespoon peanut oil
½ tablespoon low-salt soy sauce

FOR THE LAMB
1. Preheat oven to 160°C.
2. Heat oil in a frying pan, add carrot, onion and leek and cook over a low heat until soft. Transfer to a casserole dish.
3. Increase pan heat to medium and brown lamb shanks on all sides. Remove and place on top of softened vegetables.
4. Add garlic cloves, rosemary, thyme and vegetable stock. Season with salt and pepper. Place in oven and cook for 2 hours until meat is falling off the bone. Remove lamb and shred meat using 2 forks.
5. Strain meat cooking juices and vegetables through a sieve into a jug, pushing down with a wooden spoon. Discard vegetables.

FOR THE VEGETABLES
1. Soak vermicelli until translucent, according to packet directions.
2. Blanch julienned vegetables in boiling water for 10 seconds, drain and refresh under cold water. Drain again.
3. Heat peanut oil in a large frying pan over a medium heat. Add blanched vegetables, vermicelli, shredded lamb, meat cooking juices and soy sauce to taste. Heat through and serve.

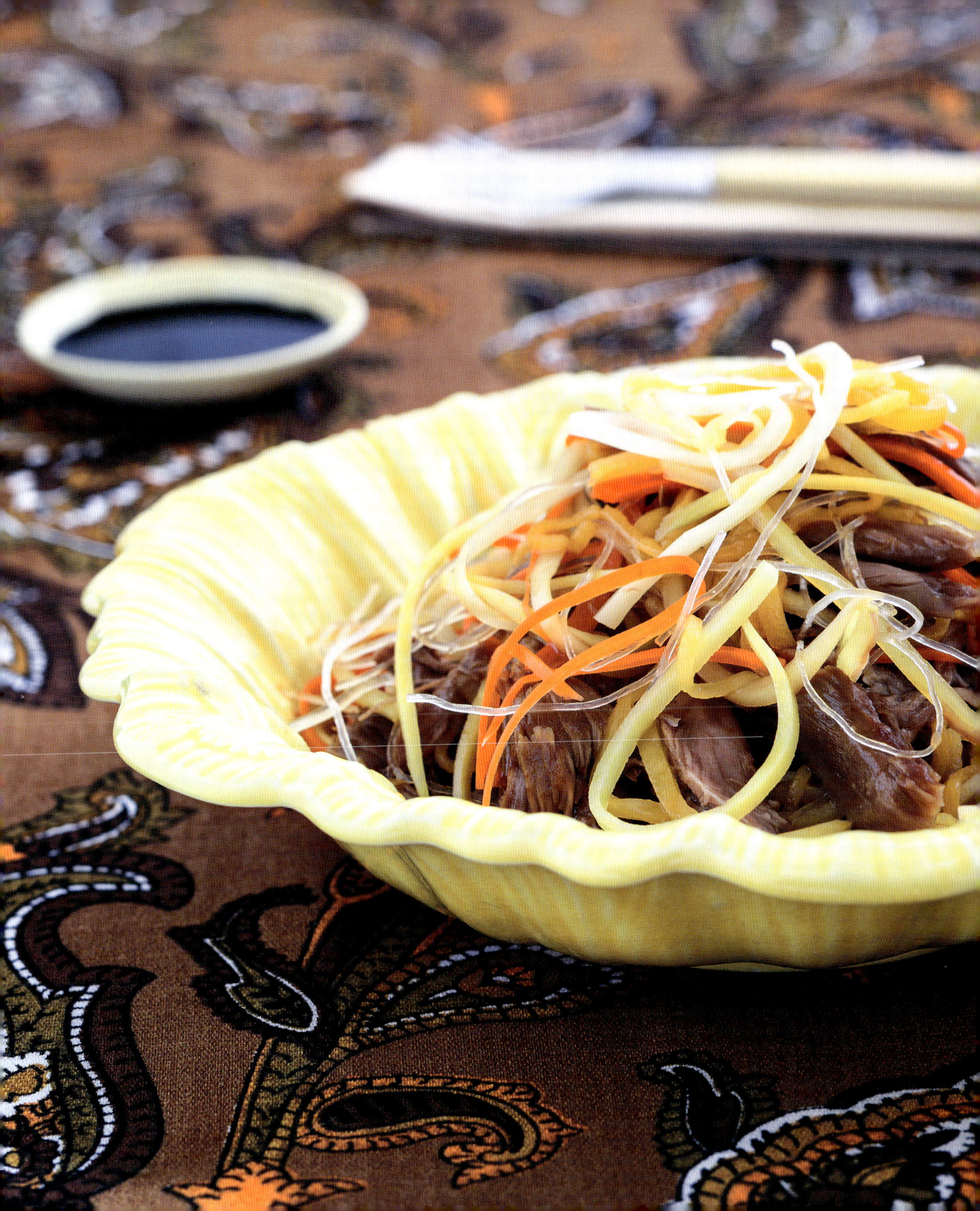

I love steaming things in little parcels. Opening them up and getting hit by the aromas is just like Christmas. I got a lot of confused reactions when I served this up as my take on the well-known taro-wrapped dish, but I think adding the fish really works.

Energy KJs	Protein	Total fat
901	23g	11g

Saturated fat	Carbohydrate	Sodium
6g	8g	219mg

Fish Palusami

Makes 4 parcels • Preparation time 20 minutes • Cooking time 30 minutes

400g skinned and boned gurnard fillets, cut into 1cm cubes
¼ teaspoon salt
juice of 2 large lemons
1 cup lite coconut milk
1 ripe tomato, deseeded and diced or cut into thin slices
½ avocado, halved, stoned, peeled and diced
½ red onion, finely sliced or diced
½ small telegraph cucumber, deseeded and diced
few coriander leaves
16 medium-sized taro leaves, rinsed well
aluminium foil

1. Preheat oven to 170°C.
2. Sprinkle gurnard fillets with salt and place in a large non-metallic bowl. Pour over lemon juice and lightly toss to coat.
3. Leave for 10 minutes, then drain fish well in a colander and place in a clean bowl.
4. Stir in coconut milk, tomato, avocado, onion, cucumber and a few coriander leaves.
5. For each taro leaf, remove tip, all of the stalk and 1cm of leaf around stalk.
6. Place a piece of aluminium foil on bench top. Layer 4 taro leaves on top, overlapping each other to form a leak-proof circular shape. Repeat with remaining leaves and foil.
7. Divide fish mixture between taro leaves. Gather edges of leaves, folding inwards to overlap and enclose palusami. Completely enclose parcels in foil.
8. Place in a shallow water bath and cook in oven for 30 minutes. Unwrap from foil and eat.

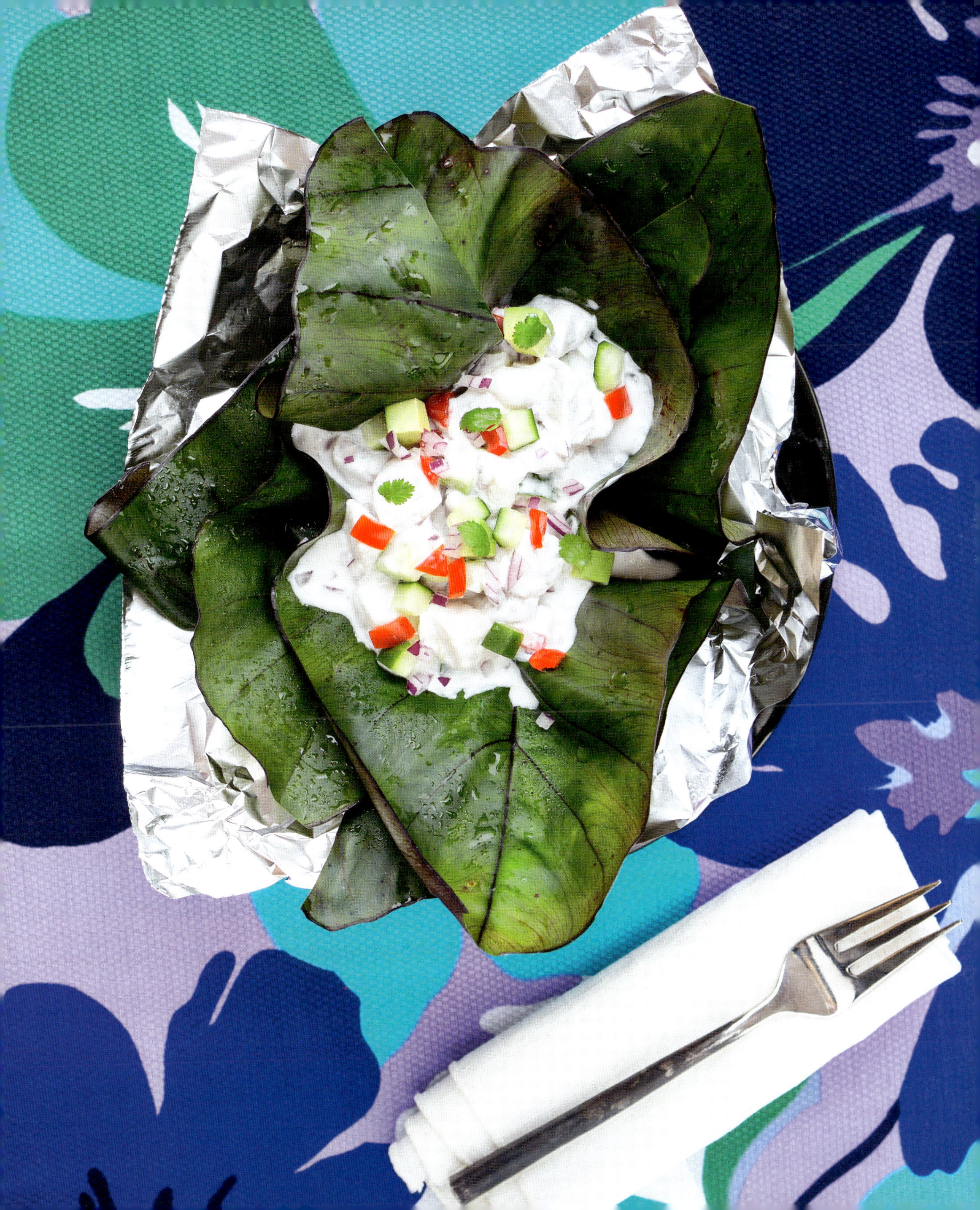

Evelina Leatio'o
Evelina's Polynesian Food

Evelina's Polynesian Food is one of the best Polynesian takeaway stores in Auckland. Evelina runs the place with the help of her family. On any given day you will find her brother, sister, son, cousins and so on all working out the back chopping taro, cooking up pigs' heads and wrapping up palusami. It may not be the healthiest, but it's simple, honest food made with love.

Evelina's
POLYNESIAN FOOD
Ph: (09) 267 7185

The infamous doughnuts. Straight out of the oven these are delicious, but don't make the mistake of saving them for the next day!

Energy KJs	Protein	Total fat
1450	9g	7g

Saturated fat	Carbohydrate	Sodium
1.7g	67g	62mg

Triple Blueberry Doughnuts

Makes 12 • Preparation time 2½–3 hours • Cooking time 10–15 minutes

DRIED BLUEBERRY MIXTURE

2 cups dried blueberries
1 tablespoon honey

DOUGH

1¼ cups low-fat milk
⅔ cup maple syrup, plus extra for glazing
7g dried yeast
4 cups plain flour
½ cup coconut flour
½ cup ground almonds
pinch each nutmeg, cinnamon and salt
2 eggs, lightly beaten
1 tablespoon coconut oil, melted
1 tablespoon grapeseed oil

FOR THE MIXTURE

1. Soak dried blueberries in just enough water to cover and leave to soften for about 1 hour.
2. Place in a blender with honey and blend until smooth. Set aside.

FOR THE DOUGH

1. Pour milk and maple syrup into a small saucepan and heat until warm (blood temperature).
2. Remove from heat and sprinkle over dried yeast and leave to froth, about 5 minutes.
3. Sift plain flour into a large bowl and add coconut flour, ground almonds, spices and salt.
4. Add eggs, melted coconut oil, grapeseed oil and yeast mixture and mix to a soft dough. Tip dough out on to a lightly floured bench top and knead until dough comes together, about 2 minutes. Add 2 tablespoons dried blueberry mixture to dough and knead for a further 3 minutes.
5. Lightly oil a bowl, place dough in, turning over to prevent a skin forming. Cover with a clean tea towel and leave to rise in a warm, draught-free place until dough has doubled in size.
6. Preheat oven to 180°C. Line a baking tray with baking paper.

Recipe continued over page . . .

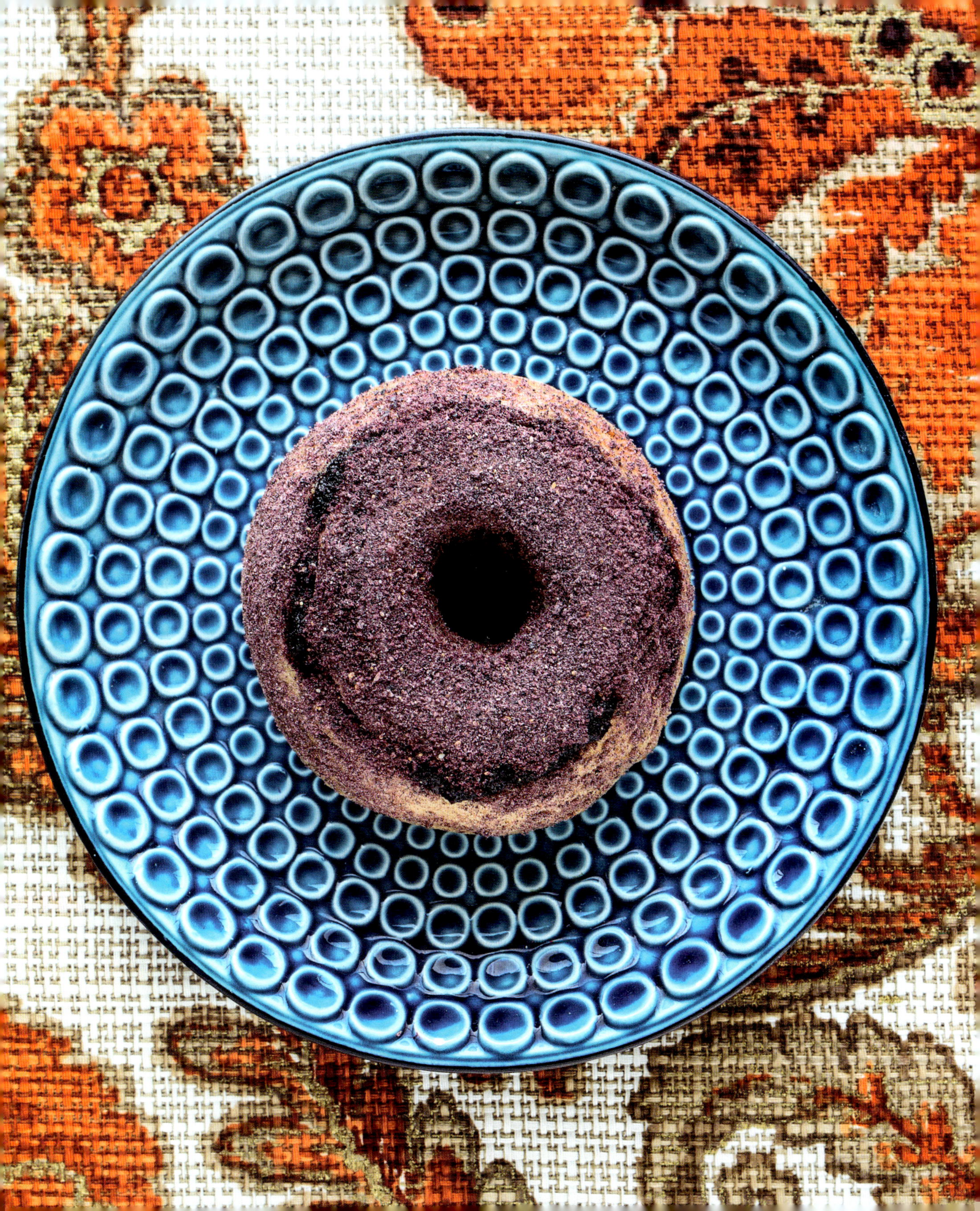

Triple Blueberry Doughnuts continued . . .

BLUEBERRY POWDER

1 cup freeze-dried blueberries
¼ teaspoon cornflour
¼ teaspoon icing sugar

7. Knock dough back and tip out onto the lightly floured bench top. Cut dough into four pieces and working with one piece at a time, roll into a cigar, about 2cm thick. Cut into 3 x 12cm lengths. Wet both ends of 12cm roll and form into a round (as you would if making a bagel), pinching the ends together. Repeat with remaining rolls.
8. Place doughnuts on prepared tray, leaving space between each doughnut, cover and leave to rise until they have doubled in size.
9. Brush doughnuts with extra maple syrup and place in oven to bake for 10–15 minutes until golden.
10. Remove doughnuts from oven and leave to cool.
11. Using a small sharp knife make an incision around the top of each doughnut and pipe in the remaining dried blueberry mixture. Sprinkle doughnuts with blueberry powder (see recipe below), and eat them the same day they are made.

FOR THE POWDER

1. Pound the blueberries to a fine powder and mix in enough cornflour and icing sugar to prevent the blueberry powder from sticking together in little clumps.

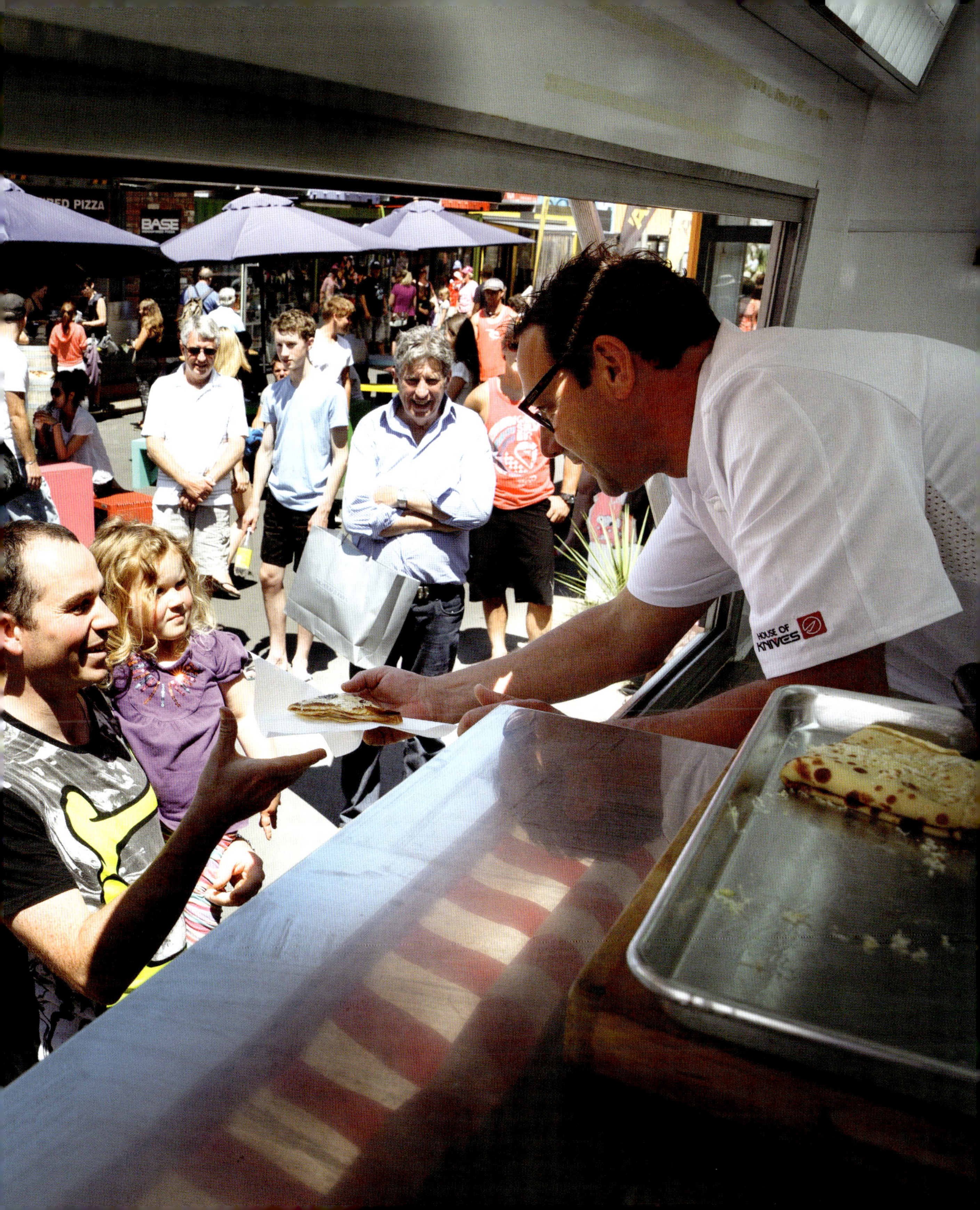
BASE
HOUSE OF
KNIVES

A totally new twist on an old favourite. Who would have thought you could make such a delicious crumble topping with so little butter?

Energy KJs	Protein	Total fat
2368	12g	26g

Saturated fat	Carbohydrate	Sodium
5.8g	81g	83mg

Baked Apple Crumble with Labna

Serves 4 • Preparation time 1–2 days for labna • Cooking time about 1 hour

LABNA
2 cups thick plain yoghurt
zest of 1 lime

CRUMBLE
70g wholemeal flour
70g plain flour
50ml grapeseed oil
2 tablespoons coconut sugar
100g New Zealand dried apricots, finely chopped
50g pistachio nuts, finely chopped

APPLES
4 Braeburn apples, peeled
2 tablespoons liquid honey, warmed
½ teaspoon ground cinnamon

FOR THE LABNA
1. Spoon yoghurt into a sieve lined with cheesecloth or a clean Chux cloth. Leave to drain over a bowl, covered, in the refrigerator for 1–2 days until yoghurt is very thick. Mix through lime zest.

FOR THE CRUMBLE
1. Preheat oven to 200°C.
2. Place flours and oil in a food processor and process until fine breadcrumb stage. Add sugar and process for 10 seconds.
3. Spread out to 1cm thick in a large baking dish and place in oven. Bake until golden, tossing after 5 minutes.
4. When golden, add apricots and pistachio nuts and cook for a further 5 minutes, but watch carefully so crumble doesn't burn.

FOR THE APPLES
1. Reduce oven temperature to 180°C.
2. Place apples in a baking dish, brush well with warm honey and sprinkle with cinnamon. Cover dish and place in oven. Bake apples until soft but not falling apart, 35–40 minutes.
3. Coat apples in crumble and serve with labna.

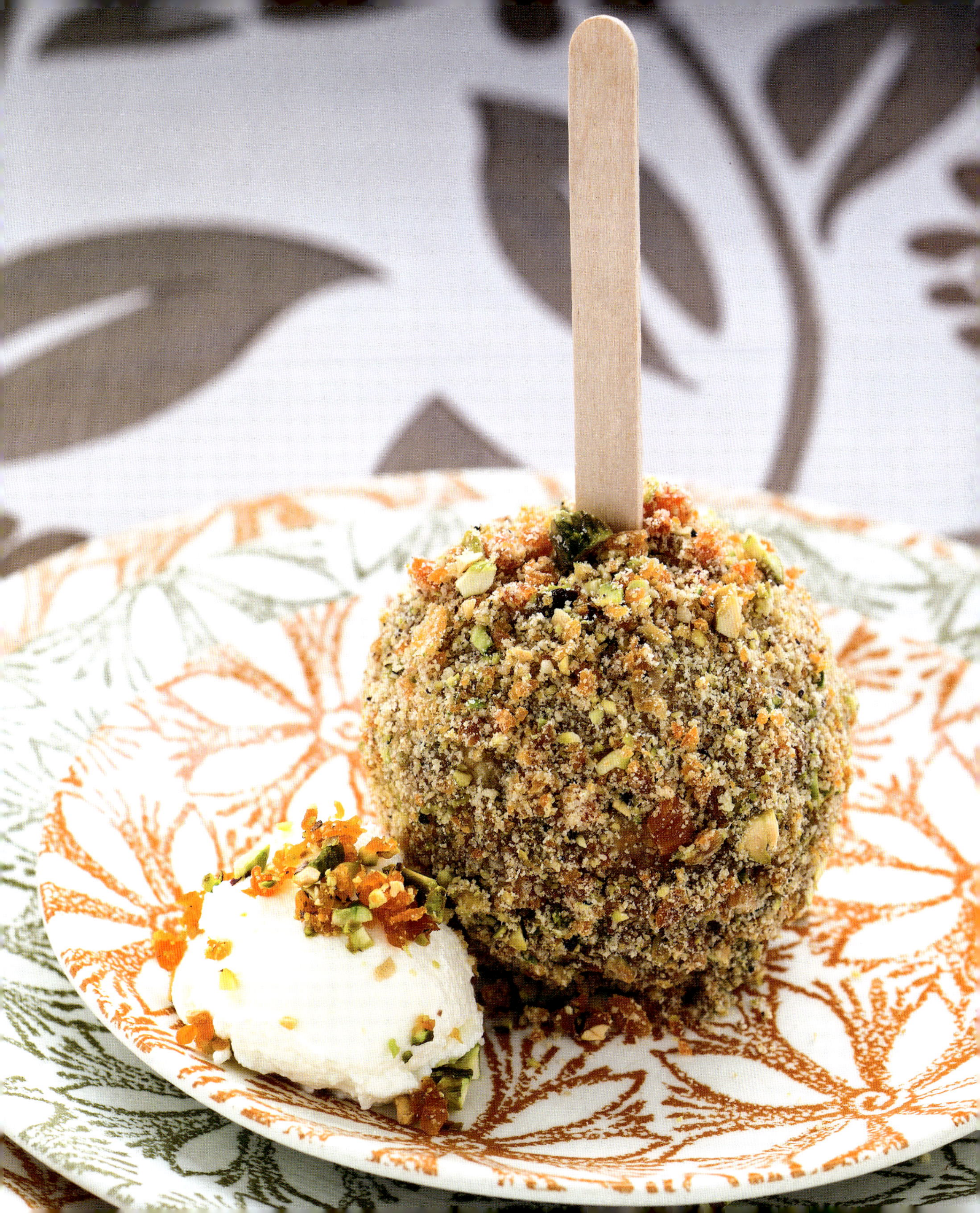

This was the first time I'd ever milked an almond. I now know that you can make a milkshake without milk!

Energy KJs	Protein	Total fat
1886	10g	24g

Saturated fat	Carbohydrate	Sodium
2g	50g	257mg

Choc Almond Shake

Serves 4 • Preparation time Soak almonds overnight

ALMOND MILK

1 cup whole almonds, skin on
3 cups water
pinch salt

SHAKE

3 cups unsweetened almond milk
1 cup pitted dates
1 large banana, peeled
1 tablespoon good-quality cocoa powder
4–6 ice cubes

FOR THE ALMOND MILK

1. Place whole almonds in a bowl and just cover with water. Leave to soak overnight. Drain and discard liquid.
2. Place almonds in a blender, add water and a pinch of salt and blend until smooth.
3. Pour contents of blender through a cheesecloth-lined strainer into a large jug. (If you intend to make almond milk on a regular basis, invest in a nut-milk bag as it is more effective than cheesecloth.) Squeeze to extract all the goodness of the almond meal.
4. Store almond milk in the refrigerator. It will last for 3–4 days.

FOR THE SHAKE

1. Place all ingredients in a blender and blend until smooth.
2. Pour into glasses and drink.

Tip: For a quick choc almond shake buy organic unsweetened almond milk.

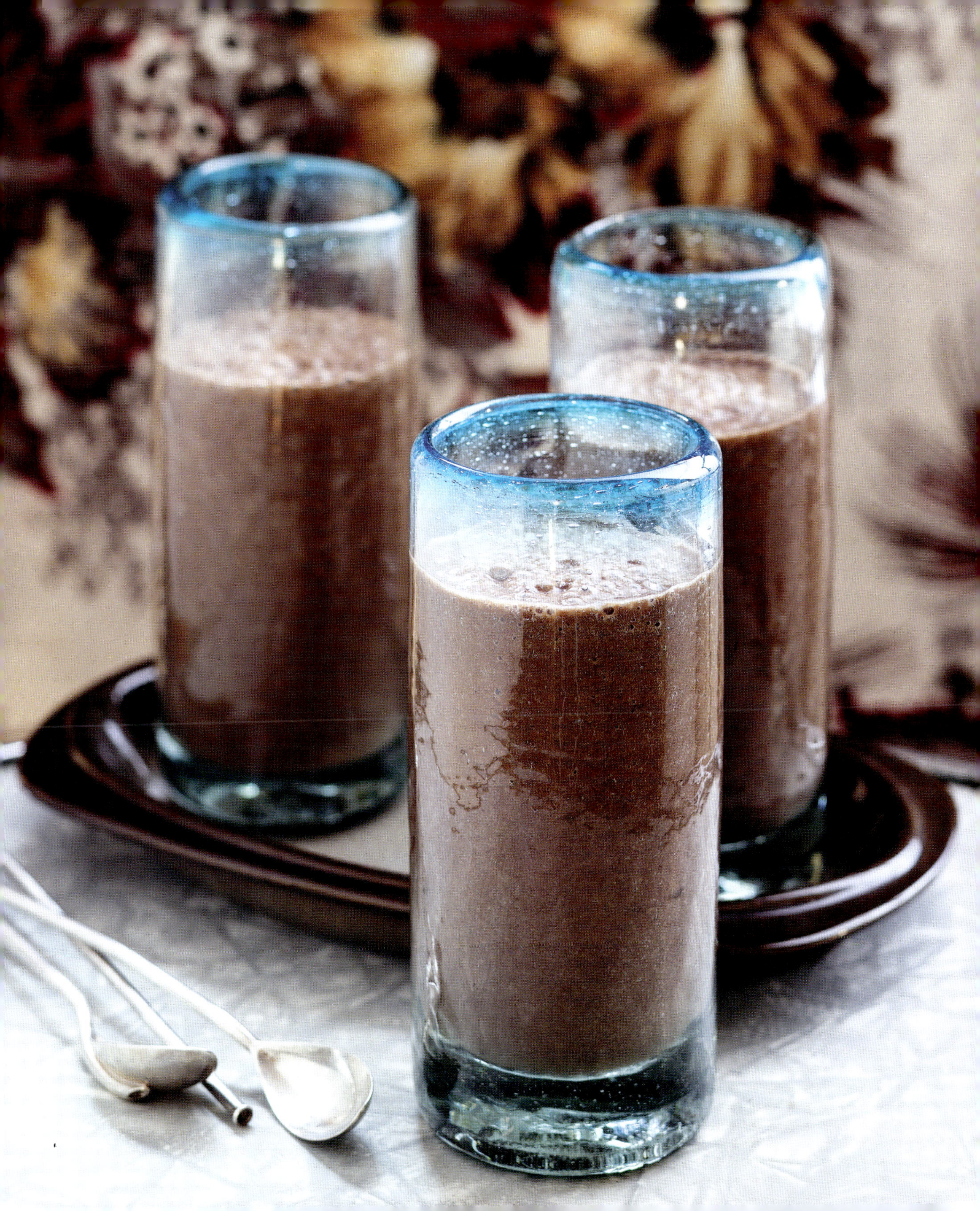

Middle Eastern Feast

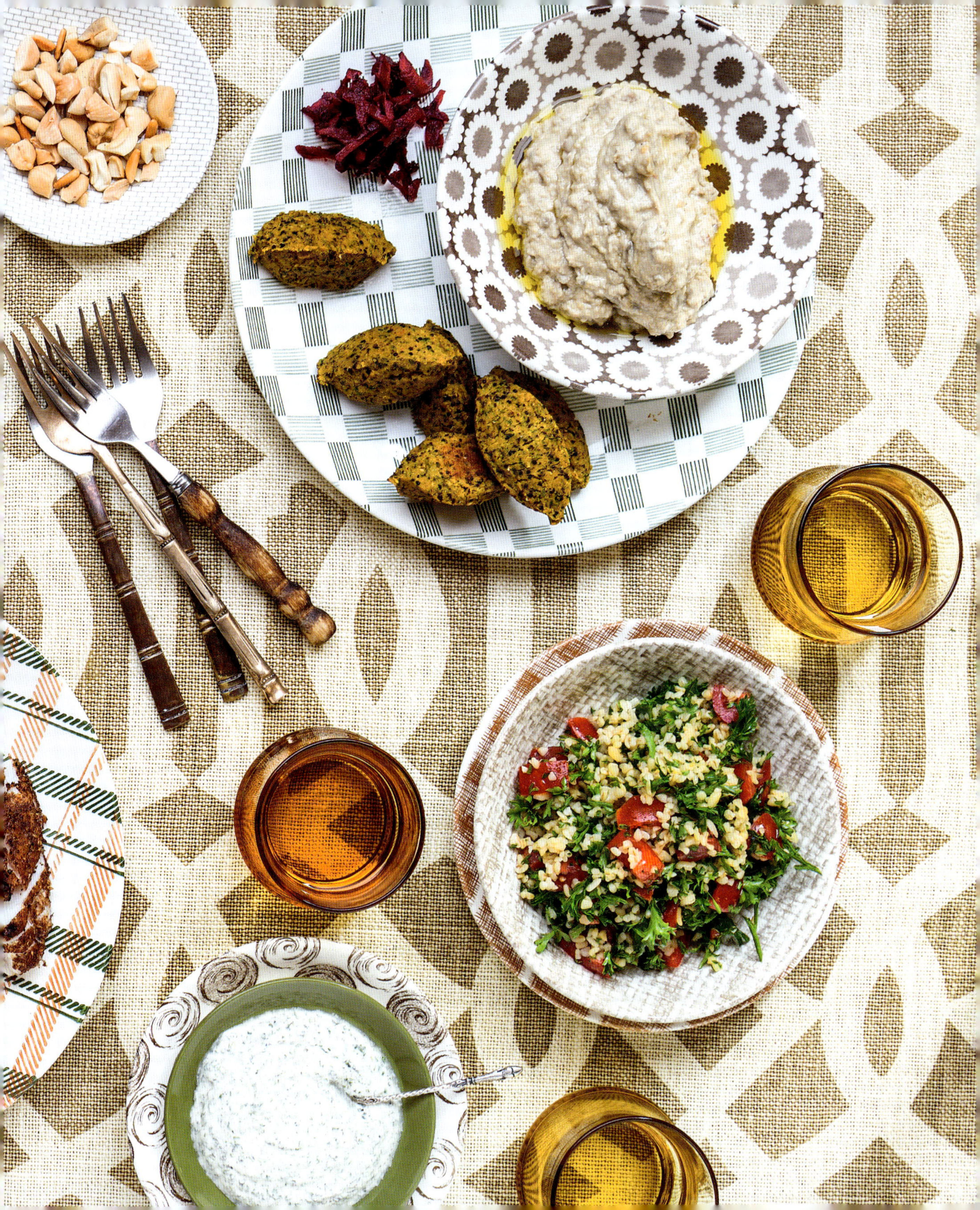

We've all nailed one of these late-night favourites, and here's my simple marinated-chicken version. Normally I would never suggest turning meat on the grill or in a pan constantly, but it is a good idea here to stop the yoghurt in the marinade from burning.

Energy KJs	Protein	Total fat
2221	28g	30g

Saturated fat	Carbohydrate	Sodium
6g	44g	490mg

Chicken Kebabs

Serves 4 • *Preparation time* 15 minutes • *Cooking time* 3–4 minutes

400–450g boneless, skinless chicken thighs, cut into 1cm pieces
3 cloves garlic, crushed
½ cup Greek yoghurt
2 tablespoons grapeseed oil
1 tablespoon paprika
1 teaspoon freeze-dried ground garlic
½ teaspoon turmeric
pinch salt
¼ teaspoon white pepper

TO ASSEMBLE

4 small spinach wraps
sunflower-seed hummus (see page 178)
cos lettuce leaves and rocket, torn
beefsteak tomatoes, thinly sliced
purple, white and orange baby carrots and celery, cut with a vegetable peeler into long thin strips
radishes, very thinly sliced — I used a mandolin
cucumber, deseeded and cut into long thin strips
grated beetroot mixed with pomegranate seeds
mixed sprouts
½ cup mixed cashew nuts, almonds and pine nuts, dry-roasted and roughly chopped

FOR THE CHICKEN

1. Place chicken in a large bowl and combine with remaining ingredients.
2. Heat a large frying pan over a high heat and pan-fry chicken pieces for 3–4 minutes, tossing chicken continuously to cook on all sides and to prevent burning. Alternatively, grill on a hot barbecue plate.

TO ASSEMBLE

1. Lightly chargrill wraps to heat to allow easy folding. Work quickly while wraps are still warm.
2. Lay one spinach wrap on a clean bench top. Spread with a thin layer of sunflower-seed hummus. Place a little torn lettuce and rocket across centre of wrap with a little of the prepared vegetables. Add either falafel, fish or chicken and a little tabbouleh (see page 178) as well. Scatter a few sprouts and nuts on top.
3. Fold over two sides, then fold side nearest to you over to enclose filling, tucking as you go. Continue to roll up tightly to form a roll. Cut in half to serve. Repeat with remaining wraps and filling. Serve with garlic yoghurt and chilli sauce (see pages 176 and 178).

HEALTHIER
CHEAPER
FASTER
TASTIER
HEALTHIER
FASTER!
CHEAPER
FASTER!
THE FOOD TRUCK
THE FOOD TRUCK
KEBAB BROS
FBQ219

Here's an alternative to the usual lamb and chicken kebabs. The sumac spice rub is fantastic with monkfish but hapuka, cod, trevally and snapper will also stand up well to the spice mix. For assembly instructions see page 170.

Energy KJs	Protein	Total fat
706	22g	8g

Saturated fat	Carbohydrate	Sodium
1.2g	2.4g	217mg

Fish Kebabs

Serves 4 • *Preparation time* 10 minutes or 1 hour if leaving to stand • *Cooking time* 4 minutes

SPICE MIXTURE

2 teaspoons dry-roasted and ground cumin seeds
2 teaspoons dry-roasted and ground caraway seeds
1 teaspoon dry-roasted and ground fennel seeds
1 teaspoon dry-roasted and ground coriander seeds
2 teaspoons sumac
½ teaspoon ground cinnamon
½ teaspoon grated nutmeg
pinch salt

FISH

500g monkfish or other firm white fish fillets
1 tablespoon grapeseed oil

FOR THE SPICE MIXTURE AND FISH

1. Mix together all ingredients for spice mixture.
2. Rub spice mixture into fish fillets. If wished, place covered in refrigerator for 1 hour.
3. Heat a large frying pan over a high heat. Brush fish fillets with oil and pan-fry for 3–4 minutes, turning once.

Tip: Dry-roasting spices — heat a frying pan and toss each spice over a medium heat until aromatic, and spice begins to darken. Cool, then crush in a mortar and pestle.

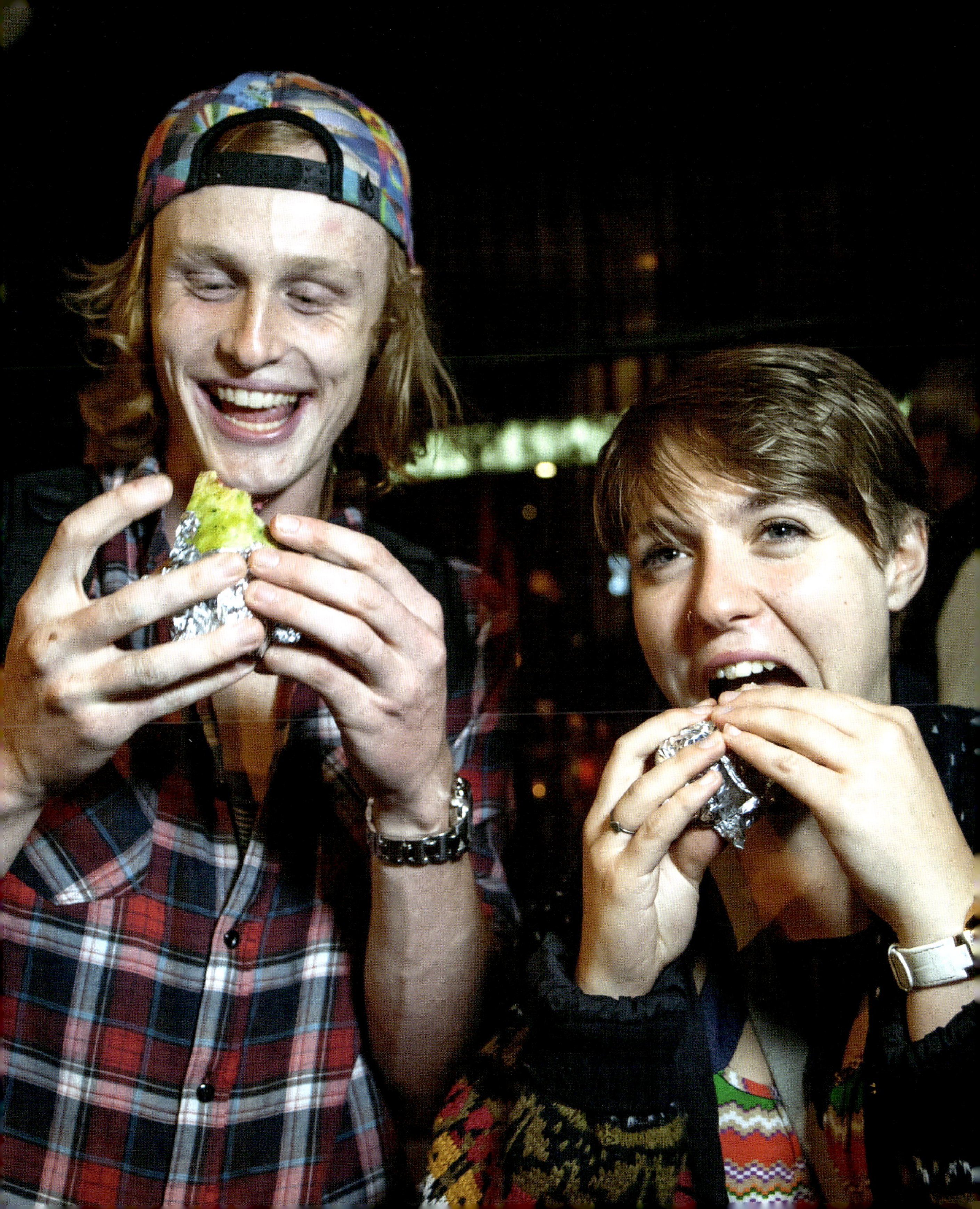

My cooking assistant called these falafel 'inspired'. Falafel are full of goodness but it's being dropped in the deep fryer that spoils it. This recipe uses some different beans, super grains and veges and works amazingly well baked in the oven. For assembly instructions see page 170.

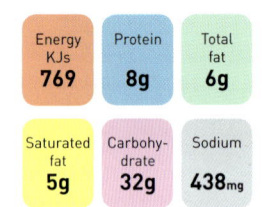

Energy KJs	Protein	Total fat
769	8g	6g

Saturated fat	Carbohydrate	Sodium
5g	32g	438mg

Falafel kebabs

Serves 4 • *Preparation time* 1 hour and 15 minutes • *Cooking time* 25 minutes

500g crown pumpkin, roasted and mashed
1 x 375g can soybeans, rinsed and well drained
½ cup cooked red or black quinoa
⅓ cup red onion, finely chopped
3 cloves garlic, crushed
⅓ cup finely chopped curly parsley leaves
⅓ cup chopped coriander leaves
1 teaspoon tahini paste
½ teaspoon baking powder
¼ teaspoon dry-roasted and ground cumin seeds
¼ teaspoon dry-roasted and ground coriander seeds
1 slice wholemeal bread, broken into pieces

FOR THE FALAFEL

1. Preheat oven to 160°C.
2. Place pumpkin and soybeans in a clean tea towel and squeeze hard to remove all moisture.
3. Place in the bowl of a food processor with remaining ingredients and process until smooth.
4. Using 2 tablespoons, shape mixture into quenelles and place in a lightly oiled shallow baking tray. Place in oven and cook for 25 minutes until hot.

Tip: You will only need to squeeze pumpkin and soybeans in a tea towel if pumpkin is a little watery after roasting.

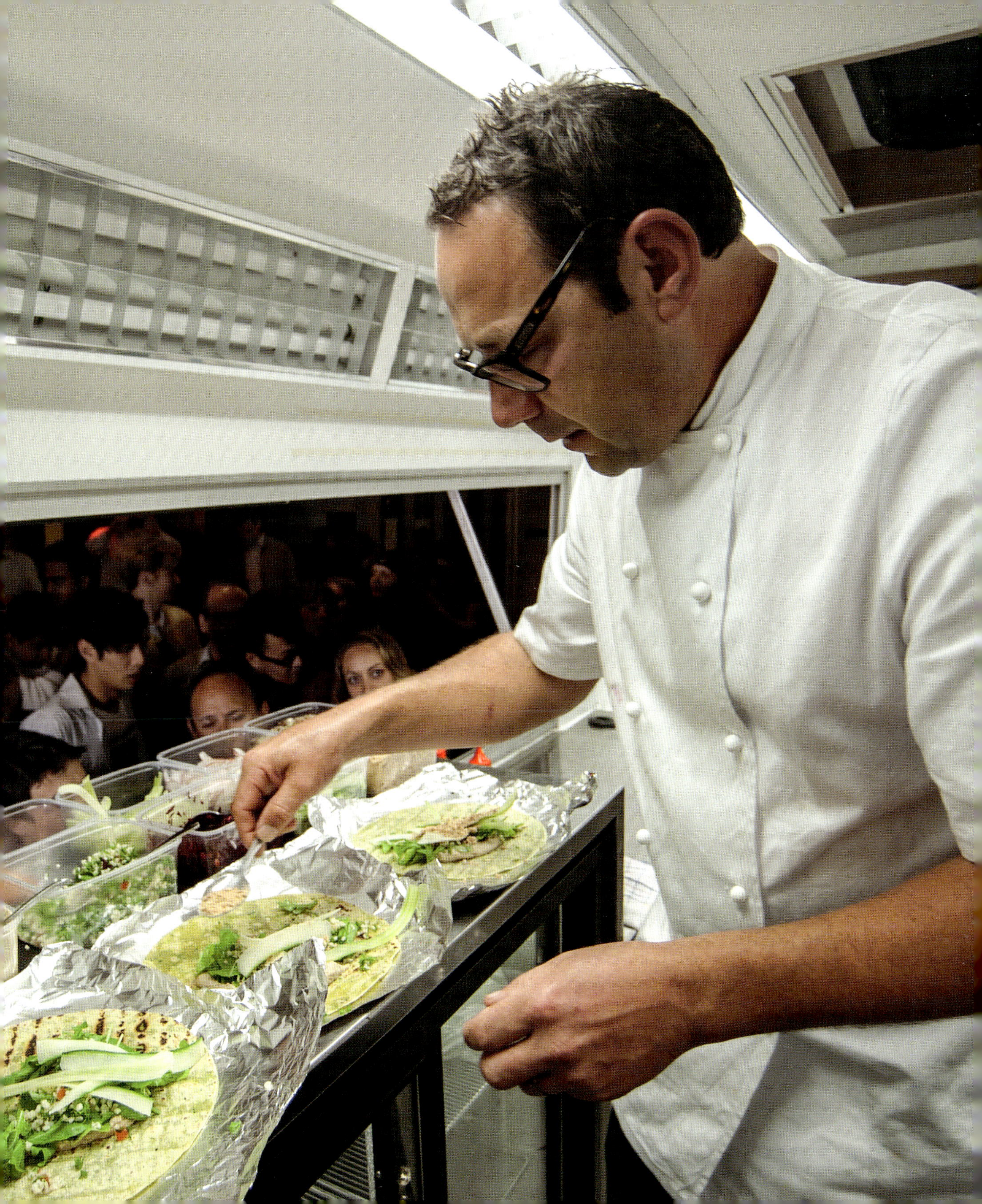

Chilli Sauce *Mild*

Makes 1 cup • Preparation time 10 minutes

1 red chilli, deseeded and roughly chopped
1 cup tomato juice
2 tablespoons cider vinegar
1 tablespoon honey
¼ teaspoon ground allspice
pinch salt

1. Place all ingredients in a blender and blend until smooth.

Chilli Sauce *Hot*

Makes 1 cup • Preparation time 10 minutes

1 yellow Habanero chilli, roughly chopped
2 Serrano chillies, roughly chopped
1 cup tomato juice
2 tablespoons cider vinegar
1 tablespoon honey
¼ teaspoon ground allspice
pinch salt

1. Place all ingredients in a blender and blend until smooth.

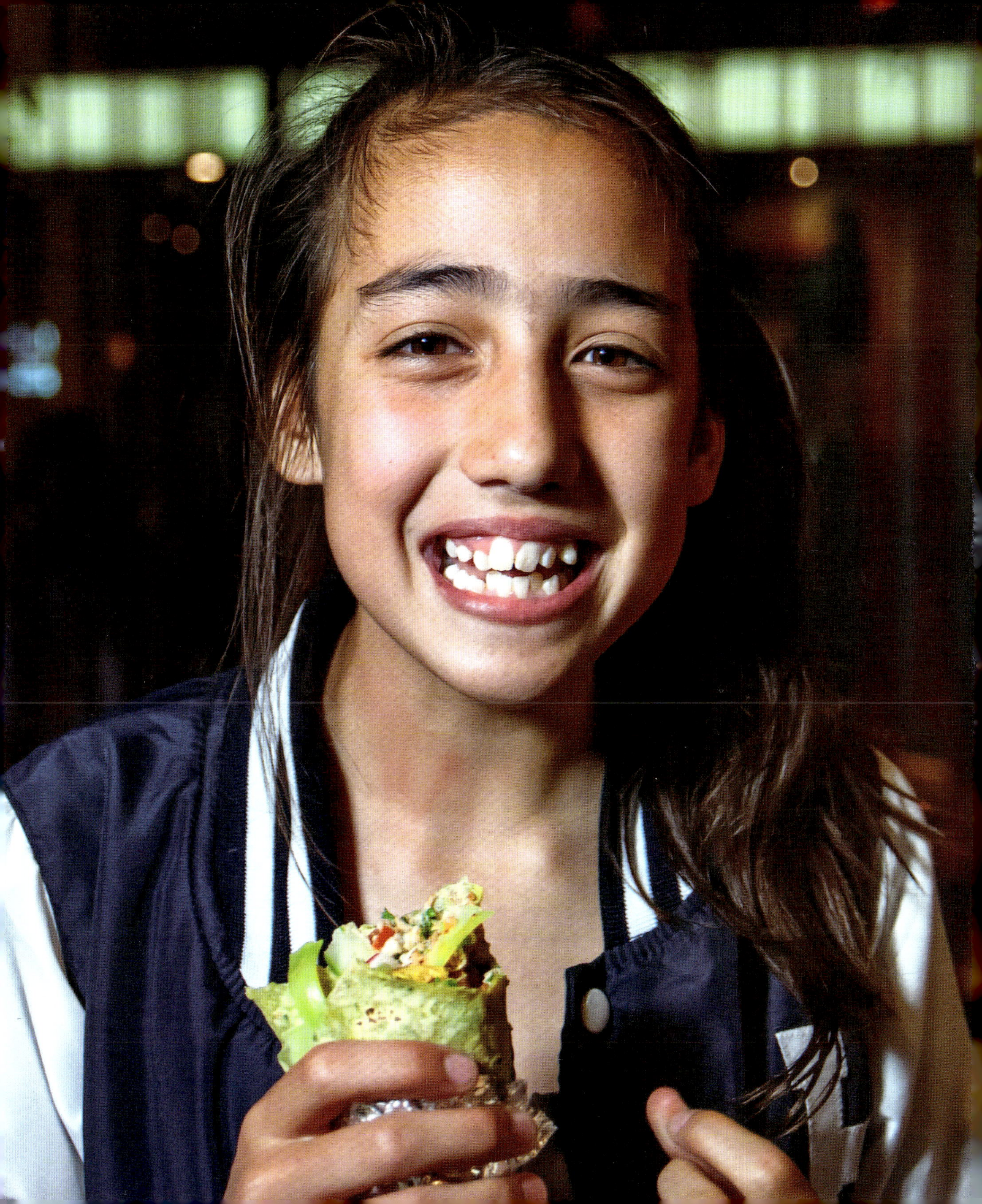

Energy KJs	Protein	Total fat
1008	8.8g	17g

Saturated fat	Carbohydrate	Sodium
2.5g	16g	357mg

Sunflower-seed Hummus

Makes 2 cups • Preparation time 1 hour • Cooking time 40–45 minutes

1 small lemon, cut in half
4 cloves garlic, peeled
1 x 400g can chickpeas, rinsed and drained
1 cup dry-roasted sunflower seeds
1 tablespoon tahini paste
100ml water
pinch salt
¼ teaspoon white pepper

1. Preheat oven to 160°C.
2. Place lemon and garlic in a small roasting dish and roast until soft and golden, about 45–50 minutes.
3. Place roasted lemon and garlic, chickpeas, sunflower seeds and tahini paste in a blender. Blend until smooth, drizzling in water with the motor running. Add more water if hummus is too thick. Season with salt and pepper.

Energy KJs	Protein	Total fat
1383	16g	23g

Saturated fat	Carbohydrate	Sodium
15g	29g	139mg

Garlic Yoghurt

Makes 1 cup • Preparation time 10 minutes

1 cup Greek yoghurt
4 cloves garlic, crushed
½ cup chopped mint leaves
½ cup chopped coriander leaves
2 tablespoons chopped fennel or dill

1. Place all ingredients in a blender and blend until smooth.

Energy KJs	Protein	Total fat
767	4.5g	7.6g

Saturated fat	Carbohydrate	Sodium
.6g	30g	107mg

Tabbouleh

Serves 4 • *Preparation time* Soak bulghur wheat for 10 minutes

1 cup bulghur wheat
1 cup boiling water
1 cup roughly chopped curly parsley leaves
½ cup chopped tomatoes
grated zest and juice of 1 lemon
2 tablespoons grapeseed oil
pinch salt
¼ teaspoon ground black pepper

1. Place bulghur wheat in a bowl and pour over boiling water to just cover. Leave to soak for 10 minutes until soft and all liquid has been absorbed.
2. Place bulghur wheat in a large bowl with remaining ingredients and gently toss with a fork to combine.

George Gewargis
Kebab King

George Gewargis is a kebab-making machine. He has been part of Wellington's late night kebab chaos for well over 20 years. The night of our challenge, George knew every customer who came in by name, and exactly what they wanted. He cares a lot about his food and believes so much in how good the product is; it has, after all, been around for thousands of years he kept telling me. I couldn't argue with that. George told me I couldn't make a falafel without deep-frying it and I could only use chickpeas. So what did I do? I will never learn.

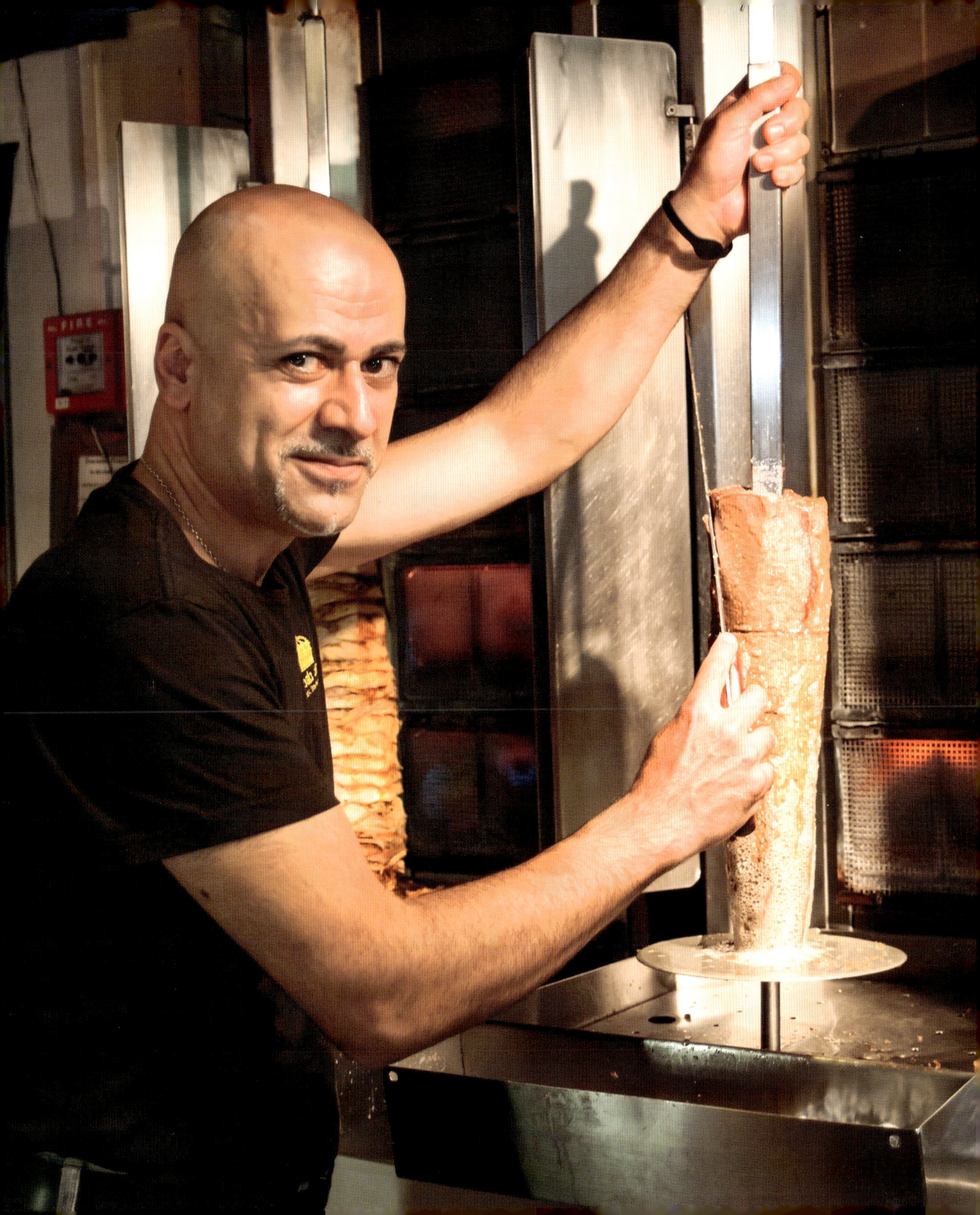
FIRE

A short history of
food trucks and street food

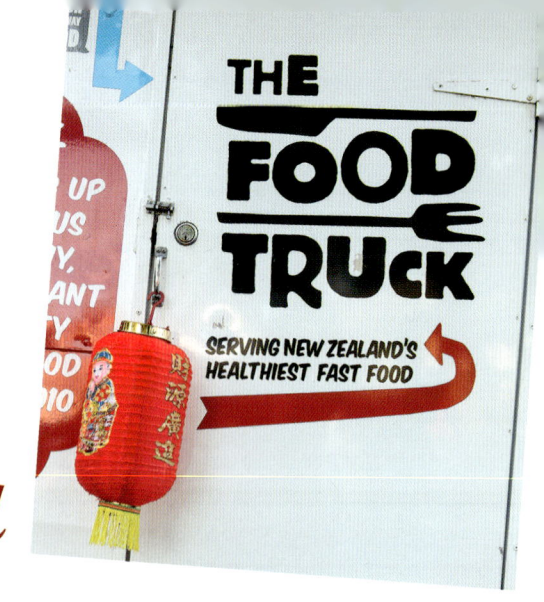

THE FOOD TRUCK AS WE KNOW IT HAS ITS ORIGINS IN — WHERE ELSE? — AMERICA. THE FIRST FOOD CARTS APPEARED IN THE 1690S IN NEW YORK, THEN KNOWN AS NEW AMSTERDAM. SKIP SOME SEVERAL HUNDRED YEARS TO 1866, WHEN THE AMERICAN WEST WAS BEING OPENED UP. CHARLES GOODNIGHT, MOVING A HERD OF CATTLE FROM TEXAS TO NEW MEXICO THROUGH DRY, INHOSPITABLE COUNTRY, NEEDED TO FEED HIS COWBOYS. SO HE BOUGHT AN ARMY SURPLUS WAGON AND TRICKED IT UP AS MOVEABLE KITCHEN WITH STORAGE. HE BUILT A BOX ON THE BACK FOR CONDIMENTS, WHILE A FOLD-DOWN BENCH DOUBLED AS A WORK SPACE AND SOMEWHERE TO EAT. HIS MEN CALLED IT A 'CHUCK WAGON' — CHUCK BEING SLANG FOR GOOD FOOD.

By the 1890s, vendors had started selling food from wagons around the universities of the east coast, including Yale and Princeton. They were known as 'dog wagons' or 'lunch wagons' by day, and 'night owls' by night. Then, as public transit improved, vendors bought up obsolete horse-drawn streetcars and turned them into the modern version of the food truck. By the middle of the 1930s, mobile food carts were a fixture in Los Angeles, and by the 1950s, ice-cream trucks were found all over the country. Then, in 1974, Raul Martinez converted a former ice-cream truck into the country's first taco truck and parked it outside an east Los Angeles bar. His friends thought he was nuts, but he'd launched a revolution; by the late 1980s the taco truck had become a fixture in Los Angeles, and Martinez's King Taco had three taco trucks, a bunch of taco stands, 10 restaurants and $10 million in sales.

Then, in 2008, chef Roy Choi opened Kogi BBQ, a food truck serving — yes — Korean tacos, driving a circuit through LA and informing its hungry citizens of his whereabouts by Twitter. It helped launch a food-truck revolution. Within a couple of years, all over the country, food trucks went from greasy to hip, serving everything from tacos and papaya salad to grilled cheese sandwiches. The timing couldn't have been better: a country and a world plunging headlong into recession, restaurants closing, chefs being put out of work — and serious eaters looking for more frugal options.

And in New Zealand? We've had food truck equivalents for quite a few years. Sometimes they're parked up rather than mobile, good examples being Nin's Bin and Kay's Crays, which have been selling freshly cooked crayfish on the side of State Highway 1 on the Kaikoura coast for decades. Not only are they parked at two of the country's most spectacularly wild spots, but you can also hunker down in a blustering wind, fight off the seagulls and eat crayfish with a stack of buttered white bread. It's totally fresh, and it's magnificent. At rugby games and A&P shows, meanwhile, caravans might sell burgers and chips and Coke.

But the most significant street food vendor in New Zealand's history is, in fact, the humble pie cart, for years a fixture of towns and cities alike. Pies go way back — they first appeared in medieval Britain and in many ways, they are the perfect street food: they use cheap ingredients and the pastry acts both as a sort of container for cooking the meat inside, as well as making it highly portable. A pie can be eaten comfortably standing up, without utensils. (More ghoulishly, early pies contained whole birds, the legs of which stuck out the sides to give the eater something to hold.) By the nineteenth century, as well as pies you could buy tripe, pea soup, pea pods in butter, whelks and jellied eels on the street.

Not surprisingly, English settlers brought pies with them to New Zealand, and by the 1930s — when the Great Depression created a need for cheap, accessible food — pie carts were common around the country. For decades, they were virtually the only thing open late at night, serving coffee and tea, pie and pud. Their boom time was the 1950s and 1960s; it's no coincidence that these were the years of the six o'clock swill, when pubs closed at 6 p.m., forcing drunk patrons out onto the street. Restaurants couldn't get liquor licences, so you drank at the pub, soaked up the booze at the pie cart and then went home and slept both of them off. Through the 1970s, they were popular with marijuana smokers, for obvious reasons.

Food historians have pointed to the democratising nature of the pie cart, which is fair enough. What's possibly more interesting is the fact that it kept the idea of eating on the street — and eating late — alive in a country not particularly known for such delights. Street food might be commonplace around the world, but in Anglo countries — New Zealand as well as Britain and the United States — street food has carried a whiff of danger. By the beginning of the twentieth century, as the emerging middle class began to buy their food from restaurants and shops, rather than markets and stalls, street food became low-brow. Anglo food culture became obsessed with the cleanliness of food, rather than how it tasted.

And so, the noble pie cart was the one place you could get a late-night feed in small-town New Zealand — or in big-town New Zealand, for that matter. While we might have looked down on pie carts and food trucks, they have always served everyone, from lawyers to prostitutes, the glitterati to the down and out. Most were family-run businesses, whose owners worked long into the night for a small profit serving our favourite takeaway food. And these carts suffered some of the same issues as street-food vendors around the world — some, for instance, were required to move once every half an hour.

These days, the pie cart is something of an endangered species. There are still a few to be found in the bigger cities — The White Lady is still going strong in downtown Auckland after more than 60 years in the business, for instance, and is still owned by the same family. But pie carts around the country have been squeezed by fast-food chains, with the golden arches and the flame-grilled and the finger-lickin'-good eating into their late-night market. At the same time, the ever-increasing bureaucracy around food has made their existence ever harder.

But what has transformed New Zealand's eating habits in the past few decades is mass immigration from countries with venerable traditions of street food, particularly in Asia. That's brought the world's cuisines to our streets. Anyone who has ever stood in the late-night soupy heat of Shanghai or Bangkok can attest to the delights of eating standing up. It might be rows of charcoal braziers, cooking bright red crawfish over red hot coals, which are then slathered with chilli that you will only find in a certain Shanghai street. Or it might be simple bowls of bun bo xao, vermicelli salad

> *Street food is a wonderful collision of easily accessible taste explosions, at an affordable price.*

with beef, or the classic bun cha, chargrilled pork patties with vermicelli noodles in the Old Quarter of Hanoi. Or assam laksa in Penang. Or prawns flash-fried in chilli and garlic with greens stir-fried with garlic or oyster sauce at the Temple Street Market in Hong Kong.

Lucky for us, our new wave of immigrants come from places where food is crucial to identity and social life. They've brought their food with them, cheerfully revitalising entire shopping districts, festivals and markets, recreating their food culture at the same time as giving the residents of their adopted country something new and exciting. In this, street food is doing what it has always done, from New York to Melbourne: giving new immigrants a much-needed leg up in a time-honoured way. By cooking.

Instead of being suspicious of new food, as many of us once were, New Zealanders now seek it out. In Auckland, they find it at the Glenfield or Pakuranga Night Markets — both held in the car parks of Westfield malls, in the most basic of conditions imaginable. Here you'll find Chinese dumplings, Filipino stews and Malaysian laksa. The same is true of Wellington's Southeast Asian Night Market, held each year on the city's waterfront.

But what's particularly delightful is how New Zealand's familiar favourites are now being served as street food, too. Up and down the country at farmers' markets, wonderful incubators of small businesses, you'll find wave upon wave of vendors. Who Ate All the Pies, say, at the Otago Farmers' Market; famed Wellington chef Martin Bosley serving bacon butties at his City Market each Sunday; and glorious whitebait fritters in thick white bread at the Nelson Market. As we've discovered new street food, we've also rediscovered the old.

Street food is a wonderful collision of easily accessible taste explosions, at an affordable price. And these days, an increasing number of food trucks bring great street and world food to us, wherever we might be: at the races, at an A&P show, at a festival. As well as Mike Van de Elzen's Food Truck, in Auckland there's Waiheke Island's El Sizzling Chorizo, Mexikai, and a host of others including The Lucky Taco, run by graffiti artist Otis Frizzell. They can be found from one end of the country to the other — from terrific Vietnamese at Matakana to the venerable Kai Kart, a caravan selling fish and chips and Glory Bay oysters in Oban, Stewart Island.

All of them celebrate the bare-knuckle joy of eating standing up, and this is what fascinates Mike and *The Food Truck* — throughout the country people are creating a street-side experience, sharing the food they grew up eating, in New Zealand or elsewhere. It is food that acts as both a reminder of where we've come from — whether that's Haast or Mumbai — and where our community is now. It is a grand tradition, one that reaches back through thousands of years of human history to the very beginnings of cities and civilisation, and one we should be very grateful for.

Simon Farrell-Green

Healthy options*

There are lots of ways you can achieve the flavour and taste of takeaway-style food at home — and indeed with all your cooking — without piling on the fat, the sugar and the salt.

To reduce salt use

- In general, reduce the amount of salt used but if using it, make sure it is *iodised*. To add flavour use herbs, spices, lemon juice and pepper in place of salt.
- Make sauces with low-salt stocks, water, fruit juice, low-fat milk and yoghurt. Thickening with flour, cornflour or arrowroot will reduce fat use too.
- Use low-salt varieties of soy, fish, oyster and other Asian sauces, and in general *reduce* the amount used.
- Instead of stock cubes and commercially made stocks use *home-made* stock and reduced vegetable cooking water.
- Use canned vegetable varieties that have no added salt.
- Use low-salt varieties of peanut butter in place of regular peanut butter.

To get more fibre

- Instead of white flour use wholemeal flour or half white and half wholemeal.
- *Replace* white bread with wholemeal pita bread or wholegrain bread, and use wholemeal breadcrumbs in place of white.
- To thicken and extend braises and stews, add rice, barley, oats or red lentils.
- Use wholemeal pasta and brown rice *instead of* pasta and white rice.
- Peel vegetables and fruits only when necessary.

To use less sugar

- *Instead of* regular canned fruit use canned fruit in light syrup, non-sweetened or canned in its own juice.
- Instead of icing a cake, dust it with icing sugar, *or use* a layer of fresh berries on top. Replace cream-cheese icing with ricotta, yoghurt and honey, or make it with lite cream cheese.
- *Reduce the use of* sugar, honey and golden syrup and substitute natural fruit, fruit purée or fruit juice as sweeteners.
- Instead of regular yoghurt use natural or unsweetened yoghurt.
- Stew fruit in a little water only, with no added sugar.

Watch the type of fat you use

- Use margarine, table spreads or oil *rather than* butter.
- Hummus, mashed avocado, mayonnaise, tahini or pesto also *make great alternatives* to butter on bread.
- When making pancakes, pikelets or fritters, spray the surface of your pan *sparingly* with cooking spray.
- Instead of shortening and lard use margarine or vegetable oil.
- Rather than cheddar cheese *substitute a lower fat* cheese, e.g. Edam or Mozzarella. Add extra flavour with a small amount of mustard.
- *Replace* full-fat soft cheese, sour cream or yoghurt with lower fat varieties such as cottage cheese, ricotta, quark or lite cream cheese.
- *Instead of* full-fat milk use low-fat skim milk or trim milk (1.5% fat or less).
- Use reduced fat cream if it doesn't require whipping; or replace with low-fat natural yoghurt or Greek yoghurt; or if suitable, use custard instead.
- Instead of full-fat coconut cream or coconut milk use a lite version; or lite evaporated milk with coconut essence; or low-fat yoghurt mixed with *small amounts* of desiccated coconut diluted with low-fat milk.
- Toast pita bread chunks or tortilla wraps cut to size, or bake slices of French bread in the oven until crispy to serve with dips instead of chips and crisps.
- Instead of regular mayonnaise and salad dressings use reduced-fat varieties and/or dilute with low-fat yoghurt or milk.
- Choose *lean cuts of meat* and trim off visible fat before cooking.
- When cooking meat, grill, stew, bake or roast on a rack, with no added fat.
- Use only very small amounts of salami and bacon to flavour dishes. This adds less salt too.
- If cooking sausages or sausage meat, *reduce the amount used* and extend with rice, pasta, legumes or vegetables. If using pre-cooked sausages, choose lower fat varieties.
- When cooking fish, poach, grill, microwave or steam rather than deep-frying. Baked crumbed fish has far less fat than deep-fried battered fish.
- Use fish canned in water rather than oil or brine. It contains less salt too!
- When cooking vegetables, steam, boil or microwave in a little water, avoiding overcooking. Sauté, bake or stir-fry by brushing the pan with a small amount of oil, or use an oil spray then add a little water or fruit juice.
- *Bake, microwave or mash* potatoes rather than roasting in animal fat or deep-frying. Mash with low-fat milk or lite evaporated milk, and a small amount of light margarine. If needed, add extra flavour with mustard, horseradish, herbs or caramelised onion.
- Instead of creamy sauces use tomato-based sauces and use *low-fat* milk or *lite* margarine in white sauces.

Cooking methods

Baking

- Oven-bake foods, without adding fat.
- Replace butter in baking recipes with a healthy oil, margarine or spread. (Spreads contain more water than butter or margarine, so choose a variety that has at least 60 per cent fat when substituting for butter.)
- Use fruit purée as a replacement for half the butter or margarine.
- Use silicone sheets or baking paper instead of greasing dishes with butter or cooking spray.

Pan-frying and stir-frying

- Spray the pan with an oil spray instead of using oil or butter.
- Choose vegetable oils with a higher smoke point for frying such as sunflower, soybean, canola or rice bran.

Deep-frying

- Deep-frying is not recommended because it produces food that is especially high in energy.
- Many foods that are traditionally deep-fried, such as chips, can be oven-baked for a healthier result.

Roasting

- Use a rack when roasting meat and lightly spray baking trays with a little oil when roasting vegetables.

Stews and braises

- Use milk in place of cream, lite coconut milk instead of coconut cream and low-salt stocks.

✳ With thanks to Heart Foundation NZ

Credit roll

A huge team was involved in making the TV series that sits behind this book, and in making the book itself. Thanks heaps to the guys at Two Heads, Nick and James, for giving me the keys to the truck again, the film crew, my glamorous assistant Marie, who helped out on game days, and TVNZ for once more backing the show. I got to work with my good friend photographer Babiche Martens again at the Auckland game days and on the food shots, and this time Kathy Paterson helped me out with the prep and the cooking and turned my ingredients lists and methods into proper recipes. Pip Duncan ran the nutritional analysis.

Thanks to my publisher Random House. Thanks to the photographers who came along to shoot me in action in Rotorua, Blenheim, Wellington and Christchurch.

Thanks to all the great cooks who let me in on their trade secrets and who didn't mind me competing with them for the day. Thanks once again to Belinda, who this time was left behind with two little children while Beddy and I roamed about the countryside.

And, most of all, thanks to everyone who came and tried out my food. I loved the smiles on your faces and the fun you had with us.

Mike

Index

A
Almond-crusted pork schnitzel, 120
Argentinian
  Chargrilled lamb shoulder chops, rubs, 32, 34
  Chimichurri salad, 36
  Smoked mushroom & garlic breads, 38
Asian-inspired slaw, 56
Autumn rice paper rolls, 90

B
Baked apple crumble with labna, 164
Banana leaf salmon, 74
Banh Mi, 86–89
Beef
  Braised beef salad, 66–68
  Ravioli Bolognese, 110–112
  Spicy beef burgers, 136
  Tacos with shredded beef, 46–48
Braised beef salad, 66–68
Bratwurst with curry sauce, 124–126
Burgers
  Cajun-spiced goat sliders, 132–134
  Spicy beef burgers, 136

C
Cajun-spiced goat sliders, home-made mustard, tomato sauce & roasted garlic aïoli, 132–134
Chargrilled lamb shoulder chops, wet & dry rubs, 32, 34
Cherries with olive caramel, 28
Chicken
  Banh Mi, 86–89
  Healthy meatballs, 24
  kebabs, 170
  pie, 144–146
  Tequila chicken tortillas, 45
Chilli sauce, mild & hot, 176
Chimichurri salad, 36
Chinese
  Asian-inspired slaw, 56
  Chop suey, 154
  Choy sum with oyster sauce, 58
  Vegetable dumplings, 52–54
Choc almond shake, 166
Chop suey, 154
Chorizo paella 'n' stuffed peppers, 22
Choy sum with oyster sauce, 58
Clam & noodle skewers with eggplant pickle, 80
Croque Monsieur crêpes, 100

D
Desserts
  Baked apple crumble with labna, 164
  Hazelnut crêpes, 98
  Tiramisu profiteroles, 114
  Triple blueberry doughnuts, 160–162
Drinks
  Choc almond shake, 166
  Thai tea bag, 70
Duck cassoulet crêpes, 102

F
Falafel kebabs, 174
Fettuccini & green pesto, 106–108
Fish kebabs, 172
Fish palusami, 156
French
  Croque Monsieur crêpes, 100
  Duck cassoulet crêpes, 102
  Hazelnut crêpes, 98

G
Garlic yoghurt, 178
German
  Almond-crusted pork schnitzel, 120
  Bratwurst with curry sauce, 124–126
  Pretzels, 118
  Sauerkraut aïoli, 122
Goat
  Cajun-spiced goat sliders, 132–134
Golden kumara mole, 44
Grilled courgette & tomato crumble pizza, 138

H
Hazelnut crêpes, 98
Healthy meatballs, 24

I
Italian
  Fettuccini & green pesto, 106–108
  Ravioli Bolognese, 110–112
  Tiramisu profiteroles, 114

J
Japanese
  Banana leaf salmon, 74
  Cabbage salad, 82
  Clam & noodle skewers with eggplant pickle, 80
  Salmon skewers with teriyaki sauce, 72
  Shiitake mushroom & prawn skewers with wasabi mayonnaise, 78
  Watermelon & tofu skewers, 76

L

Lamb
   Chargrilled lamb shoulder chops, rubs, 32, 34
   Chop suey, 154

M

Melon balls with crispy Serrano ham & spiced yoghurt, 30
Mexican
   Golden kumara mole, 44
   Tacos with shredded beef, 46–48
   Tequila chicken tortillas, 45
Middle Eastern
   Chicken kebabs, 170
   Chilli sauce, mild & hot, 176
   Falafel kebabs, 174
   Fish kebabs, 172
   Garlic yoghurt, 178
   Sunflower-seed hummus, 178
   Tabbouleh, 179

P

Pad Thai, 64
Patatas bravas, 20
Pies
   Chicken pie, 144–146
Pizza
   Grilled courgette & tomato crumble pizza, 138
   Potato pizza, 140–142
Polynesian
   Fish palusami, 156
   Taro chips with mango sauce, 152
Pork
   Almond-crusted pork schnitzel, 120
   Potato pizza with pickled fennel, green apple, sheep's feta & rocket, 140–142
Prawn & trevally pho, 92
Pretzels, 118

R

Ravioli Bolognese, 110–112

S

Salmon skewers with teriyaki sauce, 72
Sapasui, 154
Sauerkraut aïoli, 122
Sausages
   Bratwurst with curry sauce, 124–126
   Chorizo paella 'n' stuffed peppers, 22
Seafood
   Banana leaf salmon, 74
   Clam & noodle skewers with eggplant pickle, 80
   Fish kebabs, 172
   Fish palusami, 156
   Prawn & trevally pho, 92
   Salmon skewers with teriyaki sauce, 72
   Shiitake mushroom & prawn skewers with wasabi mayonnaise, 78
   Smoked fish with tomato & cucumber panzanella & salsa verde, 148
   Squid skewers with romesco sauce, 18
   Thai fish cakes, 62
   Tuna croquettes, 16
Shiitake mushroom & prawn skewers with wasabi mayonnaise, 78
Smoked fish with tomato & cucumber panzanella & salsa verde, 148
Smoked mushroom & garlic breads, 38
Spanish
   Cherries with olive caramel, 28
   Chorizo paella 'n' stuffed peppers, 22
   Healthy meatballs, 24
   Melon balls with crispy Serrano ham & spiced yoghurt, 30
   Patatas bravas, 20
   Squid skewers with romesco sauce, 18
   Tuna croquettes, 16
   Vegetable tortilla, 26

Spicy beef burgers, 136
Squid skewers with romesco sauce, 18
Sunflower-seed hummus, 178
Sweet stem broccoli crunch, 150

T

Tabbouleh, 179
Tacos with shredded beef, 46–48
Taro chips with mango sauce, 152
Tequila chicken tortillas, 45
Thai
   Braised beef salad, 66–68
   fish cakes, 62
   Pad Thai, 64
   tea bag, 70
Tiramisu profiteroles, 114
Tofu
   Asian-inspired slaw, 56
   Pad Thai, 64
   Watermelon & tofu skewers, 76
Triple blueberry doughnuts, 160–162
Tuna croquettes, 16
Turkey
   Banh Mi, 86–89

V

Vegetable dumplings, 52–54
Vegetable tortilla, 26
Vietnamese
   Autumn rice paper rolls, 90
   Banh Mi, 86–89
   Prawn & trevally pho, 92

W

Watermelon & tofu skewers, 76